This is Home

STORIES OF GOD'S FAITHFULNESS IN MY LIFE

WRITTEN BY KARI ANNE ADAMS

EDITED BY LYNNE RIFFENBURGH

This is Home

ISBN-13: 978-1983695285

ISBN-10: 1983695289

First printing March 2018/Printed in the United States of America.

Thank You

For my God, my Redeemer, my Hope, this is my witness of what You have done so far in my story. Thank you for teaching me life is so much more than living for You. It's all about the journey of living life WITH YOU.

For my husband, partner for life, who walks with me and gets to witness God's faithfulness along side of me. You constantly point me back to Jesus when I start to lose hope. I love you always.

For all of my sistas, who have come along side me in different seasons of life. I am so grateful for the times I got to talk and pray and hope and dream and grieve and take walks together and eat Moonstruck chocolate, fro yo & ice cream. You are all the flowers along the path making this life painting of mine all the more beautiful. I love each one of you.

My family who loves me and points me to Jesus. Thank you for practicing faithfulness. I love you.

My children- I am looking forward to watching and witnessing God start bringing the stories He wants to write in Your life to fruition. I guarantee it will not always be easy. I hope you can glean from what your dad and I have learned and take it with you. That these lessons would be reminders of a God who is ready to do this life WITH you too! I love you FOREVER!

Dedicated to my children, and my children's children
Josiah William—My fire of the Lord and Resolute Protector
Ava Mae Hope—Filled with Life, Gift, Hope in Jesus
Lena Grace—High Tower, Favor, Benevolence
Mallory Joy—War Counselor, Rejoice

Table of Contents

My Roots

The First Season of Waiting

Our Season Together Begins

The Unfolding of Our Family

God's Gift Continues

Broken Places

The School Paths

He is Our Stability...He is Our Home

Introduction

Psalm 71:18 (NASB)

And even when I am old and gray, O God, do not forsake me, Until I declare Your strength to this generation, Your power to all who are to come.

Deuteronomy 6:1–9 (NASB)

"Now this is the commandment, the statutes and the judgments which the LORD your God has commanded me to teach you, that you might do them in the land where you are going over to possess it, so that you and your son and your grandson might fear the LORD your God, to keep all His statutes and His commandments which I command you, all the days of your life, and that your days may be prolonged. O Israel, you should listen and be careful to do it, that it may be well with you and that you may multiply greatly, just as the LORD, the God of your fathers, has promised you, in a land flowing with milk and honey. "Hear, O Israel! The LORD is our God, the LORD is one! You shall love the LORD your God with all your heart and with all your soul and with all your might. These words, which I am commanding you today, shall be on your heart. You shall teach them diligently to your sons and shall talk of them when you sit in your house and when you walk by the way and when you lie down and when you rise up. You shall bind them as a sign on your hand and they shall be as frontals on your forehead. You shall write them on the doorposts of your house and on your gates."

This book was birthed in my heart over five years ago—the dream of writing out the stories of God's faithfulness in my life to share with my children and the future generations to come. Through the journeys I've walked along, I have learned there are no guarantees about the way your life will go, and while I still have time ahead of me, I want to take my todays to share about my yesterdays—to share lessons I have learned in good moments, in seasons of waiting, in times of having to grow up, the days lived in darkness, and in all of it, where I have fought to find hope.

Philippians 4:12–13 (NASB)

I know how to get along with humble means, and I also know how to live in prosperity; in any and every circumstance I have learned the secret of being filled and going hungry, both of having abundance and suffering need. I can do all things through Him who strengthens me.

My children are all in full-time school now, and I have been avoiding starting this the last two months. I had writer's block for a while, living in a fear not from the Lord and unsure if I could really write this all out and do it well. I have spent much time trying to pursue other directions of how to spend this extra bit of time I have each week. As each door closes in my face, I wonder why. And then a quiet voice speaks into my soul, saying, "I already told you what to do..." But it seems so meaningless. Isn't it better to be hands-on in relationships, Lord? And then a close confidant says, "But if the words you spend a few hours each week writing impact even one person, it's important." But Lord, I am so afraid. I don't know how to share after battling depression and darkness these last few years...and He reminds me of His promise from the verse He gave me a year ago: "I will not forsake you—you need to share the story I am writing in your life."

I remember being asked years ago in regards to struggling with infertility if I would ever go back and change any of it. I paused for a moment and responded with, "No, because of the work God has done in my life, and the character He has built through it, I would never want to go back to how I once was."

More recently, as I walked through a different season that brought about brokenness and deep depression in my life, I asked myself the same question: "Would I go back and change any of it?" The answer was very different, because in that circumstance, I would go back and change everything if I could...but the reality is I can't. However, what I can do is pick up and start again, with God holding the pen with me, and we can start to write together what He has done in the midst of it all.

"This is Home," is where I want to live. The here and now of where He has me, the discord of the desires deep inside longing for eternity, where there isn't all this hurt and pain, and yet being at peace with where I am, and where He has taken me, and where He wants to take me. I like the Hallmark movies where every challenge in life is wrapped up like a beautiful present within two hours, and the perfect life is about to ensue off screen. But that is not how life is here. No one likes to live on these unresolved notes—it's unsettling. I am learning to live with the peace that only God can give over and over in those moments, and see His faithfulness once more. I know this isn't my forever home, but I want to live with His redemption plan in mind while living here.

Philippians 4:4–7 (NASB)

Rejoice in the Lord always; again I will say, rejoice! Let your gentle spirit be known to all men. The Lord is near. Be anxious for nothing, but in everything by prayer and supplication with thanksgiving let your requests be made known to God. And the peace of God, which surpasses all comprehension, will guard your hearts and your minds in Christ Jesus.

My prayer for all who read this is that they will be encouraged through these stories to realize that God is faithful, and that they will start to see His faithfulness in their lives as well. I hope to share the fingerprints He has left on my life that remind me He is with me.

My Roots

❧ MY HISTORY ❧

I am going to start with the background of my family and the pieces of information I know.

My mom was raised on a farm in Eastern Oregon. Her ancestors traveled the Oregon Trail to settle there, and became wheat farmers. I remember as a little girl we would go there for the summer to see Grammy and Grandad. It was approximately a 3-hour drive, the last 45 minutes of which were brutal with winds and turns in the road that brought about feelings of dizziness and nausea.

Grandad was a quiet man who loved music and art, and worked hard on the farm to provide for his family. My favorite moments with him occurred when I would wake up early and we would take his collie dog on a walk to the town drive-in diner. He would pick up apple fritters to take back for the family and would buy me an ice cream cone for breakfast. He couldn't hear very well at the end of his life, but I always had a special connection with him. The week that he passed away, I had been working and planned to take a day off to go see him at the hospital. I knew I had been procrastinating, but I didn't know if my heart could handle seeing him in his final days. I know I will always regret not getting to say goodbye, as he passed away the day before I could see him. Every time I eat a twist cone, I remember those moments with him. He died the summer before we were given our first child.

Grammy was a jovial lady. She always had stories to tell and loved to laugh. She grew up in Hollywood, moving there as a little girl. She was raised by her mother after her parents got divorced. She lost her little brother, who died at three years of age, being struck by lightning while trying to save one of their toys, which was left outside beneath a tree during the middle of a thunderstorm. She had so much sadness in her childhood, but she was a woman that did her best to find happiness in all that brokenness. She tells stories of how she went to high school with Judy Garland, although she only saw her a few times, since a lot of the time Judy was not in school. Grammy raised five children—three boys and two girls. Visits when all of the siblings were together were always lively and fun. My mom was her middle child.

My Grammy always wanted to be a Great Grammy—and for the first four years of my marriage with Nick, she kept hoping for a baby. In the last year of her life, God granted her that dream, and she got to hold her first great grand baby. She was always telling us when we would visit to take anything we wanted out of her home—things we would use that she didn't need. I chose some beautiful crystal goblets and serving bowls that I use to serve ice cream and desserts for special occasions, and I always remember her when I use them.

During our summer trips to the farm, my mom would drive us up and we would stay for a few weeks, then my dad would follow, taking vacation time for the last week we were there so we could all be together. My mom would help my Grammy prepare meals for all the farmers and workers who came in at the lunch siren bell and pile up at folding tables and chairs in my grandparents' garage. They ate and enjoyed fellowship together, before heading back out into the sun to continue harvesting the grain.

On one of those trips, I learned how to swim. I had been dreadfully afraid of the water and getting my head wet. But thanks to an instructor named Molly, who gave us private lessons, I overcame those fears. I think this demonstrates my early personality of being a girl that didn't like things out of her control. But that was an area God was going to grow me in down the road.

I am so grateful I overcame my fear. I would have missed out on the enjoyment of learning to swim and experiences like swimming in the ocean in Hawaii, beyond the waves, to snorkel. I think so often with our fears, we let them get in the way and control the direction of our life, instead of surrendering them and trusting once more.

1 John 4:18 (NASB)

There is no fear in love; but perfect love casts out fear, because fear involves punishment, and the one who fears is not perfected in love.

I remember one time while driving out to the farm, I started pelting my mom with questions of how she and Dad met. My mom was raised in a family that went to church each Sunday, but didn't necessarily see the need of relationship with Jesus as part of what they believed. She was raised to be a good girl, but it wasn't until college that she met Jesus.

She had a roommate named Jane who knew Jesus. And Jane knew my dad. My mom and Jane went over to see my dad and his roommate because they had a chipmunk in their room. My dad thought my mom was cute. But he knew she didn't know Jesus, so he held back from anything at that point.

My dad grew up in a home in Beaverton. He was born in Japan and traveled over by boat as a baby to the United States with my grandparents. My grandparents met right after World War II. My grandpa was serving in Japan after the war, helping to get the country back in order. My grandma is Japanese, and they were set up on a blind date. They got married and had a honeymoon baby—my dad. I have always loved this story because it is a picture of how God is in the business of redeeming brokenness and making it into beautiful things.

The events that brought on World War II went against everything God is for. So much sadness and loss and death and brokenness came out of that. It's one of those things that was not in God's original design for the world before the fall in the Garden of Eden.[1] However, He doesn't let those broken pieces stay where they are. He picked up those small shards and said, "I will make something new." And so, a soldier and a young Japanese woman met and fell in love, and He began creating a new story. I humbly say that I would not be here today if World War II had not happened. For the lives that were lost, I wish that had not been their story. I know that is not what God longed for at the beginning of His creation. But I have found, that even in the darkness, I know there is hope to be found.

Isaiah 61:3–4 (NASB)

To grant those who mourn in Zion, Giving them a garland instead of ashes, The oil of gladness instead of mourning, The mantle of praise instead of a spirit of fainting. So they will be called oaks of righteousness, The planting of the LORD, that He may be glorified. Then they will rebuild the ancient ruins, They will raise up the former devastations; And they will repair the ruined cities, The desolations of many generations.

My grandparents settled into life in Beaverton. They both worked very hard. I am always so impressed by my grandma, who came here and learned how to speak English. Once she puts her mind to something, she works so hard to do it.

My dad was first introduced to Jesus by a neighbor named Mrs. Mead, who would invite neighbor children to her home and tell them about Jesus. He started going to her church as a young teenager. My dad hasn't talked too much about it with us, but I know in high school and his first year of college he made some choices he regrets. He came home from school and God got hold of his heart, and he started to make some changes in his life. One of those decisions was that he would not date someone who was not on the same page with loving God as he was.

When he met my mom, he didn't pursue anything at that point. But over the following year, my mom started spending time with their group of friends. It was during the 70s Jesus movement, and I love that my parents were part of that. My mom met Jesus personally in her own life that year. And thus began my parents' love story.

Their first date was a dance-off marathon. Over the next few years they continued a courtship that led to marriage. I asked my mom to write down their engagement story when I was in my own season of engagement to Nick, as a keepsake and for remembrance. I am going to share what she wrote with you:

Our Engagement—Written by Robin Lee Kirkpatrick

On August 11, 1975, Ray asked my dad if he could marry me.

The whole summer I had been anticipating becoming engaged, when I finally got used to the idea that it wouldn't be for a while. Ray decides to surprise me and pop the question. It was a warm summer night and I thought we were just going outside to say goodnight. He asked me to marry him on this night around 11pm, as the barn cats were milling around our feet. When I said yes, we decided to sit outside for a while and talk. Guess who decides to join us? Not only the cats, but our dog, Buffy, wants to sit right between us. It was all very romantic, a night I will never forget. He gave me a necklace with half of a heart on it that said, "May the Lord watch over you and me when we are absent from one another." He wore a necklace with the other half of the heart. It was scary to think about getting married. I went up to my bedroom all numb, and talked to God about it. I poured out all my excitement and fears to Him and He filled me with a peace that passes all understanding.

We started going together in April of 1974. We entered a Muscular Dystrophy Dance Marathon and there he held my hand for the first time. After dancing 24 hours with breaks, we gave up and that evening went to church to listen to a singing group. It was then that Ray told me he had given our relationship to God. I didn't understand what this meant at that time, but I am sure glad he did.

We had many fond memories during our dating and engagement period. One is when we went fishing on the Alsea River and landed a 36" salmon. It was quite a battle but we were sure proud of the fish when we got him to shore. There were quiet times such as roasting marshmallows over a flickering fire at Avery Park after sundown. Or the many walks we went on, sharing our hopes and dreams. I'll never forget waiting up one night to watch a lunar eclipse and after a long wait, finding out it was to happen the next night. Or the time we cycled out to the fairground for Senior Steak Fry only to find out we were a week early. A big moment came for me after he picked me up from my time at Camp Adams. I had been there for a week, as a counselor for some Junior High girls. We stopped for some lunch at Benson Park, and while sitting at the picnic table, he gave me my engagement ring. At first I was afraid to open the box to see, but I gave it a peek and it was beautiful.

At the beginning of January 1976, Ray was blessed with a job in the USDA as a grain inspector. Only one problem, he had to leave for Omaha, Nebraska on February 2. Our last weekend together we drove up to Mary's Peak near Corvallis. It was a beautiful sunshiny day with snow still on the ground. We could see the ocean from there, so that was our next destination. I cried a long time after he left for Omaha, but found it hard to believe that when I would see him in June, we would be getting married.

I wrote in my Bible on the day we became engaged and realized this was the second biggest commitment I had made to anyone. I am committed to Ray for the rest of my life and forever. My first commitment was to Jesus on March 31, 1974, when I gave my life to Him. He gave me a new and wonderful life to live for Him, which is eternal. Now Ray and I are going to live this life together for Him.

My parents started off their life together in marriage in June of 1976. They had a short trip up to Seattle for their honeymoon, and then moved to Nebraska. My dad then had a job transfer to Beaumont, Texas. And that is where my life began.

I was born on September 20, 1978. My mom likes to tell the story of how I was 20 days late, and I didn't want to come out until they put her in the hospital, and she had chocolate cake the night before I was born. I must have realized then that there were great things to be had in the world! I know my dad's favorite baby story is after they had introduced me to ice cream (one of my main food groups), how the next time they served up mashed potatoes at dinner, my eyes got wide with excitement, and my dad warned me, "Kari, it's not what you think they are," but to no avail. I was sure that was a big scoop of vanilla ice cream. I shoved a big spoonful in my mouth, and my dad would not let me spit it out after I realized I had been deceived, by my own mother no less.

We lived in Texas through the first 18 months of my life. Then there were job openings through the USDA in Oregon. My grandma (my dad's mom) called the office and told them they needed to bring my dad to Oregon, because Texas was too far away for her oldest son to be from her. I love my grandma. She was determined and focused, and the word "no" is not an acceptable answer in her vocabulary.

Needless to say, in March of 1980, my dad got the job transfer. They packed us up and we drove back to Oregon. On the drive, my parents listened to CB—radios used by truck drivers, as well as other professions, to communicate with one another on the road. (This was in the world before cell phones.) My dad was bringing his little white Datsun with us—towed on the back of my parents' Magnum—and at one point some truck drivers made a joke on the CB about the little white Datsun pushing the big yellow Dodge Magnum up the hill. When we arrived in Oregon, we settled into the suburban life outside of Portland, where I spent the rest of my childhood.

Dear Children,

I hope you enjoyed this short history of some of the people you come from. You have grandparents and great grandparents who worked hard to stay together in their marriages, in their homes. But the biggest blessing is that God started His redemption work in our family, and you have grandparents who have loved Jesus and walked many years of faithfulness with Him. They have started a deep heritage that we can pass onto many generations to come. I just want you to take a moment to celebrate that gift you have been given. I have hopes that this gift will be brought with you and shared with many generations to come.

Love You, Dear Children,
Mama

Deuteronomy 4:29–31 (NASB)

But from there you will seek the LORD your God, and you will find Him if you search for Him with all your heart and all your soul. When you are in distress and all these things have come upon you, in the latter days you will return to the LORD your God and listen to His voice. For the LORD your God is a compassionate God; He will not fail you nor destroy you nor forget the covenant with your fathers which He swore to them.

⚘ MY FIRST CHILDHOOD RECOLLECTIONS ⚘

The very first memory I have as a child was laying in my bed one evening, in the first home my parents ever purchased. With a blanket of darkness surrounding me, I knew that I existed. I wondered where did I come from? I didn't recall any prior memories to that time, and yet somehow, I was here in my bed and living life now.

When I was 5, I gave my life to Jesus. Teachers at Sunday School had shared about Jesus with me. I knew I wanted to have what they shared. I asked my mom about it as she tucked me into bed that evening. We prayed together, and I knew Jesus was with me and was going to be part of the rest of my life. The first Bible verse I memorized was Psalm 23 (NASB):

> The Lord is my shepherd, I shall not want. He makes me lie down in
> green pastures; He leads me beside quiet waters. He restores my soul;
> He guides me in the paths of righteousness for His name's sake. Even
> though I walk through the valley of the shadow of death, I fear no evil,
> for You are with me; Your rod and Your staff, they comfort me. You
> prepare a table before me in the presence of my enemies; You have
> anointed my head with oil; My cup overflows. Surely goodness and
> lovingkindness will follow me all the days of my life, And I will dwell in
> the house of the Lord forever.

In a lot of ways, I am that typical "good" girl raised in church. I had a pretty easy childhood compared to many. I knew Jesus was with me, but I didn't fully understand relationship with him at that young age. The life I was living was relatively easy. My dad worked hard providing for our family. My mom stayed home taking care of our family. We had a home, food at the table, and clothes to wear.

I had a cat named Pooh Bear who would watch me go to the bus stop and wait for me to come home each day. She was a beautiful black kitty that brought us gifts like the hearts of mice and birds she caught in her adventures outside. She would also run from me when I wanted to hold her, and hide behind our wood fireplace where I got burned a few times trying to get her, or up in the shelf of my parents' china hutch. One time my parents had a casserole dish they needed to return to a friend, which crashed on my foot when I was trying to get my kitty out of her hiding spot. I had an indented scar on my big toe nail for years reminding me of that moment. I "prophesied" my kitty would live to be 21. That cat had close encounters with death, but she ended up living to the ripe old cat age of 21 years. She passed away when I no longer lived at home with my parents. I came to say my goodbyes to her and cried tears over her lifeless body. She was my childhood friend and as I grew up, she became my comforting buddy when I had hard days. Somehow she just knew when I needed her to be next to me.

We grew up with a backyard where my dad built a treehouse. We often had our neighbors over to play, all of them about my brother Michael's age (who was born a little over two years after me) or younger. I never had anyone my age to connect with. I often spent my childhood days in my own daydream world. As I grew, I liked to curl up in my room with a good book, or writing stories and dreaming dreams. I loved sitting by my window, just looking outside watching cars and people pass by.

I was not always an easy child. I was an extremely picky eater—I remember one time at a birthday party sitting with lasagna in front of me that I didn't want to eat, and having my uncle try to convince me I should finish it. I also regret all the times when my dad got paid and wanted to treat the family out to dinner, and I complained if we went somewhere I didn't want to go. Chicken nuggets and fries were my staple go-to food when we ordered out. I could not stand Mexican food as a child, and I would survive those restaurants with cheese crispies. My worst moment was when we were driving to a family camp when I was about 11. My dad wanted to stop by this Mexican restaurant that was on the way, which was supposed to have some of the best food around. I did not want to order anything. I was a bit car sick, and it was past mealtime, so I was overly hungry to the point of feeling nauseous at the thought of food. And it was MEXICAN food. No thanks, I would pass. Stubbornly I made the choice to not order anything. My poor dad, after he ordered food, which took about a half hour because of the long line for this popular place, coaxed me into taking a small bite of a taco. After the first nibble, I became ravenous, and shoved that whole taco in my mouth. My dad shared much of his meal with me that day, and he will say to this day, "I knew I should have ordered extra." As an adult in retrospect, I see how much I took away from those times my parents intended as special nights together, celebrating his hard work with an evening when my mom didn't have to cook and my dad could bless us.

Ephesians 5:20 (NIV)
Always giving thanks to God the Father for everything, in the name of our Lord Jesus Christ.

When I was in fifth grade, my parents taught my Sunday School class. It was a group of girls only. In that time, the question of baptism came up. One of the girls wanted to get baptized. Next thing you knew, we all decided to get baptized. I know that it was a public statement of my faith in Jesus. I knew I loved Jesus, but I still was just on the edge of beginning to learn what it meant to walk with Him. I stood before the congregation in the baptismal, confessing my faith, and submerged in the waters of baptism. It was a beautiful picture of my life being made into something new.

In the fall of 1988, my parents took us out for dinner. It was a little nicer restaurant than we normally frequented. They told us they had a surprise to share with us. At one point during dinner my mom took me to the restroom, and I remember as we washed our hands, I caught a look at the reflection of her face. It just radiated with joy. There was a glow about her, and her eyes sparkled with the untold secret her and my dad alone knew. She had never looked more beautiful to me.

My parents waited through dinner. Then they took us to our favorite ice cream joint: Sweet Temptations. Run by the sweetest couple, Dave and Peggy, it was the best place to get ice cream close to home. Would they tell us there? Nope, they kept their secret locked inside as the anticipation grew. I started thinking about what it could be. Was it that we would be moving? Or maybe this other dream I had wished my whole childhood...a secret too wonderful to hope for?

As they sat us down at home, they turned on a song...and as the melody began to play, and the words filled our ears, we knew the secret. My mom was going to have a baby. I was going to be a big sister again. My brother and I jumped around the room wildly. I was so excited. That dream of my mom having another baby was coming true...and my hopes for a baby sister slowly began to take root inside my heart. We waited and hoped and prayed, and excitedly anticipated the day this new addition to our family would be born.

The months went by. My mom's due date was right around July 4. Maybe she would have a firecracker baby. More exciting news came at that time. My aunt and uncle who had been married for several years found out they were expecting their first child, due in September. This baby would be our first cousin.

There is just something about the hope and joy that comes with new life. It is filled with all sorts of possibilities of what this tiny thing about to enter the world will do with it.

On June 28, in the very early, dark hours of the morning, my dad woke us up and had us get ready to load into the car. We drove along the side roads, and I remember my parents had a stopwatch to keep track of contractions. As we drove into downtown Portland on Burnside, I remember in one of the mini tunnels my dad slowed the car almost to a stop to keep track of the contraction my mom was having. There was a baby on the way.

We didn't know what my mom would be having. In those days, it was just the beginning of ultrasound tests to find out what you were having. My parents decided to wait and find out when she gave birth.

We got into Good Samaritan Hospital in downtown Portland, and my mom was moved into a room where for the next several hours my dad sat by her side, and my brother and I waited and wondered when this would happen. My parents chose to allow us to be there when my mom gave birth. I still remember my brother, who was eight at the time, covering his eyes with his hands. He would peek for a moment and then cover them again. I, on the other hand, was very intrigued with how this worked. When it got very close and my mom had done some pushing, I remember watching her get an episiotomy, and cringing. But shortly after that my new sibling's head emerged, and out came my beautiful baby sister. She was covered with a crazy ridiculous amount of hair on that head of hers, and I was instantly in love. It was the most amazing thing I had ever witnessed.

My parents had not chosen a name yet. When they decided to talk about it, they sent Michael and me out of the room. They told us we should go think of names too. Michael and I went to the wall with all the names of babies born prematurely at that hospital. We decided to pick the most unusual names we could find to take back to our parents.

When we came back in, they had chosen her name: Abigail Lynne. This was one of those core moments that directed the trajectory of my life. In the few years that followed, my parents decided to homeschool us, which allowed me to participate in all the baby things, learning and observing all the different parts involved in parenting. And what I discovered was that more than anything else in this life, I wanted to be a mom someday. I wanted to get married and have a family, and stay home and take care of my beautiful children. Thus my career goals became firmly established in the deepest part of my being.

Last year I took a class at our church on anger and anxiety. In the class we were given an assignment to create a project that would be remembrance stones (kind of like in Joshua 4),[2] to remind us of the stories of God's faithfulness in our lives. I created a tree with many branches, and much fruit on each branch, with most having a name. Each name represented a story in my life when God has been faithful to me. So like this tree with many branches off the core of its trunk, as I write, I will be branching off on occasion, in order not to leave certain stories unsaid. As I stand at the life that was about to break forward into middle school and beyond, I realize I can continue on with the story of my life, in how God led me to start my own family. But there are so many different pieces along that path that I walked, and I know He wants me not to forget His faithfulness in each of those pieces along the way.

Dear Children,

I hope that as you begin to read the many stories to come, it can be a reminder of the foundation that God built in our family life. That it will bring hope of a God who has so many things He wants to show you and speak to you as you grow up and someday have your own stories of God's faithfulness to tell. I love you, children.

Your Mama,
Kari

⚡ THE AWKWARD YEARS ⚡

As parents, there are a lot of choices we make for our children, often hoping and praying it will be the best for them. My parents made the choice to start homeschooling me, when all my childhood classmates would be moving on to middle school. There were many ups and downs that came from this decision. I want to share a bit of my journey with you.

When I was in sixth grade, I began to feel a bit isolated. A few of my friends started excluding me. I had two friends who spoke "Double Dutch" to each other on the playground in front of me. Whenever I came around they would start speaking it so I would not understand them. One day, one of the friends slipped up and told me how the language worked. I remember laying in my bed at night over the next week, with my night light reflecting the shadows, and I would look up at my ceiling and practice Double Dutch. I had to learn it—for survival. I longed to be included. I remember the first time I walked up to them and spoke my first phrase to them. They whispered to each other in Double Dutch that I was catching on. Yet my learning that language did not change the situation. I still was not welcome among those girls.

If you are from the 80s generation, you must remember ESPIRIT bags. They were duffel bags that came in different colors, and they had the word ESPIRIT in bold capital letters written across the front. My favorite ones were the ones that had the letters in multiple colors.

Almost every single girl in my class had one, and they would line them up on the walls where bags and backpacks were hung. But not me. I had my Jansport backpack that I would put on a hook, looking longingly at those bags...wishing for one myself. My mom didn't want me to have one because every other girl had one. And apparently I was just a few years ahead of the time, as Jansport backpacks became popular when I was in high school. But in that moment, I felt like I was left out of this cool kid club.

I was also a bit boy crazy. I loved the attention from boys. I thrived on teasing and probably a bit of flirting, although I wouldn't have known that's what I was doing. I dreamed of getting my first kiss. I was so naïve and innocent, and unaware of so many things.

Toward the end of my sixth-grade year, I broke out of my "I'm a fragile girl" mentality and started playing wall ball. It was the first time in a sport that I was unafraid and willing to be free in doing the best I could. It was also a way to spend time with girls and boys and not wander the playground alone. I remember one time some of the cool popular kids heard some of my former friends making fun of me, and they stood up for me.

I had a September birthday. When I was entering third grade, there was a law that changed. It used to be that if you were 5 by November 1 you would enter kindergarten that school year. But it was moved back to September 1. Several students in my class were held back. My parents decided to keep me in the grade I was in. Academically I was doing well. But I always felt socially young compared to everyone else in my class. Even into high school I tended to be drawn to friends that were a year or two younger than me.

I look at my parents' decision to homeschool me, and considering who I was as a sixth grader, I think it was a good choice for me long term. I know who I was that year, and what I longed for, and if my parents had kept me in public school with more of the freedom that junior high would have brought, I think I could have headed into choices that would have brought a lot of turmoil into my life. Wanting to be accepted and being so naïve, I am sure I would have had multiple boyfriends by the end of junior high, and who knows what other choices I might have made. I am grateful for that part of their choice.

I also learned a lot of life-giving skills that I bring into my days now. My mom would have me make a family meal every week. I would help her out with grocery shopping. She taught me how to sew. I learned how to play piano, and I wrote many songs when I was in high school. I started babysitting for many great kids. The experience I had helping out with my sister was a huge life skill that I could bring into the babysitting jobs. I took swimming lessons and dance class. And for recess I could watch Anne of Green Gables.[3] (Okay now I am starting to sound like the cliché homeschool girl!)

But in the midst of that, I still felt isolated and alone at times. Those years are just awkward for almost anyone. For me, I mostly wore sweatpants and baggy shirts. Occasionally my grandma would take me shopping at Meier and Frank, and she would pick me up something name brand, like these Guess black jeans that I wore for a while. I remember when my mom had to take me bra shopping for the first time, we ran into a mom of a boy I had a crush on in sixth grade. I was so humiliated, trying to tuck those things half behind my back as we visited with her for a few minutes.

Often I would spend my afternoons staring out the window when all the kids were let out of school, wondering what happened to the other students I had attended school with. I didn't even get a chance to say goodbye to them on the last day of sixth grade, because I was sick and missed it.

In seventh and eighth grade, my dad started taking me to youth group at church. I loved youth group. It was my two times a week I was able to socialize with other kids around my age. I lived for youth group each week. There was a couple that started a junior high choir, and we put on plays and performances at church. It was the highlight of my week. I remember one time, there was a solo that was going to be chosen for a song called "I Love You Lord." In the quiet of my room, I prayed before God, promising that if I were chosen for that song, I would sing it for Him with my whole heart. I found out the next week that I was given the solo. My heart soared with excitement for such a special gift from the Lord. It was one of the first times I remember praying for something I had wanted so much, and receiving a yes answer for it.

There was also a small group time at our church, when I remember our leader talking to us about doing daily quiet times. At that point I was not very consistent at reading the Bible at all. But our leader said to me in front of the group, "I bet Kari reads her Bible every day…" If she could have seen inside of my heart she would have known the truth. But that was when I made the decision to read my Bible every day. I began a habit that has been by my side almost every day of my life since, reading in my Bible and writing in a journal each day.

Once I was at a friend's house. She was talking to one of the guys from church who told her he was depressed and was going to kill himself. I remember taking that to heart, and I went home and told my dad. My dad passed that on to the youth pastor, who called the guy to check in on him. The next day at church I walked up to the group that I spent time with the most, and as I approached I realized they were making fun of me for telling my dad what I had heard.

I never felt fully safe to be vulnerable with that group of friends after that. I still had those friends, but I felt so young with them, compared to where they were in life. There was the time that I went to a sleepover at one of their homes for a birthday. At the end of the evening they put makeup on me. I remember looking at myself in the mirror and crying. I didn't know if I was supposed to wear makeup, so I didn't know if I would get in trouble for it. And I was scared by the face in the mirror that I didn't recognize.

Toward the end of middle school youth group, I found a friend. Her name was Amy. We would go to the church library and check out the latest Christian fiction books there, and sit next to each other before group time and read next to each other. But Amy was a seventh grader and I was an eighth grader, which left me without a close friend when I made the jump into high school youth group—High Life.

The time came to graduate from eighth grade and move out of the comfort of everything familiar with the leaders we had in middle school, the safety among friends. I was definitely an awkward homeschooler at this point. I wore my homemade homeschool dresses I had sewn. There was loud music blaring, a lot of very tall students, and I felt very small and unseen. The other girls in my grade seemed to have no problem engaging and conversing with all the different ages of young adults. I sat in the back, feeling very lost and alone. I went to the youth group for about a month, and I would come home after church and lock myself in my bedroom and cry for a long time. I remember there was one time two of the girls that I didn't know reached out and said hi to me. I didn't know how to respond at that point—I was terrified of saying the wrong thing or doing something uncool. I went home once again and cried.

I entered into a deep struggle with depression. I found myself getting lost in the books I read, writing stories, dreaming of other realities than the one I was in. When I faced my reality, it meant much pain, brokenness. Depression is a very dark place to be. It is a lie that traps you with so many more lies about yourself. Lies you start believing and building up as a foundation of who you are. I was defining myself by those whispers in the moments of loneliness. I allowed darkness to cover my soul.

Psalm 11:2 (NASB)

For, behold, the wicked bend the bow, They make ready their arrow
upon the string to shoot in darkness at the upright in heart.

I stopped going to youth group. I couldn't handle the emotions of feeling so lost every time I went. I chose to sit with my parents at church for one of the services, and then I would help in the 2s and 3s class at our church. I loved that time with little kids. My sister was in that age group, and my mom also helped teach my sister's class. When I started I was just a helper. By the time I was in ninth grade, I was the first junior helper that was asked to teach a Sunday School class of my own. I was so nervous about it, but I was given this group that was to be my own class, that I could teach and show Jesus' love to.

And yet...conviction hit my heart. Here I was, showing them how much Jesus loved them, and then I was coming home and crying, feeling depressed and alone. And I realized something needed to change—that if I was to be an example to these little ones, I needed to believe it with all my heart, soul, mind and strength.

The Lord began to break through those walls of depression in my life. He started to shed His light in those dark places through the work of being able to take my eyes off of myself, my inadequacies and awkward tendencies, and just come willing to love and care for others more than myself. In learning that lesson, I found a mystery unlocked, the answer to no longer being under the control and influence of my emotions in those moments. A way to take my eyes off myself and see the needs of others and show them Jesus' love. What freedom I found in that.

1 John 4:11–13 (NASB)

Beloved, if God so loved us, we also ought to love one another. No one has seen God at any time; if we love one another, God abides in us, and His love is perfected in us. By this we know that we abide in Him and He in us, because He has given us of His Spirit.

By the end of my ninth-grade year, I had walked through a transformation of my mind. I found myself at a point of no longer being afraid of myself. I went to summer camp that year a different person. I made friends and lived unafraid. I started getting involved in the worship band and playing piano on the team. I was finding a place of belonging in the body of Christ because I had my eyes fixed on Him.

My Dear Children,

Depression is such a dark place to live. It can be all consuming. Lies from Satan will come at a person in full force in that lonely world. Cling to His word during those seasons. Break down those lies Satan tells you, and replace them with words of truth from the Bible. Don't let the arrows Satan wants to throw at you in those shadows penetrate the shield of faith you can carry.

Find ways to praise the Lord for the few good things each day. Turn your gaze from yourself. It is easy to feel so inadequate in those spaces of depression. Turn towards the One that wants to shine His light over you.

Days are precious. Find joy in serving others, loving those that need His touch. It is one of the best medicines out there.

I love you, my littles. Know that you have a Father that loves you more deeply than I or anyone else in your life could ever reach.

Always,
Your Mama

John 10:10 (ESV)

The thief comes only to steal and kill and destroy. I came that they may have life and have it abundantly.

Ephesians 6:16 (NIV)

In addition to all this, take up the shield of faith, with which you can extinguish all the flaming arrows of the evil one.

I had always been a bit boy crazy as a child. I had multiple crushes in elementary and middle school, and that followed right into high school. Silly schoolgirl stuff, writing the boy's last name at the end of Kari Anne... with lots of flowers and hearts. I was caught up in the romance of books like Anne of Green Gables[4] and Little Women.[5] I never liked the end of Little Women—it always disturbed me a bit, because I really believed Jo should have married Laurie, and she didn't. Anne of Green Gables always was my go-to. She was a girl with brains, she loved to write, and she used her imagination. She was everything I wanted to be, and she had the attention of Gilbert Blythe. Crazy girl, it took her forever to realize she had loved him all along, but she finally confessed the feelings for him she had buried deep. Happy ending finally ensues.

I was ready for it—to be caught up in the hopes and dreams of romance. I knew I wanted to be a mom someday, so I just needed to find the right guy to fill that role. I did things like write a love note in Double Dutch to a boy I really liked. Yes, I did. His friend intercepted that letter and poked so much fun over that letter. That was the end of the pursuit of that relationship.

Then in tenth grade, I fell for a guy that was in the two- and three-year-old class, helping at our church. He was a year older, on the quiet side, and loved kids. That is all I really knew about him. I felt very shy around him, and could barely talk to him other than things regarding the kids. I found his address in the church directory and started typing out secret friend letters. Oh my goodness, I still can't believe I would do that to this poor guy. After several months of faithfully sending my letters in the mail, I couldn't take him not knowing anymore. Then I typed a letter, put it in a bag with a random assortment of gifts I had made for him (including homemade cookies), and handed that bag to his mother at church. I turned beet red and left it with her. The things we girls do to boys!

The thing was, I had my dream given to me of what I wanted to do, when I was only 11. I knew more than anything I wanted to grow up, get married, and be a mama of beautiful children. I was on the pursuit to figure this dream out. But I was so young. My friend Amy's older sister once told me, when I was wondering why there weren't any boys interested in me, "You are the type of girl that boys would not want to date, but they would want to marry someday." I was pretty intense and determined in my dreams. That would scare most high school boys away.

After this boy found out who his secret friend was, I still felt pretty shy. We would talk a little bit and I liked getting to know little pieces about him. But he never pursued me. And I got impatient with this. I just wanted to know I was likeable by a boy. A few years before, a boy told me I was cute. But then I found out two weeks later that he had told several other girls the same thing. Yep, a player. Yet a comment like that had given my heart a boost to carry out a crush with that player boy for two years. I couldn't let it go.

As my sophomore year progressed, nothing really picked up with the boy at church. He moved away over the summer after his dad got a job in a different state. He wrote me one letter at the beginning of his senior year, letting me know he had a girlfriend. That was when it was clearer than ever. If he had been interested in me, he would have pursued me. And he didn't. I don't blame him—I probably came across as a bit stalker-esque and scary with my typed-out letters to him. He wasn't the guy for me and I definitely was not the girl for him.

My second high school crush was the brother of one of the girls in my two- and three-year-old class. (Who knew Sunday School was the place to meet boys?) This boy would help out in the Sunday School on the weeks he was there. He came every other week when he was with his dad. His parents had split when he was younger. He was a year younger than me, I thought he was pretty cute, and again, guys that are good with kids was a number-one seller for me.

Once more, I didn't really know too much about him. What I knew was that I wanted a boyfriend. I wanted to experience a first kiss and have a boy hold my hand, to be special to someone. A crush developed, and he seemed like he might have been interested in me too. That was a first for me.

What I also didn't know was what my rules were in the area of boys. My parents had made it clear they really would prefer me not having a relationship with a boy, unless I was considering marriage. Being too young for marriage meant I was probably a little young in their books to be having a relationship. But nothing was ever really spelled out directly. It was done by taking me to courtship seminars for homeschoolers. There was a big movement in the homeschool world in my teenage days based on a book called I Kissed Dating Goodbye.[6] I thought the idea was an interesting one; however, it was not my own personal conviction.

I had a deep longing for attention. After a few months of exchanging looks and talking a few times, that boy asked me out, and I said yes. I didn't ask my parents. I didn't want to know their answer, and I figured if I didn't ask, then I wasn't disobeying them—just going behind their back instead. Totally okay, right? I experienced a boy holding my hand for the first time, and a few days later, my first kiss. I was in a dream world, a happiness that I believed would not be broken.

As I write this, my heart breaks over what I did to this boy. To my parents. And to myself. I used this boy for attention and affection. I wasn't thinking of him. I was thinking of how good it felt to have him like me. Pay attention to me. I was so selfish. If only I had handled things differently. A few weeks into this, I remember giving him a kiss goodbye at church, and I came home to my dad telling me we were going to take a drive. My dad was not happy.

He drove silently. As the tension built, he told me that I needed to share with him what was going on, and the longer it took for me to say whatever it was I needed to say, the worse my punishment would be. As he drove around back roads waiting for me to speak, I was afraid. I knew that once I spoke, everything I had loved about the last few weeks was going to come to an end.

Once the fears were broken through, I confessed. I told him about having a boyfriend and holding hands and kissing. I'm sure my dad's heart broke just a little to hear me confirm the truth that he had been informed about through my younger brother. I know it must have hurt him to find out his daughter had been going behind his back and not talking through this area with him first. It was what it was. There was no changing the past.

My parents grounded me for a month from all the things a homeschool high school girl would never want to give up. I was forced to break up with him. No friends, no phone calls, no youth group. My dad said no worship band either. He told me it was not okay for me to be doing something behind my parents' backs and then going on stage and leading worship at the same time.

The one allowance they gave was that I could still go to summer camp at church. The summer camp that would change my life.

My boyfriend was able to go on the trip too. I call him my boyfriend because even though I had "technically" broken up with him, I had not broken up with him in my heart. We sat next to each other on the bus. I was not going to hold his hand. I was not going to kiss him anymore. I planned on that trip to obey my parents. But then his hand found its way to mine, and I broke the promise I had made my parents. It felt so good to have his hand on mine. But I was breaking my promise to my parents and through that, dishonoring God.

That was how the course of the camp went. The first night one of the youth leaders even told me how proud he was of me for obeying my parents. A half hour later I went and kissed my boyfriend in his tent. We pretended in public that we were just friends, but in the shadows we were acting like much more. I knew I wasn't obeying God, and that made me sad. I just didn't know how to turn back.

On Thursday night there was a campfire for us. We were asked to go before the Lord in a time of communion, making things right before the Lord. I will share more about this night in my story about my husband. But I want to conclude this relationship first. I sat there next to my boyfriend, heart breaking that I wasn't right with the Lord. I knew what I wanted and didn't have. I couldn't have both.

That night I went back and made out with my boyfriend under the stars. And the next morning I knew I had to stop. I needed to get right before the Lord.

I actually got dehydrated. I was crying hysterically with my youth leader, feeling sick deep inside, and as I cried, in between taking gulps of water from a hose she had found for me, I knew I had to break up with him. Me, myself. Not just because of my parents, but now my heart knew it was the right thing to do. So I did. I officially broke up with him. I apologized for what I had done. Oh, if I could go back and return all the kisses and times holding hands with this guy. As this is written, my heart is heavily reminded of what I took from him. How selfish I had been. What I took from his future wife. I wish I could apologize to her. I wish I had saved my first kiss for my husband. I wish, I wish, I wish...but I can't change it. This is part of the brokenness in my story— I brought sin into my life in a way that affected others.

There is a beautiful conclusion to this. Once I made the choice to honor God by honoring and obeying my parents, something happened in my heart. It felt lighter and freer than I had felt in a long time. I drew closer to the Lord once more. When I came home, I immediately told my dad everything that had happened at camp. And I apologized. In the following weeks I had times of sadness and crying over the loss of the relationship. Moments when I would see him at church and talk briefly with him, knowing the relationship needed to move on. We attempted friendship afterwards, but there wasn't too much we could do there. I finished my grounding period that month of August and was ready to start my junior year.

Proverbs 28:13 (ESV)

Whoever conceals his transgressions will not prosper, but he who confesses and forsakes them will obtain mercy.

James 5:16 (ESV)

Therefore, confess your sins to one another and pray for one another, that you may be healed. The prayer of a righteous person has great power as it is working.

Colossians 3:20 (ESV)

Children, obey your parents in everything, for this pleases the Lord.

My Dear Children,

I want you to know that if you struggle, or make choices that aren't wise and bring heartbreak, you are forgiven and redeemed and chosen. Jesus always wants you back. As your parents, we hope that we can be there to walk alongside of you when you need support. Don't be afraid to find accountability and support. Also, as your parents, if we don't always make sense to you in these areas of your life, if we seem old to you and outdated in our advice, please respect us anyway. We are doing our best to help you live well.

If I could share one piece of advice from my own experience, love others with God's love. When we start loving in such a way that we can get something for ourselves, it is not real love at all. It is selfish and has the potential to steal and take what is not ours. And that is not from God, but from an enemy that would steal and devour you in a heartbeat, as well as those that you might take from.

We Love You Always!
Mama

Ephesians 6:1–3 (ESV)

Children, obey your parents in the Lord, for this is right. "Honor your father and mother" (this is the first commandment with a promise), "that it may go well with you and that you may live long in the land."

1 John 2:15–17 (ESV)

Do not love the world, or the things of the world. If anyone loves the world, the love of the Father is not in him. For all that is in the world— the desires of the flesh and the desires of the eyes and pride of life—is not from the Father but from the world. And the world is passing away along with its desires, but whoever does the will of God abides forever.

1 John 3:16 (NIV)

This is how we know what love is: Jesus Christ laid down his life for us. And we ought to lay down our lives for our brothers and sisters.

❧ THE MAN GOD HAD FOR ME ❧

Back in the middle of my sophomore year, in February, we had student leadership team meetings on a Wednesday night when youth group was normally held. I was on the worship band, so I was there to meet with our group. In walks this new guy who was barely my height, and I was such a snob. I remember thinking to myself, "What kind of guy shows up on student leadership team night for his first time at youth group?" I went home that night, and apparently my brother had met his brother at middle school youth group. We found out they were homeschooled just like us. They were in the area homeschool directory! Nick and Sam were their names. Great. A nerdy homeschool boy showing up at our youth group on a night meant for regulars. I had a thing about homeschool boys: that I would never like a homeschool boy. Never like a homeschool boy, *ever*.

A few months later on a bus ride to a youth group event, my friend nodded over at Nick. She whispered to me, "He kind of looks like your younger brother..." Case closed. Done deal. I told God that night, "I will *never* like Nick Adams."

Early that summer, we ended up in the same prayer group together. Really it was him, and a female leader, with several other girls. I wanted to make sure that Nick Adams knew I was not available, so I asked for prayer that evening for the boy that I liked, that we would be able to figure our relationship out. Just to make it clear to Nick that I was off the market.

Apparently that is when Nick decided he had no interest in some girl who would talk about liking another boy, in front of him, when he didn't even know her. He felt it was very inappropriate. So there you have it... deal done for him too.

Well, that is what we both thought, anyway.

At the summer camp I went to, mentioned in the previous chapter, one of the leaders came up to me. Remember, my boyfriend and I were giving the impression that we were obeying my parents and were no longer together. One of the youth group leaders, Alden, came over to me as he was having Nick and a few other guys set up volleyball nets for later that evening. He asked if I was still with my boyfriend, because, Alden said, "There is this boy that I think would be a great fit for you, but…" To which I responded, "We still like each other…we are just friends…" But suspicious and curious about whom this boy might be, I had to ask, "But who is this boy?"

Alden smiled, and—no big surprise to me—said, "Nick Adams."

"Oh, yeah…Nick. He's a nice guy. But no."

Over the course of that summer camp, I noticed little things about Nick. Not in an "I'm interested in him" sort of way. But I found him to actually be a very nice guy. He was always looking to help where needed and seemed pretty upbeat and friendly.

Thursday night came. The big night when God had prepared to show me under the veil of the darkness and stars what it was that I was missing. As the whole youth group circled around the campfire and we were asked to search our hearts before the Lord, I looked around at all the students, many of them goofing off, making jokes, not paying attention. But straight across from me, my eyes landed on Nick. There he was, his head bowed, praying before the Lord with a look on his face that said he truly was before the Lord searching his heart and asking Him to work in his life.

And as I looked at him, I knew I wanted that. Not Nick. I wanted to have that in my life. That deep, close, beautiful space before the Lord. To have Him fix what I had broken. To find sweet communion with Him once more.

And that is where I found myself the next day when I broke up with my boyfriend. This is the other part of the story of God doing something beautiful and big in my life in the midst of the brokenness.

That Friday afternoon, I was sitting talking through things with one of the leaders while she was playing cards with Nick. I was sorting out the choices I had made and the things I needed to do when I went back home. She got called to help with the boats and left Nick without a card partner. I took her place, and for the next hour Nick and I played cards and talked about life. What I found with Nick was a comfortable place to talk through things, and I also found a guy whose parents had a strict set of rules that sounded very similar to mine. I enjoyed our time together. It was probably the first time I had ever hung out with a guy, just me being me and him being him. I liked that a lot.

But I was not interested in him. Not at that point. I had just broken up with my boyfriend, and was just beginning to recover from a broken heart. The rest of the day I found myself talking to several different guys. Just talking and being friendly and not being afraid of boys anymore.

When I went home to my family, I first confessed everything to my parents, and apologized, this time with sincerity and a changed heart. I finished up my grounding period over the next few weeks. I did a lot of babysitting. And I went to church on Sundays, sitting in the junior high group with my dad that month during youth group time. The last Sunday I was grounded, I ran into Nick Adams again, who was with a few other guys. He asked me where I had been. He knew I had gotten in trouble for going out with a guy behind my parents' backs, but he had never heard of the idea of parents grounding their child from youth group. (For the homeschooled girl I was, it truly was a punishment.)

Nick asked if I wanted to go with his family to a homeschool day at Oaks Park, a local amusement park. His line was that he knew lots of other homeschool girls that he could introduce me to. I had been grounded for a month and was up for anything, but I told him he would need to ask my dad. There was no way I wanted to do anything to rock the boat again with my parents. "Honesty is the best policy" was my new motto. I took him with me (he will say I dragged him by the arm, which I don't really recall) and found my dad. My dad said he would like to meet Nick's parents. We walked across the parking lot in search of them, and my dad met Nick's mom. My dad and mom decided to take a day to think on it. I remember the next day they told me I could go. I was so excited to have something to look forward to after being grounded.

On September 6, 1994, Nick's family took me to Oaks Park. Now I will tell you, Nick did not introduce me to a single homeschool girl. However, we went on every ride together (which is amazing in itself because I hate amusement park rides), and we talked the entire time. We couldn't stop talking. Apparently his mom followed from a distance the whole time as well. Nick would say now that I had tricked him into thinking I was a girl that liked amusement parks. I didn't mean to trick him—I think it was just the response of letting loose after being holed up for a month. Truly anything that my parents would say yes to sounded great to me. I still didn't think much more than that he was a really nice guy, but God was opening my heart to a friendship only He could make happen.

For my Sweet 16, my parents put on a very nice formal dinner for me and my friends. It was the first party since kindergarten that I was able to invite boys to. My grandma took me shopping, and we found a beautiful soft pink dress on clearance at Meier and Frank for me to wear for the occasion. The weather couldn't have been better for that late September day. My mom played fancy classical music in the background, and my parents, brother and Abbie helped serve us our courses around the dining room table. Nick was included on the invite list. I remember after the party was all over, sitting out in the grass on the side of the yard talking with a few of my girlfriends. They were asking what I thought of Nick. I remember acknowledging to them that I thought of him as a friend I would like to get to know better. But that was the first time the thought of something more came into my mind. I let that thought settle and began to process it.

Within a week I received a letter in the mail from Nick. It was a very short letter, about three sentences long, thanking me for the invitation to the birthday party. He shared later that it took him over three hours to write it. This was a big deal for him. It was starting to become a big deal for me. I wrote him a note back, thanking him for coming. A few days later, he wrote me a letter back. Out of this was birthed our letter-writing friendship.

Nick grew up in Scappoose, which is about a 40-minute drive from Beaverton. Back in the day before cell phones, when home phones connected to the wall were the only way of contacting people, calling each other brought on long-distance charges. As we got to know each other, we talked on occasion over the phone, which caused charges of over $20 a month on my parents' bill. They handed that part of the bill over to me, and after a few months of paying for that with my hard-earned babysitting money, we stuck mostly to letters as our main form of communication. Stamps were just so much cheaper. And now we have decorated shoe boxes sitting in my hope chest filled with several years' worth of letters.

We saw each other at church and youth group twice a week. And there was the occasional homeschool event.

There was a place called Skate World. Sadly it shut down last year, but when I was growing up it was the place to have parties and skate in a circle under a glittering disco ball for cheap. Once a month they would have homeschool date day. Nick asked if my family wanted to join his family there about three weeks after our Oaks Park outing. We decided to go, and Nick and I skated around talking about anything and everything. Then the music slowed, and the DJ announced that it was time for couple skate.

Nick looked at me and asked if I wanted to couple skate. I looked at him and asked, "What's that?" Mind you, I knew exactly what couple skating was. When I was in sixth grade I still have a memory of my friend throwing me under the bus, telling a boy at our graduation party that I wanted to couple skate with him, which I had never said! I had walked off the skating rink in a huff, so humiliated! I was not going to let Nick in on that secret. Instead, I looked at him expectantly, waiting for him to explain it. He fumbled around with his words a bit, and I responded with, "We probably shouldn't..."

I had just gotten grounded for a month for holding hands with a boy—no way was I going to agree to hold his hand in a public setting with my mom and his mom and a bunch of other homeschool moms watching, setting off a string of gossip. We exited the skating rink, and I think maybe we went to get a Slurpee or licorice, something of that sort, while we waited for the awkwardness of the couple skate to end.

In October we had a pumpkin carving party with his family. I still remember his fingers faintly touching mine while we were working on our pumpkin as a team with my dad. This was so different than what I had created over the summer behind my parents' backs. This was supported by our parents, both families getting to know each other, providing opportunities for Nick and I to get to know each other too.

As Nick continued to write to me, he never communicated what his feelings might be towards me. Writing all this down now, I see it so clearly in the way he was intentionally looking for ways to pursue spending time with me. I should have left it as it was, but I was getting a little confused by what was going on between us, so I made the decision that I was going to find out what he was thinking.

On November 12, 1994, his parents invited my family and another family from church to dinner at their home in Scappoose. I was filled with hope and anticipation. Maybe this would be the day when Nick would say something to me about what he was thinking, what his feelings were. Instead, I watched him and his brother and the other guys set up the board game Axis and Allies, and I was left tinkering around on their Clavinova, occasionally checking in to see how the game was going. My frustration began to build as I watched the evening pass away with barely any time or attention given to me. About 15 minutes before I knew my parents would want to leave, I finally interjected and asked Nick if we could talk.

Outside to the front of the house we went. I took the lead, taking full charge of this conversation. I so badly wish I had just waited for Nick, but I wanted an answer...so I asked the question every teenage boy would love to be pounded with: "What are your intentions towards me?"

Talk about a loaded question. I think I needed some godly wisdom from an older woman about then...probably 10 minutes prior, to stop me from this craziness. But no, that did not happen. Nick stood there for a minute. Then something amazing happened. Through that conversation, we both admitted with words our feelings for each other. We knew we didn't want to have a casual relationship where you go out and break up. But we also knew that we would have a long road ahead of us in thinking of marriage. I knew in my heart that this was the real deal, and I started to believe that this was the man God had chosen for me to marry someday.

I will always wonder what would have happened if I hadn't initiated that conversation. I wonder if it would have made Nick work harder to communicate with me the thoughts and feelings he had for me. Nick told me later that he had no idea he needed to verbally tell me that he liked me.

For that moment though, that evening as my family loaded back into our blue Dodge van, I found my seat and landed on cloud nine. Nick liked me. I was the type of girl he would marry if we were older. He wanted to continue to get to know me. My heart was beginning to fill up with something so much more for this guy.

The first year of our getting to know each other did not involve many dates. We started taking turns going to each other's houses on Sunday afternoons. We would take walks outside together. Sometimes Nick's mom would send us on a walk to the grocery store for her, and we would get Dairy Queen and eat our ice cream together. That was the closest thing to a date we had that first year.

One day in December, Nick's mom invited me to come with her and Sam and Nick while they ran errands around town. Nick and I sat in the back seat of his family's Nissan Maxima during these errands. As we drove, Nick slowly put his hand over mine, and next thing I knew he was holding it. I was unsure what to do, because I wanted to hold his hand too. I wondered what his mom would think—how could she miss her son's hand on mine?

At the end of the trip, I told him that I thought he should ask my dad if it was okay to hold my hand. Once again, I didn't want to do something that my parents would not be supportive of. He agreed and said he would ask my dad.

Nick's mom was putting together a Christmas party for homeschool teenagers on a Friday evening. Nick was a wreck at the party. Earlier he had asked my dad if he could hold my hand, and my dad asked Nick why he wanted to hold my hand. Nick was unsure how to answer, so he asked my dad if he could have time to think about it. And my dad said, "Okay, but it's going to cost you." Now, Nick didn't know this, but my dad was teasing him. Nick took it so seriously and was so afraid that his asking for time would truly cost him.

He asked me if he could talk to me for a moment. At first I thought he had an answer about what my dad had told him; however, as we stood on the side of the room and Nick opened up his heart, I realized he was sharing something so much deeper and more painful than I ever saw coming.

"Kari, I just found out that my best friend as a kid was hit by a car and died two weeks ago." I stared at Nick and watched his face slump down in despair. "Kari, the worst part about it is that three weeks ago, God put it on my heart to call him...that I needed to call him. And I didn't...I just read it in the paper today."

Nick and I didn't have a chance to talk more that night. His mom said later that his heart was in deep turmoil and he could not sleep that evening, but spent much time talking and crying with her.

Over time, Nick shared more about his friend, Jeremy. He and Jeremy used to sing together in school. They did everything together until they entered middle school, when Jeremy got deep into drugs and alcohol and girls, and they went down separate paths. The brokenness he felt for his friend was so painful.

This was a huge turning point in Nick's life. It was one where he had so clearly heard the Lord speak to him and he didn't obey. I know Nick would have jumped at the chance to go back and change that decision...we don't know what each day brings. He learned a very hard lesson, which he took with him in future decisions: If the Lord speaks to you, *obey*.

The following week, Nick brought back an answer about the hand-holding. He told my dad that holding my hand showed me that he trusted me.

My dad gave us permission to hold hands.

The Sunday before Christmas at youth group, Alden teasingly asked me how things were going with Nick. I told Alden I was going to marry Nick Adams someday. Now, Alden didn't criticize my naive notions or put them down. He just gave me a knowing smile and then went on to teach us a lesson. It was about how God told Mary something at a young age, that she was going to carry His Son, and how she believed and treasured these things in her heart.

Afterwards, Alden told me this: "Kari, when you said you were going to marry Nick someday, I kind of laughed at the idea of it, with you being so young. But if God has shown you that is what He has for you, treasure it in your heart, and see what God does." I never forgot that.

My Dear Children,

 I pray for days as you grow older when you will draw close to the Lord. Truly, He is the only one that can satisfy. If you come close to Him, and know Him more intimately, He will start dreaming with you of things He wants to do with you in this life. I am excited to see those dreams come to fruition. If the Lord gives you a vision, don't be afraid of it. Keep drawing closer. He has made each of you so unique and full of gifts and abilities that He has for you. Listen to those words, pay attention to those cues. Give those dreams to Him. You may find in those dreams that you have to lay them back down before the Lord, because it is important that He is your everything, and that those dreams do not take His place on a pedestal. They are not made to take the place of Him and become something to worship. They are made to be something you can use with Him for His greater purpose in furthering His kingdom. So whether it is a relationship that God puts upon your heart, or a job, or a way of serving, He is longing to do those things with You. Take Him with you on the greatest journey of following those paths and places He will lead you. I'm so excited to watch!

Love You Always,
Mama

Luke 2:19 (ESV)

But Mary treasured up all these things, pondering them in her heart.

The First Season of Waiting

I want to take the next few chapters to write about my life over the six years Nick and I waited for marriage. As I write, it may not all be in chronological order. Each story has separate, challenging, and yet beautiful lessons that can be shared, and yet some may overlap or appear out of order.

❧ GOD WHO HEALS ❧

This isn't my favorite part of the story of my life. But it is what happened and real, and it brings sadness to go back through some of it. It was an underlying area of struggle in our relationship, and I hope that my sharing might be of encouragement to those that are at a place of making decisions in their relationships, that they might make different ones and be wiser than we were…

Nick and I set some rules for our relationship early on. My family was not supportive of marriage until a man is able to provide for a family. Nick and I agreed with this. We wanted to make sure that if we got married, for the lives of our children to come, we would be able to provide a home, and I could stay home and care for our children. I also had a personal conviction that when I got married, I wanted to allow the Lord to provide as many children as He would give us, and I would not use birth control. We knew we were in for a long haul of waiting.

My personal rule, after my first relationship, was no ring, no kissing. I had experienced how quickly kissing could become intense, so I wanted to make sure that the next man I kissed would be my husband. For me it was a physical guard I wanted to set.

Nick's personal rule was he would not tell a girl he loved her unless he was proposing to her. He had seen friends use those words with many different girls, and for him, those words were something of high value and meaning. He didn't want to use those words lightly. For Nick it was an emotional guard he wanted to set. My second rule, stemming from his rule, was that I didn't want to initiate the words "I love you" first. We both were going to wait to say that.

Nick and I started meeting together after Sunday night church to pray with each other. Maybe it wasn't the wisest decision, going upstairs to a corner of a church that not many people used, to be by ourselves to pray. Our hearts were in the right place, but maybe choosing a more public spot would have been wiser.

In my mind, Nick was this amazing, perfect, too-good-to-be-true guy. He was a servant, kind with his words, a gentleman, thoughtful of others. But there was a struggle he was dealing with, and on one of those nights we met to pray, he opened up about his struggle.

Nick was very serious when he told me there was something he needed to share with me. I didn't know what to expect. He started to tell me a story of when he was watching a certain movie with his parents, and he saw something in it that caused him to lust. He now found himself in the middle of a struggle with pornography and masturbation. He hated it. He hated himself when he did it. He wished he had never fallen into it. He kept trying to give it to the Lord, and found himself stumbling over it again and again.

I had had a boyfriend prior to Nick, but I was still very naïve and innocent about this struggle and what it entailed. As he sat there next to me, tears in his eyes, asking for my forgiveness, I told him of course I forgive you. Relief flooded his face, and he told me thank you. Nick had found a place of safety in sharing that with me.

For the first few years, we treated each other with much respect. In regards to our rules, we are both firstborn, headstrong children, and when we make a decision, it is rock solid. However, we found ways to work around those rules. As far as not saying I love you, I found very creative ways to express those words without actually saying them. And when it came to kissing, we didn't kiss. But slowly, as time went on, and especially at the end of high school into the college years, we started pushing boundaries and limits, mistreating each other in this way physically. We wanted to be close...we cared deeply for each other. But we were not married, and not planning on getting married for several more years, and we began to stumble. I am grateful to say as I write this that we never had sex outside of marriage. I am so grateful for that. But we did sin in various ways that were not right before the Lord. We knew it. It followed the same pattern as Nick's struggle with pornography and masturbation. We would lust for it, then stumble, and then I would hate it, and hate myself for not stopping it.

I had my own struggles with wanting attention from other guys that began to surface at the end of high school. Nick was so busy, and there were other guy friends that were around more. I longed for that attention that Nick did not have time to give. He even broke up with me for a week after I started to pursue a relationship with someone else. I broke his trust. It was one of the most painful weeks of my life. It was also a really good time of leaning into the Lord like never before and trusting Him. I found myself at a place at the end of that long week, recognizing I would be okay whether Nick took me back or not. When he saw I had surrendered myself back to the Lord, he ended the separation period. Sadly, the passion that we felt from that short separation drew up even stronger emotions that led to more physical struggling.

Nick began to pull away from me. By the time his sophomore year of college came around, he had started making excuses to avoid seeing me or taking me home, claiming he was tired. Then I would hear later how he went and hung out with his friends. I would get so frustrated. We were terrible at communicating through this. Instead of being straightforward and truthful about what was going on, so we could work through it, he avoided me like the plague.

I felt lonely during those times of my life. I wanted his attention so badly, and I didn't know how to get it. I started taking it out on my hair. The first time was when he went away for a weekend to see his high school best friend who had gone away to college. I was upset that I couldn't go with him. In response, I decided while he was gone to chop my hair off. Not just a few inches, but the shortest I had ever cut it. I knew he liked it long. I wanted something different. I will never forget his words when he returned from his trip: "That is the ugliest haircut I have ever seen!" Oh, he was mad. But I had his attention.

My struggle for attention turned into wanting to be "beautiful." I thought maybe if I could get my hair lighter, that would do the trick. I would try box kit after box kit—my dark hair did not get lighter. I would pay to have highlights done. But then they would grow out. My "darkest" moment in my hair coloring addiction involved Nick's mom Sue helping me strip my hair color—turning it to a clown-colored red, and then recoloring over the top of it a lighter brown. But eventually it grew in dark again. There were weekends when I would color it three times, trying to achieve the right color, hoping it would catch Nick's attention. I was abusing myself in a very unhealthy way. And it was not getting Nick's attention.

I felt completely stuck, and as I kept trying to recolor and cover my hair, deep down it was an attempt to recover and fix my mistakes and struggles and hurts. I think that is what we do with sin. We try to cover it up and make it beautiful, but it really does not look beautiful. My hair was terrible looking while Nick was in college. It had its moments, but mostly, it was pretty bad. This struggle went on for a couple years and was a very expensive addiction (especially when I would apply several boxes in one weekend).

During Nick's junior year, our physical struggles had gotten so bad that we decided we needed to take a month and pray about whether or not we should permanently break up. During that month, Nick's mom Sue invited me to go on a retreat with her. It was not the type of retreat I was accustomed to. It was called an "aglow" retreat. I will say I did not agree with certain aspects of things that went on during that time—you could definitely call it charismatic to the fullest—but it was a retreat where God did a major healing in my life.

It is hard to explain in details, but one of the nights, the speaker was inviting people to come and be anointed with oil. As other ladies had their hands anointed with oil. I knew I needed to go. When I came to the speaker, I knew I didn't want my hands anointed. I pointed to my hair. And she looked at me with these eyes that were as if the Lord were looking right into my heart, and nodded, and said, "Yes, yes," as she anointed my hair with oil. I went outside and fell into Sue's arms and cried for 15 minutes...15 minutes of releasing all the hurt and pain and sin that I had piled into this struggle of dying my hair over and over again.

God used that weekend to teach me to forgive myself. I had so many times fallen and struggled with Nick, and instead of trying to change, I hated myself for it and used the hair dye to cover it up and heal the hurt, which it never did. I wasn't really aching for attention, I was aching to be healed and to be forgiven...and the person that wasn't forgiving me was myself.

I left that retreat changed. When I came back, Nick and I still had our times of struggle, but when we did, I knew that I had a Savior who still loved me and wanted to help me change. And that set me free. We chose to keep pressing ahead and trying to finish the waiting period that remained before us as Nick wrapped up his junior year and headed into his senior year of college.

But the coolest part of this time of healing was yet to come. Two weeks later, I was going to meet my friend after work to hang out. While she finished work, I wandered into Albertson's next door. It had been a month since I had colored my hair. My roots were starting to grow out a little, showing a little color variance, and I found myself wandering down the hair color aisle. I thought to myself, "Well, maybe just to cover the grow-out..."

As I reached for the box and picked it up, this voice behind me said, "You don't need that." What? I turned around to see a guy named Shane. He was a guy that had come to our college group at our church a few times, and was a single dad. I didn't know too much more about him. I smiled and rambled something about how I was thinking of covering my hair color. We chit-chatted another minute, and before he turned to go, he looked me in the eye and said to me one more time, "You don't need that." Then he walked away. As I turned back to the shelves of hair color, looking down at the box, I smiled. I put it back and said to God, "You are right, Lord, I don't need that." And I walked away.

Now that I am older, I do color my hair for gray coverage. There is nothing wrong in the act of hair coloring. The problem lay in the reason why I was coloring my hair. I know that back then, God completely healed me of that struggle. It was something I could not have done on my own. It was something that was completely out of my control. And I am so grateful for that healing.

We do have a God that heals. And I love that because I was set free from that struggle, my hair grew out long and healthy by the time I got to walk down the aisle and take my vows to marry my husband.

Now whenever I think of others that may be struggling, I remember that voice telling me, "You don't need that." And I pray if there is a struggle, an addiction in your life, an area where you are trying to cover up hurt and pain and sin, that God may set you free and that you can hear a voice tell you, "You don't need that!" Because you don't. You need Jesus.

My Dear Children,

As you will continue to read into this story, you will see how this area is of deep concern and how much pain can come from it. Purity of heart is an area we long that each one of you would carry with you in the decisions you make in relationships and how you treat others. Just remember that each girl and boy is someone's sister, brother, daughter, son, maybe someday to be someone's father or mother. And most importantly, that each one is a creation of the Living God.

When I was growing up, my parents gave me a nameplate. On it was my name, the meaning of my name, and a verse with it:

Kari ~ Pure One

Proverbs 4:23 (NASB)

Watch over your heart with all diligence, for from it flow the springs of life.

I pray that you can learn what it means to set a guard over your heart with all that you watch and listen to and see and feel and think, that you would give the Holy Spirit a place to stand guard over your heart, protecting and filtering what is brought inside of you.

I pray this because I know just a tiny glimpse of the type of hurt that can come from it. Ultimately in James 1, lust conceived brings sin that is accomplished, and brings forth death.[7] It may seem good in the moment, but please know that you need to fight against these temptations.

I pray, Josiah, that you will care for any girls that God brings into your life as fine treasures, to be cherished and saved for the one that God may have them marry. Be sensitive to how deep their emotions can flow, and don't use those emotions to get things that are just so temporary. And Ava, Lena and Mallory, you are treasures to the Lord. It can feel so wonderful to have love and care, but save your vulnerability and intimacy for the one that you would commit to on the altar.

I also just want to tell you, my children, that if you ever do stumble in this, know that your father and I understand, and we want to be here for you to walk through it and give you support that you need, bringing you back to the One that does not want to heap shame on you. Satan would have you believe lies in those dark places, that you are unforgiveable, but know that it is not true. You have a Savior who wants you to be free and live in His Light and Truth, where freedom is found.

I Love You, Dear Littles of Mine,
Mama

1 Corinthians 10:13 (NASB)

No temptation has overtaken you but such as is common to man; and God is faithful, who will not allow you to be tempted beyond what you are able, but with the temptation will provide the way of escape also, so that you will be able to endure it.

1 Corinthians 6:18 (NASB)

Flee immorality. Every other sin that a man commits is outside the body, but the immoral man sins against his own body.

Romans 12:1–2 (NASB)

Therefore I urge you, brethren, by the mercies of God, to present your bodies a living and holy sacrifice, acceptable to God, which is your spiritual service of worship. And do not be conformed to this world, but be transformed by the renewing of your mind, so that you may prove what the will of God is, that which is good and acceptable and perfect.

❧ COLLEGE CHOICES ❧

As I approached the end of our junior year of high school, I did not know what I was going to do once I finished my high school education. My grades were average; my SAT scores were average. But sadly, I made the choice to cheat when I was homeschooled, in the subject of math. I was really good at math back in elementary school days. I would sit under the teaching and I understood what I was learning; I was in the top math groups when they broke us up into school.

This would be where I would say homeschooling didn't pan out so well for me. When I got into pre-algebra, I didn't understand what I was learning. My mom tried to help the best she could, but she didn't understand. There were not a lot of choices in curriculum back then like there are now. I was stuck with this Saxon math book, and when I tried to go back to find foundational building blocks for whatever new problem I was working on, I could not figure it out. One thing I have found is that I do well watching problems and then copying the patterns. I am definitely a hands-on person—you can tell me a thousand times how to do something and it will go in one ear and out the other, but once I am doing something with my hands, I pick it up pretty quickly.

This whole trying to read it in a textbook and learn it did not work for me. I would spend hours a week trying to figure it out. Then when my mom couldn't help me, it meant my poor dad had to spend his evenings after working all day trying to help me—taking up most of the evening just to figure one thing out. After a while, falling so far behind and not understanding concepts, I cheated. I knew it wasn't right. I wish I had not cheated. In the middle of high school, I confessed to my parents that I had been cheating for several years, and that I had no idea what I was doing in math. My parents were saddened by this, and we started in half algebra again. But at that point I was beyond discouraged by this deep hole that I could not climb out of.

It is my one regret with being homeschooled.

However, God had put a dream in my heart, and it was to get married and have a family. And although I wasn't equipped in the area of math for college, I did learn plenty in the areas of cooking, cleaning, sewing, crafting, childcare...life skills that I am so grateful I was trained in while at home.

When the question of college started surfacing, I wasn't sure what I should do. Nick and I had talked a lot about how we wanted to figure out ways to do school debt free. We didn't want to go into huge debt that we would have to carry into the next stage of life, so we started looking at our options of how we could do this. We prayed over it and asked the Lord to show us how to do it, and for His provision and direction.

Nick is kind of a genius, so he had no problem teaching himself math and other subjects at home, and getting very high SAT scores. He played soccer for his school, was in marching band for many years, and we both volunteered in high school for Habitat for Humanity, so he was an all-around dream student for most prospective colleges.

I, on the other hand, had no idea what direction I would take in school. I was a dreamer, a creative type, and although there are great schools out there for things like that, they are very costly, and jobs that come from those things, don't often have a high return on what you can make doing them.

I knew I wanted to be a mom, but I also loved music and writing songs in high school. I remember talking to Nick about this, and he gave me an ultimatum, pointing out that pursuing music didn't necessarily go with the life of being a mom someday...so I gave up that dream, because I wanted the wife and mom dream more. I will tell you later how God gave me a small gift back in that, when we helped plant a church later.

I thought about doing beauty school—I always loved to do hair—but my dad didn't think this was a good idea for me, because he felt I would get discouraged if someone didn't like how their hair turned out. I dropped that dream too. Once again, God took that dream and gave me a small gift back in that now, with three girls, I get to use my hair-styling abilities every day.

I don't think my parents meant not to help me in these areas. I think they were frustrated too, and not sure what to do with me. My dad was a hard worker and provided all that he could give for his family. He worked many overtime hours to make ends meet and allow my mom to stay home and care for us kids. I am sure if they could, they would have loved to provide a financial way to help me with school. But it just wasn't an option. And I didn't have good enough grades to get scholarships, so I was at a point of feeling very directionless my senior year.

As Nick started to visit different schools his senior year, we started to think through what our life would look like, apart from each other. He took weekend trips with his mom to visit schools in Idaho and Seattle. He also considered Portland State. The schools that were away from home both offered him partial scholarships, but it was still more expensive than staying local. He decided after much prayer and consideration that he would choose Portland State.

Looking back at how those four years of college went for him, I don't think our relationship would have lasted if he had gone away to school, so I am grateful that he ended up in Portland. As he began meeting with a counselor at the school to prepare for the following year, she was sure he would get a scholarship that would cover most of his tuition. He turned in all the paperwork required for this scholarship and waited. When he found out he did not get the scholarship, his counselor was shocked, and commented that unfortunately, because of the homeschool high school umbrella program we had done through a private school that was not accredited, he got overlooked.

But then, a short time later, his counselor called to say there was another scholarship she was going to submit paperwork for on his behalf. A few weeks later, Nick found out he had a full ride scholarship from Walmart to attend Portland State. We were shocked and amazed and blessed. We had been praying for Nick to do school debt free, for a provision and a way for it, and the Lord honored that request.

I turned in paperwork to attend the local community college and tested into math at a level that would have required an extra year to catch up to college level. I decided I would take classes to obtain a one-year business certificate. To help pay for it, after a seven-year career as a babysitter, I retired and started working at the local Burgerville.

Plans made, we started plugging along at what was in front of us. Nick worked part time all the way through college on top of his 18-plus credit terms, to pay for gas and food, etc. I worked at Burgerville for more than eight months. It was a fun job working with other kids my age. But the days started early. I would get up at 4:00 in the morning to be at work by 5:00. My shifts were typically 5:00 a.m. to 1:30 p.m., and then I would head off to my afternoon classes, finding myself in bed by 8:00 most nights. Toward the end of my time there, they started mixing up my shifts, having me work some 5:00 p.m. to 9:00 p.m. shifts, and then come back at 5:00 in the morning. After doing that for a month, I decided it was time to move on.

I moved on to working at a local drug store. It was closer to home, and the hours were better than those at Burgerville. I did my best to keep my register organized, but somehow my till would always be off by a few pennies here or there. I rang up customers' purchases and tried to be friendly and efficient. It was not a long-term career job, but it paid the bills.

In the beginning of March, I was contacted by the father of a family I used to babysit for on a regular basis. He owned a real estate company and was looking for someone to come work part time for him as a receptionist and administrative assistant. I had been offered the same job almost a year prior. However, I had just been hired on at Burgerville, and my dad did not think it was a good idea for me to quit a job right after I started—he felt that I should practice commitment. I let it go in that season, to honor my dad, and stayed with Burgerville. When I started looking to move on from Burgerville, I inquired about a job possibility with this man, but at that point he was set.

This time when he asked, I said yes. I gave my two weeks' notice to Drug Emporium. I hoped they would slowly release me of hours, but instead they loaded my last two weeks with an extra 10 hours each week.

In February I had gotten my first credit card from my bank. It was my own decision—I felt it was a grown-up decision. However, as grown-up as I may have felt when using my credit card, I learned very quickly when I received that first bill that I had spent more than I made. This is where grace came into play. God's grace allowed me to learn a lesson about debt that taught me very clearly I did not want to live in debt.

That month in March was one of the most exhausting months I ever worked. I was doing those 30 hours each week for my last weeks at Drug Emporium. It was finals week at community college. And then I started my new job as well, which was 20 hours a week. In the end I was very happy to be done with two jobs and school. But the blessing that came through that push was that God provided enough for me to pay that credit card bill. And after that, I cut that credit card up and decided, "I don't need that!"

My job at the real estate company felt like a transition into the grown-up work force. I learned a lot about myself through that job. I loved being a helper and getting to answer phones for the real estate company and the sister mortgage company downstairs, take messages, make sure messages were transferred over to agents, make photocopies, send out mailers, file, create books and spreadsheets. All of those little tasks I thrived and excelled in.

One day, driving home, my dad's black Dodge Challenger that he had given me to drive to and from work broke down. Black smoke followed me into the Chevron gas station on the side of the road, and I waited for my dad to come to my rescue. My dad was very knowledgeable at fixing cars. He purchased cars that he would be able to work on. Having my dad come to my rescue was no new thing. There were plenty of times when our affordable cars would break down, and he would bring his tool kit and his willing spirit, not afraid to get his hands dirty, and he would repair those broken parts. But this time, there was no fixing that could be done to the car. I had driven it into the ground.

As I told my boss about the dilemma of not having a car, he had his own dilemma. He was short having someone answer phones when I was not there, and asked if I would consider working for him full time. He offered me free use of a family car that was not being used, as long as I insured it, as part of my working full time for him. As I sorted through this decision of coming to work full time, I realized that a business certificate from school would probably not get me any further than what I was being offered now.

I made the decision not to continue my education, and I became a full-time receptionist and administrative assistant to my boss. I worked hard and was a helper. I even started doing errands for him, like taking real estate signs out to different locations. On one such occasion, I accidentally took off an electric side view mirror of his car. My hard-earned paycheck and my awesome dad went to work to find a replacement mirror at a car junkyard, and he helped me fix it. But that being the only casualty, the situation worked out well. I slowly started setting aside money to save for a new car, and eventually I was able to return the car to my boss and purchase a red Toyota Corolla. It chugged at a snail's pace up hills, but it was my very own first car.

About the time of my one-year anniversary with my grown-up, professional job, some rough changes came to the company. My boss ended up leaving the company and moving away, turning over what remained to his father, Dave, and his father's business associate. At this time, the mortgage company, run by my boss's mother, Patti, moved upstairs as well, so I started to get to know the ladies that worked there on a face-to-face basis.

Originally, I had been promised a raise after the first year, but as my former boss had to leave, he was not able to fulfill that promise. Dave and Patti made mention of the possibility of moving me over to work for the mortgage company side of the office. Nothing was happening, though, and I started to get a feeling maybe I needed to move on and start looking for another job. It turned out they were looking for an administrative assistant at our church, so I turned in an application and was called in for an interview.

I went to ask Dave and Patti if I could leave an hour early that day. They said, "Sure, as long as it's not an interview for another company." My face could not lie. I told them, "Yes, it is." They let me leave early, and in I went for the interview.

 The next morning, Dave and Patti brought me into the conference room. There they shared that they did not want me to leave, and if I would take the job as a loan processor, Patti and their daughter Susan would train me and they would give me a raise. I did enjoy working with them and felt loyal to them, so I accepted, turning down the job opportunity at the church. That very day they moved me to a desk in the back and set me to work for the mortgage company, hiring a receptionist to take my place within two weeks.

I ended up working for them for the next two years, while Nick wrapped up his sophomore year of college, all the way through the middle of his senior year. Dave and Patti treated me like a second daughter. Patti would often treat us to lunch. I experienced sitting in the passenger seat of her car with heated seats for the first time—I had never experienced such a luxury. Dave would often show up at work midafternoon with a Taco Time choco-taco or a hot fudge sundae from McDonalds down the road. Some mornings he would bring in a box of Dunkin Donuts. He spoiled us with goodies. He had season Trail Blazer tickets, and the first time he offered me tickets to take Nick out for a game was one of many times we got to see Nick's favorite team play, as a gift from Dave. (That first game we will never forget—we were at the Rose Garden until 11 at night, because the game went into quadruple overtime.)

I was there when their daughter Susan, who was pregnant with her first child, broke her water at the office and was quickly escorted by her mom and dad to the hospital, where she gave birth to her son Jacob. They were my work family.

During that season I prayed much for those I worked for. I tried my best to show the love of the Lord in my actions and in my work ethic. We had people in and out of the company that I got the chance to pray for and hear their stories. I learned to work efficiently, to be organized and thorough, and do my best to make sure boxes were checked and documents signed correctly.

Unfortunately, even in the best work families, you can make mistakes. I made a whopper of a mistake and hurt them very badly with one poor decision. There was this rep that used to come in our office. He was kind of cute—at least I thought so at the time—and our secretary was always teasing me that he liked me. I don't know why I fell for that, but my history with Nick being busy, and looking for attention from him instead of looking for the Lord to be my everything, definitely was a place where I would stumble and fall. After several months, this rep asked if he could take me to lunch—he had a new business he was starting and wanted to know if I would be interested in a position. I said yes, foolishly uncertain what I was hoping for. I had been with our company for a while, and part of me was ready to grow into something new. And part of me liked the idea of getting to go to lunch with this guy. It is so humbling to admit my fault in this, but I hope that from my mistakes, others can learn.

I drove to this lunch, where it turned out to be this guy and his boss. I found myself put in a corner, being asked about everyone I worked with. What I liked and didn't like about them. Words came out of my mouth about one loan officer that I had some frustrations about. I left the meeting feeling very misled and upset at myself for the words I shared.

Those words came back to bite me very shortly after. The next day, that loan officer I had spoken of told Patti, in front of me, everything that had happened, all the things I had said, things that hurt her, words I wished I could swallow up. I wish I had not even looked in that direction. Patti's heart was broken at the thought that I had even considered going to another place of business without talking to her about it. I felt so humiliated, because I had basically lusted after the idea of attention from another guy while I was in a relationship with Nick, and I had broken my testimony of showing God's love to those that had so graciously trained me and treated me like family. I wish I could have taken the one choice back that led to another choice that led to another choice. To shut those words down from a voice that said, "He might like you..."

The next six months I felt humbled like never before. Things were not the same between my boss and me. I could see the lack of trust she felt towards me. Over time it healed, but it is a regret I carry with me. I stayed there until the economy started to change in 2000, when refinances came to a halt, and the business had to be brought to a close. But it was a job that carried me through all of my waiting for Nick to finish school. A job that helped me pay for date nights with my broke student boyfriend, purchase my first and second cars, and save for my wedding. I will always be grateful for that season in my life, and the experiences and learning that the Lord provided through it.

My Dear Children,

I know someday you will be out in the world having to make choices of what to do as you start your life. Sometimes you may find yourself in jobs that are hard work, labor intensive, terrible hours, or working for managers that make things challenging. I call this the Joseph opportunity in life. Joseph was a man in the Bible that was put in places out of his control, and in situations where he was a slave. Three times Joseph, at his lowest, is brought up to help those in the midst of his affliction. He steps in where he has been placed to do his very best for God.

He helps bring clarity to a dream Pharaoh had, and he is quick to point out that the Lord is the one revealing the things he is showing Pharaoh, not Joseph. This leads Joseph into the third time God is going to raise Him up into a position of high standing. This time, it's to save the people of the world and to save the very family that sold him into slavery in the first place. God made him forget his hardships and made him fruitful in the land of his affliction.[8]

Just remember that when we do our work with the Lord, He can use it for bigger purposes that we may not see at the time. Or maybe we will never see it until eternity. Don't downplay the small roles in life. Those are for building character and strengthening you to be the men and women He is calling you to be.

I pray that if you find yourself in a Joseph situation, you will rely on the Lord to lead you into beautiful things for His greater purpose.

Love,
Mom

Ephesians 6:5–8 (ESV)

Bondservants, obey your earthly masters with fear and trembling, with a sincere heart, as you would Christ, not by the way of eye-service, as people-pleasers, but as bondservants of Christ, doing the will of God from the heart, rendering service with a good will as to the Lord, and not to man, knowing that whatever good anyone does, this he will receive back from the Lord, whether he is a bondservant or free.

Colossians 3:22–24 (ESV)

Bondservants, obey in everything those who are your earthly masters, not by way of eye-service, as people pleasers, but with sincerity of heart, fearing the Lord. Whatever you do, work heartily, as for the Lord and not for men, knowing that from the Lord you will receive the inheritance as your reward. You are serving the Lord Christ.

✎ MISSION TRIPS ✎

Starting at the time I was a senior in high school, I got to be part of three mission trips with our church. From my experiences, I learned a lot about living in humbling circumstances, trusting God in out-of-control situations, and seeing God work in ways I never would have expected. Each trip I went on taught me very valuable lessons, so I am going to take the time to write out what I learned from each one of those times.

Right after high school graduation, Nick and I went with a bunch of other students on a trip down to Mexico with our youth group. I had never been out of the country before, so this was a big deal for me. We were going to help out with an orphanage. The morning came to leave, and we loaded up in three oversized passenger vans that could hold 15 people each, with our leaders each taking turns at driving. We made stops along the way to get sleep for the night.

The world was barely entering the age of cell phone technology, so instead, we would make comments back and forth on CB radios. The vans were blue, red, and white, so we named them Blue Dog, Red Dog, and White Dog. On the trip down, I rode in Red Dog. That was the van driven by Nick's parents, who came along for the ride to help on the trip. Along the way, we got the awesome idea to practice being in Mexico's hot weather by rolling up the windows and blowing the heat on high for five minutes. At the end of that time, we went to turn on the AC to give us the much-needed relief. But in that moment, something happened. The AC stopped working. In fact, the heat would not turn off, and the rest of that trip Red Dog was a heating machine, affectionately, or maybe not so affectionately, christened "Hot Dog."

Working at the orphanage was hard work. We were doing a lot of labor-intensive jobs that required much energy and strength. We were all exhausted by the end of each night. It challenged each one of us in learning how to work together with others that maybe we would not have normally gotten along with. The fun part was getting to spend time with the kids that lived there.

We fell in love with those kids. Sue, Nick's mom, fell in love with a sibling set there. I could tell she would have done anything to have a way to take those beautiful children home with her. Back at home, Nick's parents were in the process of getting approved for adoption through the state, working with DHS. Caring for the fatherless was near and dear to their hearts. Later the following year, they would bring into their home Rachael, a beautiful 10-year-old girl to complete their family, giving them a daughter and Nick and Sam a little sister.

Many of the lessons I learned in Mexico revolved around contentment. There were families and children there that did not have much of anything, yet they seemed so happy with the little they had. It stretched me way past my comfort zone into areas that were hard but good for me. Being around a big group of people in close quarters, using unusual bathroom situations, and being surrounded by poverty, I found I had so much to be grateful for in my life, and I am glad I experienced that.

I am going to share about the third trip I went on next. I want to come back to my second trip at the end, so I'm not skipping it—just saving it for last. This trip was to Costa Rica. We were going to be visiting a family who served in Costa Rica, supported by our church. In the beginning I was debating whether or not I should go on this trip. A friend from our college group decided she would go, so I chose to sign up too. It wasn't necessarily something I felt like I had to do, but something I thought I should do. As it turned out, she was not able to go, so I was the only girl my age on this trip.

Nick's parents and his sister Rachael went on the trip as well. When we arrived, we stayed in this hotel that to me could have been a five-star resort from what I had ever experienced in the past. It was a large home with lots of columns and pathways, beautiful fountains and a pool. I remember being so excited and exploring the place with Rachael. It was a refreshing way to start off.

The plan for this trip was to head out to the jungle with the missionary family. They lived in the city part of the time and the jungle part of the time, where the father was working at Bible translation for a village close by. Their jungle home had some repairs that needed to be done, so part of the time there would be those needs to be cared for. The women that went on the trip were looking to spend time with the wife and mother, to encourage her and provide female fellowship.

We explored the city for one day before we left for the jungle. I was amazed at the sights to be seen in the local mall. There were TV monitors throughout the food court, and hundreds of people crowded in that area to watch the World Cup. It was a community affair. The little shops were different than anything I had ever seen. Some held authentic items made in Costa Rica, some not so authentic. Lots of bright colors greeted us left and right as we perused the city. The next morning, we packed up from that little resort and took all we had to the jungle. When we arrived, the missionaries' home reminded me of a tree house—it was raised up six or seven feet off the ground for when the rainy season hit. Inside the home, hammocks hung throughout, inviting anyone looking for a good nap or a place to read a good book to curl up there. The Williams family had three boys and two girls, so Rachael and I stayed on the designated girls side with their twin girls, Anna and Christina.

Our first morning in the jungle after breakfast, I headed out with all the men on the team to do the hard, labor-intensive work. I felt so out of place. Working in a dress was just awkward. All the other women stayed inside chatting away and the kids played. I struggled to figure out where I belonged. After that first day of working hard and wrestling through if that was the place for me, I found myself assigned the task of "babysitter." It wasn't what I planned on doing when I signed up, and I struggled, thinking about everyone who had paid for me to go on this trip, wondering if I were doing enough. Guilt shadowed my mind, telling me I should be out laboring with all of the men. Not having a female companion my age on the trip brought feelings of loneliness at times.

I did love my time with their kids while I was there. I enjoyed every moment I had with them on our adventures in the jungle of Costa Rica. Taking hikes, smelling the scents only to be found in the beauty of the rainforest. Swimming in a local stream,  where a short-lived sickness worked its way through my body from whatever extra was in that water. Seeing beetles and centipedes the size of my hand (the memory still grosses me out)! Trying to knock coconuts off of trees. Observing the roasting of meat over a fire, and getting to enjoy it later in amazing handmade tamales. Tamales with a flavor unrivaled here in the States. Playing spoons, a game I absolutely hate, but loved playing with all of them. Having girl talk with the twins and Rachael at night. I will always cherish those times. I am glad I got to be part of that trip.

Being a mom now, I look back on that time and I see the need I was meeting for that missionary homeschooling mama who just wanted to have adult conversation and fellowship with the other women on the trip. Through my taking on the task of spending time with her children and taking them places, I was able to help provide freedom for that. But at the time, I felt useless and really struggled with my identity on the trip. I think there were good lessons I learned along the way. Sometimes the jobs in front of us may not be as defined as we think. It can take a little sorting and wrestling to figure out exactly what our role may look like. And it is good to find contentment in the midst of uncertainty—learning to rest in those places where it may seem like we are not enough. By whose standard and rule was I judging myself? Was I meeting the expectations of the leaders on the trip? I had many doubts throughout the trip.

When Jesus went to work, it was all about the people: spending time with them, eating with them, doing life with them, listening, praying, sharing, and fellowship with those that needed it. That was essentially my purpose on this trip. For a doer like me, it was a hard task to take on, but it was exactly what He wanted me to do. Nothing else but to be. I think it is ironic, but so true, that often God's purpose for mission trips is not necessarily about the people you are serving, but to put you in uncomfortable situations that are out of your control, to mature and grow you and teach you to lean deeply into Him.

Between Nick's freshman and sophomore years, Nick and I decided we would like to do another mission trip. We looked into what was being offered at the church and decided to apply to go on the trip to Poland. They were looking for students to help out at youth summer English camp, which would involve times of talking with high school and college Polish students, practicing English with them, as well as doing Bible time together.

As it turned out, we were the only two that applied to go on the trip, and with it fast approaching, there was a decision to be made. It would not have been wise to send an unmarried, dating couple on a mission trip across the world. We began praying, and then the Lord provided Andrea, a sweet gal who was a few years older than us, to be the third member of the team.

Then, it started to rain. An extensive amount. It was labeled the 1997 Central European Flood, and later renamed the Millennial Flood. The Oder River, which runs through Poland and Germany, overflowed into much of the southern region of Poland. Buildings were covered up to three stories high in some areas. The missionary from Poland was unsure if the camp would be able to take place. With only a few weeks before our scheduled departure, we prayed again for the Lord to intervene and provide a way. He did, and on the day of our departure, I found myself flying on my very first, very long overseas international flight.

We were filled with anticipation and adrenaline. Switching planes to a Lufthansa plane, I found myself intrigued by words in another language throughout the plane. I wrote down the word I found next to the toilet—splukiwanier—which later I was told by one of my Polish friends was pronounced "svookivaniey." As the flight progressed we began to feel exhausted and slowly drifted in and out of sleep. Landing in Germany, we were on the hunt to find our next flight to our final destination: Wroclaw, Poland. Wroclaw is pronounced *nothing* like it is spelled in English, which we found out after several attempts asking for help getting to our next gate. The attendant looked confused until we showed him our ticket, when he pronounced with recognition and enthusiasm, "Ahh! Vroatswaf!" Nothing like it is spelled. But it was our first introduction to the differences between the Polish language and the English language. We were exhausted at this point, overwhelmed by the smells of cigarette smoke and musky perfumes for sale in the "duty-free" area nearby.

When we arrived in Poland, I learned that one of my bags took a tour to Germany and would arrive in a few days. Thankfully I had packed evenly in both bags and was good to go until it arrived at the camp where we would be staying. We did our best to stay awake as we met our Polish hosts, missionaries Doug and Lila and their two children, Natalia and Philip. They took us to their residence—I remember standing in awe as I looked at their home on a higher level of the building, never having witnessed someone living in a downtown area in an apartment-like building. It was very foreign to what I considered a home for a family at the time.

They packed up their final belongings, and we began our drive to the countryside where the camp was going to be held just outside the town of

Lwowek (pronounced "Levovek"). Doug pointed out along the way where water was higher than it should have been. He mentioned concerns of how many students might actually make it with all of the flooding. He warned us there might only be two or three. Our heavy heads could not absorb much more, and we slowly began to catnap in the car. We made it to our destination, ate a meal, and were escorted to our sleeping arrangements. There was a building for all of the male students, and a separate one for the females. Andrea and I found our bunks and very quickly fell into a state of deep sleep for the evening.

The next morning when I awoke, everyone else was still asleep and it was very quiet. I remembered briefly from the night before being pointed to where we could take showers. I brought what I had down to that spot, and to my shock was sprayed with icy cold water. I washed my hair in record time and thought to myself in a martyr-like way, "This is ALL part of the missionary experience." Later at breakfast Doug asked if I had taken a shower. I nodded and he looked at me with a confused expression. He then informed me that the hot water had not been turned on yet. I then understood that Polish people are just as able to take hot showers as we are in the United States. No matter, I will always remember that sacrifice I thought I was making, serving in Poland. And I also learned very quickly how to turn on hot water for future showers to come!

Students started to arrive at the camp in the days that followed. In time we had over 20 students, a bigger success than the three Doug had anticipated. In the beginning, they had us play a game where we all had to say their Polish names. They sounded so unfamiliar to me. Tomasz, Agatta, Markieta, Krzysiek, Justyna, Ania...some of the many friends we made on this trip. We would do English and Bible classes in the morning, then go on adventures throughout the day. Our times included exploring a castle in the town of Lwowek, swimming at a nearby pond, and climbing up a "mountain" that was really like a very big hill. (Nick and I found their idea of a mountain humorous, when the mountains we have in Oregon are a bit more majestic.) A few days into the trip, a team from Ireland joined our group, and we got to learn some Irish folk dancing.

God had moved some big obstacles for us to get to Poland. We were about to see why.

There was a girl named Justyna that came to the camp. She did not know very much English and seemed to be a quiet, shy girl at first. As we got to know her, we found that she seemed to have conversations with herself quite often. She was always mumbling and muttering. She was labeled a schizophrenic.

Doug started to talk to Nick about some of his greater concerns with Justyna. The possibility of her potentially having some sort of demon possession in her was circling the conversation. So on one of the days of outings, Nick stayed back with Doug and Lila to talk through and figure out what they should be doing. When I came back from the outing with my new Polish friends, Nick was outside sitting by Justyna, and he asked me to come over to them. Nerves started to get at me, as I was unsure what I was walking into. Nick said to me very clearly, "Kari, this isn't Justyna." I looked at Justyna in the eyes, and with no fear in her face, she looked back and said in very clear English, "Are you scared?" As the words entered my ears, a shudder went through my body. The Holy Spirit spoke through me and stated, "No, because Jesus is stronger than you."

Justyna was demon possessed. I have in my life never witnessed anything quite like it. She would at one moment be just Justyna, and then the next minute be one of the demons. I say one, because over the course of our time with her, we found out she had two demons inside of her. The one we were aware of was loud and spoke very clear English. The second demon was harder to see at first and we didn't find out right away. Whenever Justyna spoke English very well in conversations, I could tell it was no longer Justyna that was present. Nick told me that she had worn a ring with a Satanic symbol on it, which Doug had taken and crushed.

Doug, Iris (the team leader from Ireland), Nick, and some missionary ladies that lived next door to the camp took Justyna in a room that night to pray over her. Pray, they did. I prayed while they were with her. They came out, announcing that the demon had left Justyna. We were all very happy and praised God for that. But the next day, she was still acting a bit shifty. There was a change that would happen in her eyes. She would be fully present, and then her expression would change. She did this flip of personalities all day long.

That night we determined there was still another demon inside of her. At this point, Doug went before all the students in the camp. He told everyone what was going on. Some of the same group went back into a room to pray with Justyna. We all waited, some prayed, and we wondered what would happen, as we heard cries from the room they were in. There were some who were very uncertain and afraid of what was going on, and others who didn't want to sleep in the same room with her at night, and moved into a different room.

The change came the following day. When they went to pray with her again, there was something different in Justyna. She wanted to be free as well. They asked her if there was anything in her life that might be giving the demon power. Justyna got rid of a necklace that she had been wearing. She found CDs that she had. Nick said he watched her break and crush them with her hands. Justyna claimed Christ in her life and she was saved, and no longer could the second demon stay there. It left her.

Justyna had to shut out the voices that were no longer inside of her. She said she could hear them outside of her body still. The only way she found to quiet those voices was to read the Bible. And she read it all the time. So much so that when she first returned home after the camp, her mom thought she was a bit crazy.

Some of the students who saw what happened to Justyna chose to follow Jesus for the first time. There were a few recommitments to the Lord. And then there were those who were shaken by the whole thing, uncertain about a lot of things, and left the camp sorting through their time there.

The number-one thing that was most impactful in my life about Justyna's story is how she was introduced to the world of demons. It was indirectly through her mother. When she was a child, her mom would hold séances, or do Ouija board with friends, downstairs in their home. Justyna was not part of this, but it opened a huge door in their home that Satan walked through, and two of his demons took over her mind, body and soul. As a mom, it has made me so cautious of what I allow in my home with my children. Some might think of me as overly protective, but when it comes to things in the spiritual realm, items that might bring in occult influence, I don't think you can be too vigilant in keeping watch over your children. There is a real battle out there.

The second takeaway for me was coming face-to-face with someone who was demon possessed. I had that moment, when the demon spoke to me, to decide if I were going to choose fear, or His love. Not on my own power or ability, but only by His Spirit in me, did love conquer, not allowing fear to fall on my soul.

The third remembrance for me is reflecting back on all the ways Satan tried to take down this camp, and how our God said no way! He provided Andrea so we could all go, He stopped the rains, drew back flood waters, and got each student there safely that needed to come, so He could save a precious girl from these demons that had taken over her soul, and show His power to everyone at that camp. He moved mountains to do His work. And we got to watch.

At the end of the trip, Nick, Andrea, and I were very exhausted in more ways than one. We were offered a very beautiful gift. One of the girls, Dorota (which is Polish for Dorothy), invited us to come stay our last night in her home. They had a home of modest means, but they sacrificed their cozy beds for us, where we slept soundly. The next morning, we woke up to a table filled with assorted pastries that they had purchased for us from a local bakery. They loved us and poured into us, using their gift of hospitality to fill us back up before we headed back home.

As we arrived back at the airport at the end of our stay, many of our new friends met us there to say their final goodbyes. We wrapped our arms around them tight and said our farewells, and we left a piece of ourselves in Poland with them. Poland changed my heart forever. I learned the beauty of walking around places and exploring local villages, living in townhomes, a different way of living that I am still drawn to today. It is a beautiful country, and I am so grateful the Lord provided the opportunity for me to experience that.

One fun last thing to share: One of the students thought I should learn a Polish tongue twister: Stół z powyłamywanymi nogami. This means, "The table with broken legs." It's pronounced "Stu, spovewa, meova, neyme, nogami."

Dear Children,

I love you so much. I am so grateful for the lessons I learned on these mission trips I have gotten to take. I pray someday the Lord might take you to places that would stretch you and put you in uncomfortable situations that would push you to lean on the Lord in ways that you would never learn here in the States.

If you do go on trips like this, here is my prayer for you: That God would give you an attitude of gratitude for all that we have, and a desire to use it for His purpose. That He will show you identity in Him, no matter what the circumstances. For you to not live in fear, but freedom found in His love. To be able to see our God work in big ways. That you are able to witness His amazing power and love. That you may someday have many of your own stories of His faithfulness to share with generations to come. To love Him the most.

I pray for a guard over your heart, so that no matter what darts the evil one may send your way, His shield of faith will guard you and not allow them to penetrate. May our God have victories in your lives.

Your Mama Always,
Kari

1 Peter 4:10 (NASB)

As each one has received a special gift, employ it in serving one another as good stewards of the manifold grace of God.

Daniel 7:27 (NASB)

Then the sovereignty, the dominion and all the greatness of all the kingdoms under the whole heaven will be given to the people of the saints of the Highest One; His kingdom will be an everlasting kingdom, and all the dominions will serve and obey Him.

Leviticus 19:31 (NASB)

Do not turn to mediums or spiritists; do not seek them out to be defiled by them, I am the Lord your God.

Acts 19:19–20 (NASB)

And many of those who practiced magic brought their books together and began burning them in the sight of everyone; and they counted up the price of them and found it fifty thousand pieces of silver. So the word of the Lord was growing mightily and prevailing.

Acts 26:18 (NASB)

To open their eyes so that they may turn from darkness to light and from dominion of Satan to God, that they may receive forgiveness of sins and an inheritance among those who have been sanctified by faith in Me.

Ephesians 1:15–22 (NASB)

For this reason I too, having heard of the faith in the Lord Jesus which exists among you and your love for all the saints, do not cease giving thanks for you, while making mention of you in my prayers; that the God of our Lord Jesus Christ, the Father of glory, may give to you a spirit of wisdom and of revelation in the knowledge of Him. I pray that the eyes of your heart may be enlightened, so that you will know what is the hope of His calling, what are the riches of the glory of His inheritance in the saints, and what is the surpassing greatness of His power to us who believe. These are in accordance with the working of the strength of His might which He brought about in Christ, when He raised Him from the dead and seated Him at the right hand of the heavenly places, far above all rule and authority and power and dominion, and every name that is named, not only in this age but also in the one to come. And He put all things in subjection under His feet, and gave Him as head over all things to the church, which is His body, the fullness of Him who fills all in all.

OUR COLLEGE GROUP YEARS

Sometimes, in reflection, I wish I could have gotten to go away to school to experience the college life. I remember visiting a friend who went to Oregon State. It was in the fall, so the beautiful autumn leaves had fallen everywhere, and the romantic idea of carrying my books to and from classes, learning more about music and writing, just seemed so desirable to me. The practical, wise, frugal side ruled over my romantic dreams and tendencies, so it was something I had surrendered.

Nothing about my middle school, high school, and college age years was conventional. It was not by the book to stay at home with my family, to find a job straight out of school, and to work instead of more schooling. But it was what I had been provided, what I had to work with. And one of the best gifts of that season came because I was at home, and not away at school: our college group.

When Nick and I finished high school, we started visiting the college group at our church. At the time, there were probably about 10 to 12 people attending. I remember feeling out of sorts again. Nervous about fitting in. They had a day trip to the beach planned, which I hoped to attend so I could get to know the other students better. But it happened that I spent that weekend fixing a car with my dad that I had gotten into an accident with earlier in the week. My anxiety started to rise as I wondered, would I fit into this group? Where would I belong?

Over the course of the summer, we started to have some planning meetings. One of the needs was for someone to lead worship at the beginning of each Sunday School time. I had been in the worship band in our high school group, and if we had access to a piano, I would be happy to play songs for the beginning of our times each week. Nick had never led worship before, but he had a good strong voice, so that is where we landed, playing worship songs together and bringing the class into a time of praise and prayer together.

Then more things started to take shape as we dreamed and envisioned what our group could do and be. We began planning a college group winter retreat. Then a beach retreat. The more we were around each other, the more these friendships and relationships grew.

Weekly meetings were introduced at Dairy Queen on Monday nights. We would pack that Dairy Queen out with all of us college-age students, talking together and eating treats. For two hours we had fellowship there. We decided to add a prayer time prior to Dairy Queen, so we would meet at the church for a half hour each week to pray before we headed over to Dairy Queen.

On Wednesday nights, one of the gal's parents opened up their home every other week during the summer so we could play volleyball in the backyard. It was a great opportunity to have friends come that didn't know Jesus, just to hang out. We decided we wanted to find a place to serve together, so every other Wednesday night our group would go to the Oregon Food Bank and help for a few hours. Then we would go eat after at a Shari's or Red Robin.

Sunday nights, our adult leaders would host small groups for the guys and girls. It was a great time of praying together and studying different books. Often we would once more end up at a local restaurant together to end the night.

Our church talks about missional living—a place where your church community is your family. You eat together and do day-to-day life together. You pray for each other and support one another. If one in your group has a need, you rally around that person to provide. It's not just inward focused, but outward, welcoming anyone that has need of community, to show them love, and serving the community around you in whatever needs present themselves.

This is exactly what we had with our group during the four years of Nick's college season. We were a family. What was unique about this family was there were a lot of boys in the group. The girls were a little on the low side. But the boys became my brothers. They all treated me with respect, because they respected Nick and wouldn't have approached me in any way other than as a sister. The few girls that were there were sisters to me. Three to five girls attended most of the years, and summers fluctuated with a few more girls when they were home from school.

Our retreats would range from worship and speaking, to just being plain silly—we had games we would play, skits to perform, pranks against the boys or the boys against the girls. It was an emotionally safe space where we could just be real and build relationships together, loving Jesus, loving each other, and having fun. Sometimes I felt like on our own, we were just a bunch of misfits, but when we were put together by our God who loves all of His misfits, He made us into a beautiful family that made sense.

Some of my favorite memories:

The first winter camp. I was supposed to help lead worship, but I lost my voice and I couldn't sing. The Lord taught me how to worship without a voice. We sat in a circle our last evening there, starting with just a few songs, and ended in a cappella singing that went over an hour long. I remember Paul, who seemed to me like the quietest boy in the group, breaking through one of the quiet spaces in between songs with the words to "Awesome God."[9]

Celebrating Valentine's Day together. Our leaders put on a beautiful banquet where we had the opportunity to dress up, no dating relationship required, to be family together.

Working on teams to dress up Nick and our friend Paul as Christmas trees at a party in December.

Dipping salty Dairy Queen French fries into my twist ice cream cone with friends each Monday night.

Marshmallows in the boys' tennis shoes at a winter retreat, although they didn't appreciate it as much as we anticipated, due to their shoes being wet from snow, and the marshmallows became a soggy mess.

Putting Fourth of July poppers under the toilet seats at a retreat.

The last beach retreat. We decided to take one last trip to the beach, and one of the gals suggested with much jubilation the idea that we should all start singing songs together. We broke into an impromptu time of worship, on the golden sand, with the sound of the waves crashing around us, and the sun shining warm as if to promise beautiful blessings of summer just around the corner. Three other people approached our group, and it just so happened that one of them had a guitar. We joined voices with our new extended family, praising His name. This was Nick's and my last retreat before we were married, and an unforgettable way to end it.

Our college group, our family for that season, was the best gift God could have given me and Nick in our years of waiting for school to be finished, and to start married life together. We didn't get the on-campus experience that we both would have liked, but there is no comparison to what we experienced or what the Lord did in that time. Some of our lifelong friends have come out of that group, where two or three were gathered in His name.

Dear Children,

I want you to know that there is something to be said for having community and relationship where Christ is at the center of everything you say and do. I pray that as you grow and encounter relationships in school, church, and work, the Lord will provide communities for you to be part of, where He can do His work in your life. I pray for a place for you to be Jesus lovers, to praise His name together, praying for one another, encouraging one another, breaking bread together, sharing joy and laughter in the happy times, and mourning in the breaking times. His Holy Spirit can unite people that wouldn't have anything else in common, other than Him, in unexpected ways. Missional living like this is a gift and a beautiful thing to find.

Friendships like these are gifts. Cherish them and commit them to the Lord.

I Love You, Babies!
Mama

Colossians 3:14–16 (NASB)

Beyond all these things put on love, which is the perfect bond of unity. Let the peace of Christ rule in your hearts, to which indeed you were called in one body; and be thankful. Let the word of Christ richly dwell within you, with all wisdom teaching and admonishing one another with psalms and hymns and spiritual songs, singing with thankfulness in your hearts to God.

Ephesians 4:15–16 (NASB)

But speaking the truth in love, we are to grow up in all aspects into Him who is the head, even Christ, from whom the whole body, being fitted and held together by what every joint supplies, according to the proper working of each individual part, causes the growth of the body for the building up of itself in love.

Acts 2:42–47 (NASB)

They were continually devoting themselves to the apostles' teaching and to fellowship, to the breaking of bread and to prayer. Everyone kept feeling a sense of awe; and many wonders and signs were taking place through the apostles. And all those who had believed were together and had all things in common; and they began selling their property and possessions and were sharing them with all, as anyone might have need. Day by day continuing with one mind in the temple, and breaking bread from house to house, they were taking their meals together with gladness and sincerity of heart, praising God and having favor with all the people. And the Lord was adding to their number day by day those who were being saved.

✁ THE CAR/DEBT LESSON ✁

I wanted to take a chapter to talk about my lessons with cars. Growing up, my dad always got the affordable vehicles that he would be able to fix up, to save on the expenses car maintenance could bring. I experienced many moments when my dad would come meet us on the side of the road with his toolkit handy and fix the ailings of our current method of transportation. I appreciated that my dad was able to make these repairs. However, I did not like the many times our plans got changed because of a failing car problem. He always wanted us to come out and spend time with him when he was working on a car, but honestly, it was something I had zero desire to spend my time learning.

As I approached 15, I was excited about getting my driver's permit. I studied for the test, and the morning of my birthday my mom took me down to the DMV to take the exam. Sadly, I failed my first time. Not the best way to spend a birthday. But after more studying in the book, the next time I took it, I was able to pass, and thus began my year of lessons from my parents. My dad took me out for the first few times with his manual transmission car. After the second trip out, getting stuck on a mini hill and not able to get going again, I threw the towel in and said, "No more!" He drove us home that day. I took a break for a bit, then my mom let me drive her in our passenger-size Dodge van. This van was christened the "party van" by many high schoolers who my dad drove around in it—it was bright orange with a gray stripe down the middle. As you stepped inside, you were greeted by thick shag carpet, dark wood paneling, and multicolored ceiling lights encased by a wooden beam that my mom hit her head on many times. The back five-person u-seat could be turned into a bed. It had storage underneath and a marble table with cup holders. It was a one-of-a-kind classic. I got very comfortable driving an automatic, and eventually gave my dad's manual transmission a try one more time. At 16, I took my driver's exam and passed it with flying colors.

As I approached high school graduation, my dad decided to get a third car so that each driver in our household had a mode of transportation. It was a bright red Dodge Rampage. It had a front end that looked like a car, and a back that looked like a pick-up truck. He chose it to be my car. Right after I graduated, my parents went to help with a high school church camp, while I stayed home working to save up money for school in the fall. It was grand opening week at the Burgerville where I worked, and I was scheduled early mornings to late afternoons—long shifts filled with much hard work. I was exhausted by the end of that week, and I couldn't find anything in the fridge at home to eat. I decided to go out and look for something to eat, but I was overly hungry, overly tired, and very frustrated. As I was driving home without anything to eat, I looked down at the cassette player and tried to fast-forward to a different song. When I looked up, I saw the long front of my dad's Dodge Rampage driving straight into the car in front of me, which had suddenly stopped. I tried to brake, but the brakes did nothing for me, and I got into my first accident.

I felt terrible. Thankfully, the damage to the car in front of me was minimal, and they told me not to even worry about it with insurance. However, our car was a different story. I could barely get the driver's side door open. When I got home, I called my dad and told him what had happened. He was not too thrilled, and informed me I would be paying for whatever damage needed to be repaired. The Sunday he returned, we drove around to junk yards to get the parts needed for fixing things up, and all of my hard-earned money from that grand opening week went back into the car I had wrecked.

I did not like that car after that. It had such a long front end, and it was hard for me to gauge how close I was to someone. So I told my dad I didn't want to drive that car anymore. He took it as his work car, and I took over his manual transmission Dodge Challenger, which had a sunroof, and as I mentioned in a previous chapter, I drove that car into the ground. Then I borrowed my boss's car.

When the time finally came for me to buy my own car, a friend was selling his Toyota Corolla. I had saved up enough to purchase it and began taking ownership of my first car. Over time, the desire grew in me to have a newer car—one that had all the bells and whistles that my "I think I can, I think I can" chugging up a hill car did not come with.

One weekend when my parents were gone, I decided to break for freedom and find my own car. I wanted to make my own decision and not have it be something that my parents were telling me yes or no to. I started looking for cars in the paper, and found a Nissan that appealed to me. I made an appointment to see it on a Saturday morning, planning to take Nick with me. When my dad called to talk to me before I went, he voiced extreme hesitation over this decision. I told him I would be taking out a loan for the car, which he wasn't a big fan of. My dad called Nick and urged him to be extra vigilant in finding out information about the car, and told Nick different things to watch for.

The Nissan was just as beautiful as it sounded on paper. It drove like a dream. I knew I wanted it badly. But Nick looked at the title, and it read: *Totaled*. I told Nick it drove great, and I wanted the car. The records also indicated it had come from the Midwest, which had recently dealt with much flooding. Warning lights were going off, and Nick called my dad, who told me I should not buy it. I was so upset. I wanted that car so badly. I could afford it. But, a bit begrudgingly, I honored my dad's request.

The next day after church, I took a drive to Kia Motor Company, and I found myself a car I liked. It wasn't as pretty as the Nissan, but it was brand new, and clean, and it had a good warranty. I decided to take out a loan with the bank and purchase my very own Kia Sephia. I said goodbye to my red Corolla, selling it to a friend in our college group, and enjoyed the luxury of a brand-new car.

My parents weren't thrilled that I had taken out a loan, but I think they were a bit relieved that it was that car over the other one. Here is where the lessons in money started to come in for me. I had it pretty easy in my college-age years. My parents didn't ask me to pay any rent for staying there. The only expenses I had were my cell phone and insurance, prior to taking out a car loan. Yet I would find myself in a very tight spot every six months when my insurance bill came. Christmas time was also a month when I ran out of money fast. I loved to give gifts, but I also needed to pay for gas for the car in December. Talking with Nick, he looked at me as if the answer were obvious. He said, "Kari, why don't you take the total cost of insurance, divide it by six months, and set that amount aside each month in a savings account, and when your bill comes, you can pay it off." He also suggested saving each month for Christmas gifts. At first I objected to it, because it was change. But this simple piece of instruction really was so wise.

When I took on monthly car payments, I had no issue with doing so, because my car came with a five-year warranty and my loan was five years. Any issues that came up while I paid my car off would be covered by my warranty. At the mortgage company where I worked, Dave introduced a new program for paying off house loans more quickly. It was set up so that you would make your home payments bi-weekly, adding an extra full payment when the year was done, which was a full principal amount. It would decrease how much you owed on your home, and you could pay it off several years earlier, or even more, depending on if you wanted to pay additional to your mortgage. This was ingenious to me. I decided to take that same approach with my car. There was no early, pre-payment penalty, so I started taking bigger chunks of my paychecks to put toward my loan, and made cuts in my daily expenditures with food and such. I paid that loan off in a year and a half, and decided to take the money I had been using for making car payments to start saving for my wedding.

This turned into a blessing in the end, because what I couldn't predict was getting laid off due to the rising of interest rates and reduction of refinances that had been taking place. When I was laid off in March of 2000, six months before my wedding, I had a little nest egg in my savings account. Between money that my parents gave me to contribute to our wedding expenses, and after using some of my savings to purchase furniture for our first home, we had exactly what we needed. Through wisdom the Lord provided.

I also have one side story to share, about my Kia Sephia.

I was not a get-my-hands-dirty type of girl. *At all.* So I did what any girl of that nature would do when the oil of her car needed to be changed. I paid my brother to do it. He was more affordable than Oil Can Henry and was conveniently located right at my house.

Several months after I got my Kia, my Check Engine light came on. I was confused why this was happening—it was a brand-new car. I took it in, and they looked at the car and told me maybe the fuel lid had not been screwed on all the way, so to try doing that in the future. They could not find anything wrong with it.

Several weeks later, it came on again. Once again, I went in and they checked it, but couldn't find anything wrong inside. They decided to replace that Check Engine light sensor. For a while that seemed to do the trick, and for several months I did not deal with that light on again.

In July of that year, we were scheduled to take a trip to Condon, to visit my mom's side of the family for the Fourth of July. Three weeks before that, the Check Engine light came on again, and they checked it and told me everything was fine. So Nick, my brother Michael, and I loaded our things into my Kia Sephia and headed out on the three-hour drive to Eastern Oregon.

Nick drove on the way up, and the clutch occasionally slipped out of fifth gear. He told me, "When you get home, Kari, you need to get this looked at." We spent our time with family, and on the night of July Fourth, after the fireworks, I took the driver's seat and the three of us headed back home, as we all had to work the next day. On our 45-minute trip back to the highway, we took a wrong turn and ended up on an unlit, curvy canyon road with no cell phone service. It was unfamiliar and dark, and as we drove, the car continued to slip out of fifth gear. At the end of that road, we thankfully found ourselves very close to the highway, and got on highway I-84W, leading us back home. It was about midnight at this point, and we were driving through the Dalles. All of the sudden, the car shifted out of fifth, and then fourth, and I started freaking out. Nick directed me to pull off to the side. The Kia Sephia slipped out of gear all the way to first, and then it froze. Like a very heavy solid rock, the car would not move.

I have so many praises about this moment. First, that it waited to happen until we were out of the dark, no-cell-service canyon. Second, that it was late at night, so no other cars were around to cause an accident or make it difficult to pull off to the side in time, before it locked up. Third is Nick's uncle. His uncle's family happened to live in the Dalles, and his Uncle Bill happened to be an insurance adjustor, which provided him with connections to a tow truck company that was able to move my car to a safe spot until the morning. We were able to stay at Uncle Bill's home that night and sleep, spending time the next day figuring out what we should do.

That little Kia Sephia was under warranty, so a tow truck took it back to Portland, and the dealership mechanics looked at it and determined the transmission was dead. The car had very few miles on it, and the transmission was dead? Here I thought I had avoided the mark by not buying the Nissan with the suspect Title, and instead, I had ended up with a Kia lemon? Kia was great and fixed the transmission, and I had my car back. Sort of. It never really ran quite the same after that day, and I was not sad when I sold it for a new car a few years later.

Several months later, my brother changed the oil for me. I am hesitant to write this, afraid the Kia Corporation might read it and track me down...but here goes. Michael changed the oil and was perplexed by the results. He looked at the oil level, and it showed double the amount that should have been in there. He called my dad out to ask his opinion on the situation. My dad examined the oil stick and saw the double oil level. He asked my brother where he was draining the oil from. My brother pointed below. My dad looked at him and said, "Michael, you drained the transmission oil out of this car." All of the sudden everything started to make sense. My brother had changed the oil for me three weeks before we went to Eastern Oregon. He had drained the transmission fluid and filled up my car with double the oil. For three weeks my car was thirsty, and once it used up the very last drop of transmission fluid it could find, it died.

Because it was months after the whole ordeal, we were able to have a good laugh about it. Nick wonders why Kia never checked the transmission oil. He guesses they probably never thought that on a brand-new car, they should check to see if the transmission oil was almost out. I am so grateful to God for giving us what we needed in that moment. He was our *Provider* God.

Dear Children,

As you get older and start to experience situations that may be challenging to you, remember you are not alone in those moments. We have a God that is a Provider. He gives us what we need in those moments. It isn't always situations we would want to be in. But in those times, He is the manna we need to make it for that day. For me, growing up, cars were an area where I learned those lessons. Often they would break into my world and inconvenience my life in that moment, but God used them to be part of my journey to help me grow up out of some of my childish tendencies.

I also want to encourage you to take your daddy's wisdom that he gave to me in regards to finances. Be wise with what you have. Ask the Lord how you can use it with what is in front of you. There are different ways of doing things that may seem out of the box at times, but in the big picture they are going to help you do well with what you have.

Remember God is Provider. Praise Him for that in those moments. I am so grateful for how He provided you!

Love,
Mama

Psalm 23:1 (NASB)

The Lord is my shepherd; I shall not want.

Philippians 4:19–20 (NASB)

And my God shall supply all your needs according to His riches in glory in Christ Jesus. Now to our God and Father be the glory forever and ever. Amen.

Genesis 22:13–14 (NASB)

Then Abraham raised his eyes and looked, and behold, behind him a ram caught in the thicket by his horns; and Abraham went and took the ram and offered him up for a burnt offering in the place of his son. Abraham called the name of that place the Lord will Provide, as it is said to this day, "In the mount of the Lord it will be provided."

Our Season Together Begins

My beloved speaks and says to me: "Arise my love, my beautiful one, and come away, for behold, the winter is past; the rain is over and gone. The flowers appear on the earth, the time of singing has come, and the voice of the turtledove is heard in our land." Song of Solomon 2:10–12 (ESV)

✒ OUR ENGAGEMENT STORY ✒

Six years. Too long. But we were almost at the finish line of this particular season of life.

I was patient. As patient as a little kid on Christmas day. Can I tell you opening a present early is never worth it? One year, when my brother and I were in elementary school, our parents put this *big* wrapped box under the Christmas tree. We wondered what it might be. One night our parents left me in charge, and so, out came the scissors and the repair tape. We pulled out that rather large gift, addressed to everyone in our family. Could it really be what we had hoped for this last year? We stared at it. Was it really worth it? We slowly and very carefully removed one side of the tape. Pulling down the wrapping paper on that side, there we saw it was...a Nintendo! With a power pad! We were ecstatic. Quickly wrapping the present back up and returning the gift under the tree to its positioned spot, we waited for Christmas day.

Christmas morning arrived...and as we opened all the presents one by one, we slowly worked our way through to that last box. My dad pulled that box out, and he put it in front of Michael and me. But he didn't say we could open it. You know what he did? He spoke to us: "Do you have any guesses on what this might be?" He had a sparkle in his eyes. One that showed how much he had worked hard to give this to us. One that was ready to be delighted in the reaction of his children when they opened up this gift. Trying to hide our guilty faces, we came up with every other answer in the book than what we knew it to be.

We opened it up, but let me tell you, it was not nearly as exciting as it would have been if we had just waited. If we had just been patient. Our parents didn't find out until several years later of our sneak peek confession, and we did enjoy the gift and used it all the time, but that is one moment in life when I wish I could go back and just be patient a few more days, giving my dad the full gratitude of receiving the special gift that he deserved, that both our parents deserved.

That story is a good childhood illustration of why it is important to wait. To be patient. God's timing is much better than ours. As you will continue to see, this is a lesson God has had to teach me over and over and over again.

Now for the first lesson leading up to our engagement story—one lesson from a story of many little God lessons along the way. It was the summer before Nick's senior year of college at Portland State, and I had a feeling that sometime in the next year I would be an engaged and very happy woman.

I planned a fun little outing with my mom, Nick's mom, my sister Abbie, Nick's sister Rachael, and my friend Kathryn. We went to this place in Portland called Daisy Kingdom. It was a fabric store with all sorts of cutesy and frilly fabrics. But there were also imported wedding dresses. It was a beautiful summer day, and we were having a blast looking through everything. Now mind you, this was a trip to just have fun looking. That's right, you heard it from the mouth of the not quite bride to be..."looking." There was no plan to purchase anything. I started sifting through the dresses, when I stopped. There it was. My dream dress in perfect form. A full ball gown skirt, laced up in the back, a beautiful handmade dress imported from Italy, for $250. I had to try it on. I went into the dressing room, pulled it over my head...perfection! I emerged and surrounded by so many ladies that I loved, everyone agreed that it was the perfect dress for me. It fit perfect, it was everything I had dreamed about, the price was beyond perfect. I called Nick to tell him. I just knew it was meant to be. I started to explain all the details to my future husband, when I heard one word on the other end that halted me in my dream world.

"No."

Excuse me? What did you just say to me?

"Kari, no. I really want you to wait until I propose. I want you to have fun looking at dresses once you are engaged, and I think you need to wait until after I have proposed."

"But Nick, it is the *perfect* dress—it's from Italy, one of a kind, it may not be here later."

"No, I want you to wait."

Oh, I hated those words.

Okay, fine, I would wait until we got engaged. I could be submissive. This would be a good practice for me. I didn't buy the dress. Nope, I was going to "honor" Nick. So instead, I became that drip that it talks about in Proverbs[10]...I figured we just needed to get engaged and that would allow me to get my dress. Problem solved.

Thus began the project called: "Operation Nag Nick." Bugging. Annoying. Drip, drip, drip. I didn't really care at that moment about getting engaged. I wanted the ring on my finger so I could go to Daisy Kingdom and get my princess dream-come-true dress that I had wanted all my life. A week went by...another week went by...I figured a few weeks into this the dress had to still be there. But then a month went by. Next thing I knew it was fall and my hopes of getting that dress became less and less. Soon my nagging took a turn for the nasty. I was angry at Nick. If he really did care, why hadn't he proposed? Why wouldn't he let me get my dream dress? Didn't he understand what a good deal it was?

One autumn evening I decided to let him have it. I told him everything I had told him before. When you are getting married you are a princess, and a princess should always get what she wants. I wanted him to hear me, loud and clear. I wanted to be told I could go get that dress. But when I paused for a breath, Nick spoke these words:

"Kari, it's not there anymore."

My eyes blinked and stared back at him. "What did you just say?"

"It's not there anymore. After you found it, I worked at saving up the money to buy it for you. It took me a few weeks, but once I had the money I sent Kathryn to go get the dress for you. Then when I would have proposed to you it would be back in your bedroom afterwards, waiting for you. But when she went there, it wasn't there anymore. Please stop bugging me about getting engaged, because it's not there."

Silence. So much for being a princess. I just got knocked off my royal throne and found myself sitting in the category of major spoiled brat. Those words that my amazing, wonderful boyfriend spoke to me put me in my place. It took me a moment to recognize what I had almost done, and when I figured it out, I knew from that moment on I would not be nagging Nicholas anymore about proposing to me.

I had almost ruined the thing that my heart deep down had truly been dreaming about. I almost missed out on allowing God to give us an amazing engagement story because I was obsessed with a piece of fabric. I was focused all on me. I knew my place now. I would wait. I would be patient, because my beloved, the one whom I had waited five years for so far, was doing his part in the planning of our future, and this was one surprise I did not want to ruin.

It was a lesson in submission and trusting and waiting all rolled into one. And it was a lesson that a wedding was not about me. It was about committing myself to love and to submit and to cherish my best friend for the rest of my life. About a God who loved us so much and had so much more in store for us than what we could plan on our own.

We went on plugging away at daily life. I always wondered every time we went on a date if this might be "the" date when he would ask me to marry him. But time after time passed and still no proposal.

On Friday nights that year we took swing dancing lessons. Our friends Paul and Kathryn went with us one term. Kathryn and I decided to have an old-fashioned sleepover after one of the classes, and when I came to her house she handed me a box. Inside was the most beautiful fake engagement ring with a matching wedding band marked with the price of $18.99 from Nordstrom Rack...I had to smile. She told me that I could wear that on my finger until Nick asked me to marry him, since, "You guys are practically engaged already!"

I didn't actually wear it, but the next day we were having our annual Christmas party at Nick's parents' house. My family was invited every year, filled with the fun of a home-cooked meal from Sue (either a turkey tetrazzini or a chicken in a crockpot...or maybe a lasagna—you never wanted to miss out on Sue's cooking), a white elephant gift exchange, and lots of laughs and fun fellowship.

As I pulled into the driveway, there was my mom whom I hadn't seen since the day before. Hmmm...this might be fun. I reached into my bag and pulled out my most beautiful fake ring ever. Sliding it onto my finger, I stepped out of the car and smiled at my mom.

"So, mom (pause)..."last night, Nick and I... well I forgot to tell you!" and I held that glittering, sparkling fake ring placed onto my appropriate finger right up to my mom's face.

Her eyes got wide as she looked at the ring. In shock she blurted out the first thing she could think of.

"What? No...I thought Nick was going to propose to you at the college group winter retreat in January!"

I blinked...and then stared blankly...my worst engagement fear ever had just come true. I spoiled the surprise of the when and the how in that very moment. My little prank came right back at me. Tears started to fall. My boyfriend followed me back to his room, and I told him what I had undone. Nick looked a little frustrated. Well, a lot frustrated. He had put a lot of thought into things as well...more tears fell from feeling as though I had ruined that moment for him.

But once again, God had a bigger plan, and I just love how He takes those moments that to me are so funny now to look back upon, and turns them into something better.

We forged ahead into the New Year/millennium of 2000. No ring yet on my finger. My patience was starting to get a little thin...I was hoping for a wedding in September and really would have liked six months to plan for it, which would mean a ring on my finger by March. Nick knew there was this lingering deadline over him.

We went on that college group winter retreat in January. I don't remember exactly what happened while we there, but I do remember this. We were asked to go before the Lord about some things, individually. While I was praying, Nick slid up next to me and took a seat. He looked at me intensely.

And he said, "Kari, I have been so wrong. I am sorry I haven't expressed my feelings into words. I got stuck on a plan, but I realized that God has released me to say these words to you..."

Could it be? Really, was he going to propose anyway?

"Kari, I love you." There was a pause.

Then he talked again about how he had been released to speak these words, and that he knew God had been telling him to say them to me for a while, but he was scared. But no proposal followed those words. I was very confused. See, this takes us back to the rules Nick and I had made in our early relationship years. My rule was no ring no kissing, and Nick wanted to save "I love you" for proposing to his future wife.

So I addressed that "rule" with Nick. "Kari," he responded, "I was wrong not to tell you sooner. And I want you just to be patient a little longer." There was no ring that day. Patience was beginning to feel like a dirty word again. But once again I knew, I could wait.

There was no ring at that college group winter retreat. And the funny thing to me is, after I had ached to hear the words "I love you" for so long, now that I had heard them, I didn't know how to respond. I ended up not telling Nick I loved him back right away.

Once I did get past our "rule" and opened my heart to sharing what had been true for so long, I asked him if we could maybe take some time to write out what it meant to love each other, since we had waited so long to say those words to each other. Nick agreed to it. Of course I had mine done that night—all written on pretty stationery ready to share what it meant to love Nick. I read it to him the next time I saw him, and he told me he was still working on it.

A few weeks later Nick picked me up during my lunch hour at work. We drove to one of our favorite spots in Portland, Gabriel Park, with McDonald's in bags, and found a picnic table. We hadn't had much down time since the retreat, so it was just nice to catch up. Nick seemed a little rushed to finish his fries, and for the first time ever, he finished his food before me. I soon found out why. He had completed his letter to me, and he wanted to share it with me.

He started to read that letter. As he read it and opened his heart on what God showed him, in what it meant to say he loved me, my heart soared with dreams of the future. And when he got down on one knee, I froze. All I remember are the last words he read, "...to be wholly devoted to you. Kari Anne Kirkpatrick, will you marry me?"

The moment I had dreamed of for the last six years was finally happening. And I meant to tease him when he proposed, saying something sassy like, "Hmmm...let me think about it..." But I was so stunned and shocked by the moment, the only word that came to my lips was, "Yes!" Then he brought out the ring.

Let me just take a moment to share a few details about my ring.

My ring is beautiful and special in so many ways. The stone came from Nick's Nana, and had been passed down in the family. The shape was called the Amsterdam cut, and it was made in 1885. Just under a carat in size, to me, it was a huge rock. Nick and I had done a little ring browsing. I hadn't ever seen the diamond until that moment. He knew from our window shopping that I wanted simple white gold bands, nothing fancy or flashy. Nick did an amazing job picking out a setting for my wishes. He spent a lot of work having it appraised, insured, reset in the new band, and reappraised, and reinsured.

More than that, he had purpose and symbolism behind the setting he chose. The big stone sits in the middle, and the engagement band holds another tiny diamond on the bottom right. He slid the ring on my left ring finger. As he held my hand and we looked at it, he shared that the tiny diamond on it represented me, and the wedding band held another tiny diamond that would represent him, and the big stone represents God. He told me that the reason the stone was so big was to serve as a reminder to us that we would always keep our focus on Him. And so often since that day, I have glanced down at my hand and been reminded of those words. It was perfectly designed in every way for us.

I looked up at Nick and felt like I was living in an amazing bubble of a dream come true. He actually pulled it off. He surprised me with a proposal and did it romantically and well, complete with McDonald's on a sunny day at Gabriel Park in February. It was perfect in every way. My lunch break was coming to a close, and as I started to pick up our lunch trash, Nick stood up and said, "Okay, now let's go to Seattle."

"What did you just say, Nick?"

"Let's go to Seattle! I talked to your boss a few weeks back, and she gave you permission to have the rest of the day off, so let's go!"

In that moment I flashed back to when I was getting ready to leave for lunch. I saw a knowing expression with a big smile on Patti's face, and her words came back to me: "Take your time on your lunch break today; don't worry about coming right back." And I realized she knew and had done an awesome job keeping a secret.

Before we left for Seattle, we had a few people to stop and tell along the way. The first was my family. I saw my mom and this time when I showed her the ring, she said, "What is that, a Cracker Jack box ring?" Not this time, Mom. No Cracker Jack box rings on this ring finger. We then stopped by my friend Kathryn's work place, and I held my hand up to her with a goofy grin on my face, and she screamed and hugged me. It was definitely fun to surprise people.

We headed up to Seattle, a place I had always wanted to go. I felt so out of place in my pink handmade jumper that I had been wearing during the day. Nick took me to Old Navy and bought me an outfit that I felt much more confident walking around in. I stared and people-watched as we walked through the big hilly city. It was the end of the work week for people, lots of suits, neutral colors, men and women walking around with some place more important to be. Then we walked down to our dinner restaurant—Isabella Ristorante. Nick had a reservation at a cozy little Italian restaurant. After dinner we drove to the other side of the bay and looked out across the Seattle night skyline. The night was turning cold, so we quickly snapped a picture, then back into the car to head home.

The ride back to Oregon was a little bit quieter. It was getting later, and the closer we got to home, the raspier my throat started to feel. Nick stopped at a convenience store to pick me up a Snapple to drink and help soothe my throat. We stopped really briefly in Scappoose for quick hugs of congratulations from Nick's parents, and then he drove me home. (It was a 45-minute drive between our homes). I fell asleep in lala dreamland, and the whole weekend I was on cloud nine. I was going to be getting married and soon would be Kari Anne Adams.

In all reality, you can't live in a dream world, and in real life, the little throat tickle that started the night we got engaged had turned into a full-blown sore throat. I tried all the tricks, but nothing I did was getting rid of this bug. In the midst of it, wedding planning was already beginning—appointments were being made for bridal dress shopping, and there was eagerness from family for me to start making decisions on what I would do with bridesmaid, candle lighter, and flower girl dresses. I started to feel pressure...pressure...pressure...I think the pressure that a lot of brides may feel to start working out all the details.

In the midst of everything, after a visit to the doctor I found out I had strep throat. We brought on the antibiotics, pushed ahead, and life got busy. And then interest rates went up, which meant I lost my job. I had been the only one in the office most of the time. My boss told me when I had nothing to do to just have fun looking at wedding dresses on the computer. However, after a few weeks of that, she told me the news that they were going to have to close shop. She might work from home sometimes, but at this point I had two weeks' notice. This wasn't the worst news in the world, because I had planned on stopping work right before I got married anyway. You know the plan—I was going to get married...and have kids. So why would I want to work if we started whipping out those babies?

As I mentioned previously, I had been setting aside extra money in my savings account. I didn't know that I would be getting laid off from my job when I started saving, but God knew. I tried to find a few temp jobs while on unemployment, but in the end it was hard to commit to anything because I would be quitting in four months. I remember one night being very overwhelmed and stressed about everything from the dress to cake, flowers and photography.

I went back to my bedroom with all these thoughts and plans, feeling completely out of control. And the Lord took me to the passage in Philippians 4[11] that talks about being anxious for nothing, but in everything by prayer and supplication let your requests be made known to God, and His peace which surpasses all comprehension shall guard your heart and mind in Christ Jesus. I prayed over that verse, took out my journal, and started listing all my prayers and supplications before the Lord, and I gave them to Him. I said, "You take them." He did, and being engaged ended up being one of my favorite seasons in life.

The crazy thing is that not having a job was the best pre-wedding present God could ever have given me. It gave me the last few months of my unmarried life to be home, spending time with my family and wedding planning with

them. I did things like making my veil for $30 instead of spending $100, or seeing a ring bearer pillow in a magazine for $40 and making it for $6. I had a blast planning my wedding. There were a few things that had to go, like throwing a nice dinner reception with dancing. But instead, my big splurge: I got a beautiful cake for a great deal of $600 (a year later they showed my cake at bridal fairs and were charging twice as much for it).

Truly, being engaged was a season of some of the best memories of my life, and if it weren't for the things that looked like trials to me in the moment, I would not have enjoyed it nearly as much as I did.

Dear Children,

So many times I have watched over and over while engaged couples become stressed about the planning and preparing for a wedding. Emotions can run high during this time. It is a season leading up to one of the biggest changes life can hold. I want to encourage you to know that it does not have to be this way. In any season that requires a lot of decisions to be made, we have our God who wants to be involved in all of it.

Take some time to be still with Him in the midst of the chaos and whirl of activities. Go to Him. Lay all your anxieties before Him. I am so grateful He brought me to that place, because it allowed Him to take the reins. He saw all my dreams for this day, all the details I hoped for, and He made it so much better than if I had done it on my own. It turned into a worship service, a reminder of how earthly marriage symbolizes the marriage between Christ and the Church. It pointed to Jesus in every aspect. Trust me, a God who created the earth in seven days can definitely help design your wedding in less than six months!

Go to Him. He wants you to bring those dreams before Him so much! He is definitely all about celebrating marriage. He was the one who created marriage in the beginning.

Don't forget, it's so much more than a day. Your wedding day will not be perfect. No day is capable of that. It is a commitment of the rest of your life to spending it with this person God has created—for as long as you both shall live. So let go of all those perfect expectations, give them to Creator God, Designer of all things. Keep your eyes fixed on Jesus.

Love Always,
Your Mama Kari

Psalm 33:6–9 (NASB)

By the word of the LORD the heavens were made, and by the breath of His mouth all their host. He gathers the waters of the sea together as a heap; He lays up the deeps in storehouses. Let all the earth fear the LORD; let all the inhabitants of the world stand in awe of Him. For He spoke, and it was done; He commanded and it stood fast.

Song of Solomon 2:10–12 (NASB)

"My beloved responded and said to me, 'Arise, my darling, my beautiful one, and come along. For behold the winter is past, the rain is over and gone. The flowers have already appeared in the land; the time has arrived for pruning the vines, and the voice of the turtledoves has been heard in our land."

SEPTEMBER 16, 2000

September 16, 2000. That was the chosen day. Partly because I love September. My birthday is in September, and it had only rained once on my birthday in Oregon up to that point. By scheduling my wedding day four days before my birthday, I figured there was a good chance for a beautiful, sunny day to get married in wedded bliss. I also did calculations—yes—based on my period. I had terrible periods. The first day or two, these lovely monthly visits would put me in bed, accompanied by my Christy Miller books[12] to help me cope with the pain. We are talking trips back and forth from bed to the bathroom feeling miserable. It was very important to me that I did not feel like that on my wedding day. Based on my calculations after my February cycle, September 16 was looking like the perfect Saturday for a wedding.

We were quick to reserve the church; after all, I had been planning this wedding in my head for six years! It was the first thing I officially did. We had our date, we had the church, and I had strep throat. Somewhere between the excitement of being engaged and getting sick with strep throat and taking antibiotics, my predictable period came two weeks late in March...setting me up for a menstrual cycle right around the week of my wedding. I tried not to think about this as the day drew near.

You might ask, why not use the birth control pill? I had personal convictions about the pill. I wanted to have a honeymoon baby. I was not going to "control" my ability to get pregnant, but instead set myself up to be in competition with the Duggar family! I was ready to be married and ready to be a mom, so the pill was simply not an option for me. (Funny how God would teach me about "control" in this area later on in a very different way.)

The week of the wedding came. The sun was beautifully shining every day, and we were working on final wedding touches. My dad picked out our getaway car, a Silver Dodge Sebring Convertible, and decided it really wasn't much more to reserve it for a week instead of just for the day, so he had it on hand to cart me around to all of my last-minute wedding errands and appointments.

I had my moments of last-minute wedding jitters, including going back out to look at wedding dresses one last time because I wasn't in love with the one I had purchased. I ended up keeping it. We had fun moments like the last-minute decision to play the Addams Family theme song as guests were dismissed from the ceremony to the reception. And I was anxiously waiting for my period to show up. I even skipped a trip to the beach with my parents one day because I was so afraid it would come and I wouldn't be near my bed. I wish I had just gone to the beach that day.

Rehearsal night came, and no period in sight, so the festivities began. We had a fun rehearsal, where I learned how to hold my flowers and how to slide a ring on a finger if it gets stuck (and during the ceremony, mine did!). We had a beautiful homemade rehearsal dinner put on by Nick's mom and several of her friends, with scrapbook pictures scattered across the tables of us and the people we love. Nick had to take toothpicks out of an apple and tell one thing he loved about me for each toothpick. I ate the apple at the end. Then I went home for a quiet night to sleep in my own bed one last time in my parents' home.

The next morning I woke up bright and early. The wedding was set for 2:00. We gathered up all of our belongings and headed to the church. The morning was spent doing hair—I did a lot of hair, because it was one of my secret dreams to be a hairdresser and I loved to do fun styles. I had my Mary Kay makeup that had been chosen for me a few months prior. White shoes without a black heel, in honor of Nick's Papa. (The night before Nick's mom got married, as she knelt before a table to take communion wearing her wedding shoes with black heels, her father would not stand for it and off they went to purchase shoes without black on them). My "something old" was my beautiful engagement ring, and my "something new" was my dress. My "something borrowed" was a previously worn garter from Nick's family. My "something blue" was periwinkle blue painted toenails.

My bridesmaids made me a scrapbook filled with pictures, and each of them read me a beautiful letter they had written to me that made me cry. They filled the air with singing, "Going to the Chapel,"[13] and they scurried around putting on their handmade periwinkle blue bridesmaid dresses with matching sandals. I had picked periwinkle as my wedding color because it represents royalty, and being part of God's family is as royal as you can get.

And no period. It didn't make its entrance that day.

We took separate pictures before and couple photos after the wedding, because Nick and I had chosen to wait until the ceremony to see each other. I was kept hidden downstairs while our church gym filled up with so many wonderful people who had loved and supported and prayed for us through the years.

The ceremony started with worship, then the wedding party entered. Nick's parents sang a song by Wayne Watson called "Somewhere in the World"[14]—a song about praying for your son's future wife. Then it was my turn to walk down the aisle. The last thing I remember my dad saying to me before he took me down was that his suit had been the wrong size for him and they had to get it fixed. My sweet dad who had loved me all those years walked me down the aisle to hand me into the care of my future husband.

It felt so surreal. Everything. I did not feel like it was me walking down the aisle. I did not feel like it was me on the platform stage with Nick saying my vows. I sang to Nick a song at my wedding that I had written for my future husband back when I was 16, when I was just getting to know Nick. My friend Aly accompanied me. Nick started to cry and then I choked up for a second, closed my eyes, and as Aly strongly carried the song in that moment I picked up my courage and finished it.

Next thing I knew, we were man and wife, and Nick was going to kiss me, for the very first time. All of the sudden I became very nervous and very shy, and as he went to kiss me he clasped my face in his hands and gave me a very sweet, simple first-time kiss. Then he kissed me one more time. I looked around and saw my bridesmaids wildly waving these Olympic-style rating cards for our kiss, and the groomsmen all standing very stoic and respectful, and I felt very blessed to be surrounded by such a huge crowd of witnesses to God's goodness in our lives, separately and together, to finally bring us to this moment of becoming man and wife.

We walked down the aisle and Nick kissed me a few more times, then we returned for final pictures before the cake reception.

We had a round of toasting consisting of some very sweet and sentimental words, as well as some that had everyone laughing—including one from John Price about being an Intel engineer, and a three-page toast from Nick's brother, Sam. I will never forget the words at the end of his toast. It was a hope, "that on this day, it would be the day that we would love each other the least." Those words have stuck in my heart over the years and it is so true that over time, love develops, and you can take the hard times and make things harder, or you can choose for them to be what creates beauty and depth in your love. That is my desire in my marriage to Nicholas James Adams, that we will choose the path of beauty and depth through trials and joys.

We cut our cake, and our guests had fun clinking their glasses to make us practice at kissing, then we spent the rest of the ceremony greeting everyone and thanking them for coming. We were so blessed by the love everyone showered on us that day.

We had chosen to have Nick's dad and my dad drive the convertible for us, taking us to our new home together to get our bags for our honeymoon, and then to a hotel by the airport where we would catch a shuttle the next morning and head for Disney World! Our convertible drove up for us to depart, decorated with simple "Just Married" on the windows, pop cans dragging on the ground behind (which my dad promptly removed 10 seconds after we were out of sight of the church) and little wedding bells. It was very cute and tastefully done, and my dad and Al, both dressed in their tuxes in the front seat, made a mutual agreement that all the decorations would be removed as soon as they dropped us off at the hotel, so as not to send the wrong message during their drive back to the church to pick up their wives!

We left that afternoon—that beautiful, sunny, 80-degree afternoon—filled with memories that blurred together into a really special day, and headed towards the next big thing...our honeymoon.

Dear Children,

I love you so much! September 16, 2000 was the start of two lives being joined together by the Lord, committing to spend the rest of our days together. I wore a white dress and white shoes. Your dad and I weren't perfect. But we never crossed the line completely before we were married, and I am so grateful we were able to share our kisses and intimacy for the first time after our marriage. It was a time to be grateful—we were crossing our six years of waiting into learning how to live together, to be one together, to love each other every day.

Our hope for each one of you is that you, too, will be able to celebrate intimacy for the first time with your spouse, after you are married. It is a beautiful gift that God designed for husband and wife. We want to support you in decisions leading up to your marriage that will help you live in purity, honoring and respecting the people God brings into your lives prior to your commitment to marriage. Treat them as brothers and sisters, as dear friends, because they are potentially someone else's bride or groom. And they are made in the image of God.

Your spouse is meant to be a gift to you, just as you are to them. Treat yourself this way, treat all those around you in that way.

I want to tell you that if you do stumble, it does not mean that you are unworthy to wear white, or have your bride wear white on that day. Because when we confess and repent, He has taken all of our sin struggles, nailed them to the cross, and He makes us whiter than snow. He does this for all of us that turn to Him when we fall short. Satan shames, God forgives and embraces. Always remember that. God wants you to turn to Him with your struggles. Satan wants you to turn away from God and feel unworthy of Him. Remember the story of Rahab, marrying Salmon.[15] God made beautiful things out of their story. This is not a get-out-of-jail-free card, but a reminder to my children—if you ever feel like there is no escape from your sin—that He will never stop wanting you to turn back to Him.

But I also want to tell you that if you do stumble in these areas, it will be hard work on the other end to create an environment where you can trust each other. A safe place filled with intimacy that is pure and lovely. There are consequences that follow these choices. God asks us to wait, because He loves you, He is the Creator of sex,[16] and He wants you to enjoy it to His fullest intent. He wants you to cherish your spouse He has given you. We hope and pray that someday, Lord willing you meet someone to share your life with, you will be able to make a marriage covenant with that person, and for the first time be able to truly give yourself in His love to that person.

With All My Hopes and Prayers for You in This,
Your Mama, the Wife of Your Daddy

Genesis 2:18, 22–25 (ESV)

Then the Lord God said, "It is not good that the man should be alone; I will make him a helper fit for him." And the rib that the Lord God had taken from the man he made into a woman and brought her to the man. Then the man said, "This at last is bone of my bones and flesh of my flesh; she shall be called Woman, because she was taken out of Man." Therefore, a man shall leave his father and his mother and hold fast to his wife, and they shall become one flesh. And the man and his wife were both naked and were not ashamed.

Ephesians 5:1–2 (ESV)

Therefore be imitators of God, as beloved children. And walk in love, as Christ loved us and gave himself up for us, a fragrant offering and sacrifice to God.

Hebrews 13:4 (NASB)

Marriage is to be held in honor among all, and the marriage bed is to be undefiled; for fornicators and adulterers God will judge.

Psalm 51:6–13 (NASB)

Behold, You desire truth in the innermost being, and in the hidden part You will make me know wisdom. Purify me with Hyssop, and I shall be clean; wash me, and I shall be whiter than snow. Make me to hear joy and gladness, let the bones which You have broken rejoice. Hide Your face from my sins and blot out all my iniquities. Create in me a clean heart, O God, and renew a steadfast spirit within me. Do not cast me away from Your presence, and do not take Your Holy Spirit from me. Restore to me the joy of Your salvation and sustain me with a willing spirit. Then I will teach transgressors Your ways, and sinners will be converted to You.

1 Thessalonians 4:3–8 (ESV)

For this is the will of God, your sanctification: that you abstain from sexual immorality; that each one of you know how to control his own body in holiness and honor, not in the passion of lust like the Gentiles who do not know God; that no one transgress and wrong his brother in this matter, because the Lord is an avenger in all these things, as we told you beforehand and solemnly warned you. For God has not called us for impurity, but in holiness. Therefore, whoever disregards this, disregards not man, who gives the Holy Spirit to you.

✹ THE NOT SO "HONEY" MOON ✹

I have really been thinking and praying about how to write this, because I want to be very sensitive to my marriage with Nick. But I think we both agree there is a lot we learned in this, and the reality of things not going as planned hit once again, so I will do my best. This actually will lead into a lot of areas in our marriage that we had to work through and sort out, but for now, we will just cover the honeymoon week.

We dreamed and talked about where we would want to go. We decided on Disney World, because we wanted to have fun. I remember looking through the different hotel resort options and Nick showed me the few he was thinking of for us. There was one that was very cute: Dixie Landings (it has been remodeled and named something else since). I loved the French style of the buildings, and the atmosphere seemed a little less childlike than some of the other resorts. Since we were on our honeymoon, although we did want it to be fun, we were also going for a romantic feel.

Nick took care of all the details. I think that is my favorite part of this, that he let me dream up ideas with him, and he took that and ran with it to create a very special time for us. Honestly, I had spent a lot of time planning and dreaming up our wedding and thinking about how much fun it would be to have a vacation together and to start a home and a family together. But I didn't spend much time at all preparing for the three-letter word essential to marriage. See, I didn't even type it out because that was how I felt about it: extremely shy, not wanting to think about anything of that nature before we were married, because I wanted to keep my focus on purity of heart.

In our counseling, our pastor had even asked us if we had talked about things together to prepare ourselves for the honeymoon. Of course we hadn't. No way was I about to open up about anything of that nature there. We were also the first among our friends to get married, so we didn't have a lot of advice from those that had gone before us. In conclusion to that very brief discussion with our pastor, we were given some suggestions to read up on the subject, which Nick did, but I chose not to until after we were married.

I can't really judge if this was the right decision or not, but I am going to share the outcome. We got to our hotel by the airport and said goodbye to our dads. Then we checked in and all of the sudden I was faced with the reality of what we were supposed to do next. And I got super nervous. I don't want to go into too many details, but a basic summary is that after staying up until 3:00 a.m., we did not have sex, and we got a very short amount of sleep before we had to catch our plane that morning. It was a very bumpy start.

Then, around 12:00 p.m. the next day, while we were on the airplane to Orlando, I felt a little funny, and I went to the bathroom to check things out. I discovered my period had just started. Yep, exactly what I had planned. As soon as we got off the plane and got to a shuttle to escort us to our Disneyland hotel, my cramps were in full swing, and I was miserable. All I wanted was a bed. We couldn't get checked in quickly enough. Once we got to our room, I dealt with my period pains in regular fashion in the privacy of our bathroom, and finally got into very comfortable clothes. Nick was amazing through all of this and ordered us pizza for the night. We just stayed in bed and watched the Disney channel while eating pizza. By the next day I was feeling well enough to try out one of the theme parks with Nick. But I was on my period the whole week.

Nick was patient in the beginning, but I recall one night of frustration in the intimacy area, when he told me that if I wasn't willing to try to be with him, we would need to see a counselor. I told him I would never, ever tell anyone about this and that we could just live together without ever having sex.

Slowly throughout the week the Lord helped me overcome all my anxieties and fears. By the end of the week, we were able to come together, and it was exactly what it needed to be to help me through what I was sorting through. But that first week was definitely not the best start in that area of our marriage, and so many times I have wanted to go back to Disney World to redo our honeymoon. It is what it is, and although it was a really hard week, it was really fun too.

At the end of our trip, we were exhausted and ready to be home in our new apartment. Our long flight didn't bring us back home until close to midnight. We opened our doors to find our home not only filled nearly to the ceiling with a huge, very generous pile of wedding presents, but also covered with decorations everywhere. Apparently our home had been victim to not one but two post-wedding decorating parties. My sneaky brother had at one time lifted the keys from my purse and made himself a copy of them, just in case he ever needed it. Streamers everywhere, balloons surrounding the gifts, ribbons and decorations clinging to bathroom mirrors. Rose petals leading us straight to our bed.

They did a beautiful job. Really, it was very classy. But Nick was about to get the full experience of what an OCD wife looks like at 12:00 in the morning. I couldn't handle it. It was our new apartment—and I wanted it clean. Tidy. Yikes! We spent a few hours into the early morning taking down decorations piece by piece. At one point I lost my newlywed husband to sleep, so I finished up the cleaning myself and headed to bed.

The first week back, Nick didn't have to work, so our time was filled with opening gifts, returning what we had duplicates of, and starting our family. What I mean by that is that thanks to our generous wedding guests, we had enough gift money to pay the apartment pet deposit, and Nick took me out to get us our very first cat. We searched all day trying to find a kitten. We visited local pet shelters and a pet store nearby, with no success. As a last resort we traipsed across the river in Portland and found a calico kitten inside the window of a Scamps store.

Search successfully completed. We purchased our kitty at the price of $69.95 and got the supplies we would need to care for our new baby, then headed back to the apartment. Once we got her settled in for the night, we watched her wander through our home figuring out her surroundings. We debated what we should call her. Finally, we settled on Katie. She was our Katie Kitty, our baby girl.

At the end of our second week together, I started to mentally prepare myself for the reality of Nick going back to work, and me staying home with our new kitten. Through all the bumps and ups and downs, overall, I had very much enjoyed our first two weeks as a married couple. With Nick heading to his job, I was ready to start mine as well. A job I had dreamed about my whole life. A stay-at-home wife and hopefully someday soon, a stay-at-home mom. At that moment, our life was filled with much hope and bright dreams for our future together, as husband and wife.

Dear Children,

If anything, I hope and pray our first week of marriage can help give some wisdom to you in your marriages, to help things not be quite so bumpy. First, I pray that you can take realistic expectations into a honeymoon. Know that things may not go as perfectly as you would hope, that it takes time to figure it out. Leave room for the time in your married life schedule to not be rushed. To think of the honeymoon as a season that allows you to really get acquainted with the details of your spouse. Second, it's okay to prepare and talk through expectations ahead of time, with a few trusted people that could pour into your discussion a healthy Biblical perspective of sex in marriage. Third, don't put pressure on yourself that it has to all go like clockwork that first week. Or even the first month. Honestly, you have the whole rest of your lives to figure it out together. Keep persevering and trying. Fourth, practice so much grace on each other. You both need it. Words of grace can heal insecurities in a heartbeat, and create a safe spot to try again next time.

My last words of encouragement come from a question I received from a high school student. She wanted to know if it was hard to have a pure heart when having sex with my husband. These words rang in my soul. So often, when we are told no and wait prior to getting married, it can definitely be a transition to mentally say, "It's okay now."

But let me tell you, sex in marriage is one of the most beautiful, holy experiences a married couple can share. God delights over seeing what He created enjoying this gift, in the way He designed it. My answer to her was that having a pure heart came with the territory of this intimacy we were given to share in marriage. When two people married to each other are loving God, and looking to love their spouse with His selfless love, it is one of the purest intimate moments you will ever experience.

Love You, My Children,
Mama

Ephesians 5:25–32 (NASB)

Husbands, love your wives, just as Christ also loved the church and gave Himself up for her, so that He might sanctify her, having cleansed her by the washing of water with the word, that He might present to Himself the church in all her glory, having no spot or wrinkle or any such thing; but that she would be holy and blameless. So husbands ought also to love their own wives as their own bodies. He who loves his own wife loves himself; for no one ever hated his own flesh, but nourishes and cherishes it, just as Christ also does the church, because we are members of His body. FOR THIS REASON A MAN SHALL LEAVE HIS FATHER AND MOTHER AND SHALL BE JOINED TO HIS WIFE, AND THE TWO SHALL BECOME ONE FLESH. This mystery is great; but I am speaking with reference to Christ and the church.

Song of Solomon 4:10 (ESV)

How beautiful is your love, my sister, my bride! How much better is your love than wine, and the fragrances of your oils than any spice!

Song of Solomon 5:16 (ESV)

His mouth is most sweet, and he is altogether desirable. This is my beloved and this is my friend, O daughters of Jerusalem.

1 Peter 3:1–2 (ESV)

Likewise wives, be subject to your own husbands, so that even if some do not obey the word, they may be won without a word by the conduct of their wives, when they see your respectful and pure conduct.

1 Peter 3:7 (ESV)

Likewise, husbands, live with your wives in an understanding way, showing honor to the woman as the weaker vessel, since they are heirs with you of the grace of life, so that your prayers may not be hindered.

ᴇ SERVING IN THE HIGH SCHOOL YOUTH GROUP ᴈ

Nick and I have always had a desire to be intentional to serve and care for others, and in our minds, when we were making plans to start our lives together, we did not see why we would not continue to make choices in this way. Around the time we got engaged, we began discussing what that would look like for us in our married life. We decided that when we got married, it would probably be a wise time to step back from all we had been part of with our college group. The time spent those four years had been a blessing, but once we were married, we wanted to move forward with something new. However, we still wanted to help in some way at our church, and we began to verbally process what that could look like for us.

We prayed about it and decided to meet with the youth pastor at our church. We talked about our desire to transfer our extra time to helping with youth ministries. He was very excited about this possibility for us. He mentioned the need for people to help on a middle school retreat. Nick was unable to get the time off for it, still finishing up school, but I said I would go. On that retreat I met some amazing eighth-grade girls in my bunk room. Ashley, Annette and Allison were part of that group, and at the end of my weekend, I was attached to the idea of getting to be part of their lives. Nick and I prayed about it and decided that we would go on staff with the high school youth group.

As we were making decisions about how we would serve together once we were married, one of the leaders of our college group asked if he could meet with us. He shared his concern that it might not be wise for us to commit to anything right away. He suggested that after we were married, it might be better to spend the first year just being married, and focus on learning how to love each other in that season. We appreciated his advice, but we didn't heed it. We received opposite advice from the youth pastor, who had been married a few years at that point and shared that he thought starting off your marriage with serving was a great way to use your time together. That is the advice we chose to follow.

(In reflection, I don't know which road was better to take. Looking back at what happened those first two years of our marriage, and what the needs were in the high school group, it really is a hard thing to sort through if we made the best decision or not. There are things I would have regretted missing out on if we hadn't joined the staff, but there are things I know would have been better for us as a couple if we had chosen to take that first year off. You learn and grow from these choices. This was our first big decision that would set the trajectory for our life.)

As we made the decision to help in the high school group, we went on their spring retreat to Westwind in May (this amazing piece of beach along the coast, hidden just north of Lincoln City, that you have to take a river raft to get to). Our hope was to start building relationships with some of the kids as we made the transition from our college group to helping in the high school group over the next few months. We both felt our love grow for these students who we were just beginning to meet. It confirmed our decision to be part of the youth group. A lot of the students were interested in hearing our dating/engagement story and excited with us about our upcoming wedding.

Over the summer we started attending the high school Sunday School class on a weekly basis. We also attended their Wednesday night youth group. The youth pastor had been working with high school students on leading worship. He wanted to step back from that responsibility, so he turned that role over to me and Nick to oversee. By the time we were married, we were also assigned small discipleship groups to lead, and I was ecstatic to see my list included the gals from the middle school retreat, plus two other freshmen girls that I looked forward to getting to know better.

A big announcement came one Wednesday evening during our first year serving. Our youth pastor, head of this ministry that reached more than 100 kids on a weekly basis, was going to be returning to school and stepping down from leading the youth group. There was no replacement planned for him.

Nick and I looked at what we had as leadership—nine adults for all these students—and the math didn't add up. But we were determined to keep this ministry going for the church.

All of the leaders dug deeper and stepped up in their roles, more committed than ever to provide stability, teaching, training, prayer, and fun activities to continue to give these students community. For two school years Nick and I did this together with them.

Some fun memories stem from those times...

Getting toilet-papered by some of the kids and one of the staff members who was very much a kid at heart. Nick and I were on vacation and returned to our home covered in toilet paper. But on Sunday at church, we decided to play it cool. Didn't say a word to anyone about it. Then, one of the guys, Eric, couldn't contain himself anymore. He had to ask us, "So, did anything happen to your house last week?" I pretended to think to myself, and then I responded with, "Well...like what?" And he stepped out further on his limb, "Did anyone TP your house while you were gone?"

"Hmm...now that you mention it, I did happen to notice some toilet paper in one of our neighbor's yard..." spoken with a straight face... (and being very honest as there was some toilet paper in our neighbor's yard when we returned.)

And he took it. "Oh no! We got the wrong house!" Not only that, but he continued to spill forth all the names of everyone that participated in the awesome TP job. "We almost went through a window to decorate the inside of the house, too! I'm so glad we didn't do that!"

"Me too!" I thought in my head.

Within the next five minutes, he had told everyone how they got the wrong house, and the leader that was involved came to talk to us about it. I couldn't take torturing them anymore. I smiled big and told them they got us.

It was just one of those awesome moments to go down in the books for how to respond to high schoolers when they TP your home.

Another amazing time was winter camp, when the band "Down Here" was on its way to Nashville to sign a contract with a big recording label. They stopped by our camp and did a full worship concert out in the mountains for us. I will always remember getting to play Spades with some of the band members. Good times.

One leader, Deanna, who was a travel agent, had promised to take her small group girls on a cruise between their junior and senior years. She needed a chaperone. Since I was not working, a full-time stay-at-home wife, she asked if I would be up for coming with them. Did I need time to think about it? Nope! On I went for an adventure I had never imagined. We got to visit San Diego, where some of the girls bought beach boards and one got a henna tattoo, soaking up the sun. I decided I could definitely visit San Diego again someday. When we went to Ensenada, we all got our hair braided—although my only regret was having to cover my head with a bandana the rest of the time, to avoid a burnt scalp. Catalina Island was another stop, and several of us got our ears pierced on the upper cartilage. (It was so adventurous to me at the time—but boy did that piercing hurt for the next year, and I could not sleep on that side as it healed). The food on the ship was incredible. We got to sample many varieties of options; I tried escargot for the first time, and probably the last. It was fun to try it without having to pay for it. (It tastes like slimy mushrooms, if you are wondering.) Getting to know the four girls on the trip, and have an adventure with them and Deanna, was the best gift about that time.

One of the biggest lessons I learned was from an unwise choice I made as a leader. I had invited my group over for a sleepover. It was a great time of hanging out together, talking and having girl time. But I let them watch a movie without running it past the parents. A week later, I got a 45-minute phone call/reprimand from one of the dads. His daughter had come home from my house, all excited about the time, and shared about the movie they had watched and how funny it was. Her family decided to watch it and was shocked at some of the jokes and things in this movie that they did not want to expose their children to.

Even though the movie maybe wouldn't be a big deal to a lot of families, this dad was absolutely right on. For their family, it was not okay to watch something like that. I should have thought through it more. I should have asked. But I didn't. I had to apologize to the girls and let them know I had made a bad choice.

That lesson stuck with me as I started to think through what I would allow my children to watch someday. What movies was I personally watching? Was I being vigilant to guard my heart with what came into our home? I am glad that dad was willing to take that stand for his family. We need to be voices for our kids. When you are sending your child to a church youth leader's home, you want to know that they are going to be cared for the way you would care for them. I failed that time, but what I learned from it was so valuable.

Nick and I found that with all of our time invested in the high school group, we really didn't have much time for friends outside of that. We had just a few nights at home, and with being newly married, we were trying to work through all sorts of kinks in learning how to communicate better, intimacy, and spending time together. Honestly, our first year of marriage was really hard. The second year was just a smidge better. We were thriving at serving, but empty in the friendship bank, and our marriage was not thriving.

Our youth group was going on more than a year without a pastor leading it. As staff, we were all getting burned out. After a long search, they found a new pastor for the group. Mark and his wife, Irene, were new energy and life that our group had been longing for. We enjoyed getting to know them and their heart for the students. Also, they brought with them some friends who had more experience with worship leading. Mark asked us if we would mind turning that responsibility over to them. We were happy to.

One evening at home, Nick and I got into a horrible fight. It was a repeating conversation that was filled with hurt and exhaustion and did not bring into our marriage life-giving love. I remember being on the floor of our bathroom crying, and we were trying to figure out what to do. We needed time to care for each other. So much had built up that wasn't being dealt with. We needed friendships, and although we loved the community in the high school group and the staff there, we sorely missed some of the relationships from our college group time of life. As tears flowed down my face, we both knew what we needed to do. Having been relieved of our primary ministry in the high school group, and now having a pastor to oversee the ministry, Nick and I were at peace, one that only comes from the Lord, that we needed to finish up the school year, and then we were being called to step back so we could care for what was broken in our relationship.

When we told our new youth pastor, I know it wasn't what he had hoped for. We still finished our second year strong with them. We helped chaperone a spring break mission trip to Mexico with the high schoolers, which Mark and Irene had planned. It solidified our decision, watching them engage with the students and start to build trust relationships. We knew the kids would be in great hands. My biggest loss over the decision was no longer doing a small group with my girls. I had been with them for two years and adored each one. I dealt with feelings of letting them down.

It's hard to make a decision like that, where there is so much need and relationships are involved. And that is where the questions I had at the beginning come from. Did we make the right decision by saying yes to helping with the youth group, versus taking a year to rest and be married? When I look over the two years we were there, the need was so strong, with them not having a youth pastor for a good chunk of it. We didn't know that would happen when we said yes to helping. Had we been called just for that season? I don't know all the answers. I do know now, very clearly, that we did the right thing in stepping back and taking rest time. I had no idea what was around the corner and the work that God was going to do, but I am so glad we listened to His voice and obeyed.

Dear Children,

We can't make our decisions based on what will please people. If we use that as our guide, we will always be letting someone down. The Lord needs to be our guide in matters such as these. Sometimes the answers will seem unclear, and maybe there isn't a right or a wrong in that moment. I do look back to that time when we were broken and hurting in our bathroom after a very hard night, and I can say with confidence that God was making it clear to us that we needed to step back from our commitment. In this decision, I still felt like I was letting people down. I'm sure I did let some people down.

The thing I have learned is that we can love with Jesus' love, but we can't be Jesus. We don't live on people's pedestals—that is only a place that Jesus rightfully belongs. So when we make our decisions based on His love, and His calling for us, His peace will guard our heart and mind. He is the one to care for and meet the needs of His people, and He will provide. So be available, be ready, and be sensitive to Him.

I Love You, Children,
Mama

Isaiah 26:3–4, 8–9, 12–13 (NIV)

You keep him in perfect peace whose mind is stayed on you, because he trusts in you. Trust in the Lord forever, for the Lord God is an everlasting rock...In the path of your judgments, O Lord, we wait for you; your name and remembrance are the desire of our soul. My soul yearns for you in the night; my spirit within me earnestly seeks you. For when your judgments are in the earth, the inhabitants of the world learn righteousness...O Lord, you will ordain peace for us, for you have indeed done for us all our works. O Lord our God, other lords besides you have ruled over us, but your name alone we bring to remembrance.

⋇ NOW I WILL DO SOMETHING NEW ⋇

Stepping back from high school group ministries proved to be a very wise decision for our marriage. It provided a new place to figure out just being us. We weren't rushed to go a hundred different directions, and we took our time, just easing into how we would spend our days.

During the summer months, we thought we would give the young marrieds group a try at our church. They had several outings planned, and we enjoyed the aspect of getting to know other couples in similar places in life. My favorite fun memory with that group was participating in a progressive dinner. Basically, as couples we got mixed with multiple couples at three different locations for appetizers, dinner and dessert at a home all together. There were a lot of great people that we loved being able to meet through that group. However, something didn't fit for us long term. At the time I didn't understand the lack of peace and hesitancy to commit to the group, but looking back I know exactly why. God had a very specific call on the next season of our life and He was giving us rest and refreshment to prepare us for what was ahead.

We started to reconnect with some of our college group friends. Not that we had stopped being friends, but we just had not had the time to spend with them like before. One of the guys, Brent, had just proposed to a gal who had joined the college group the day Nick and I left for our honeymoon. She reached out to Nick and me and invited us with her and Brent, along with a few other friends, to come to the beach for the weekend at her grandparents' beach home. It was such a blessing to have the freedom to do that. The summer weekend proved to be amazing as we enjoyed laying out in the sun, climbing a dune, outlet shopping just us girls, playing games, and watching movies. In spending time with this group, we remembered and cherished what we had lost a bit of when we left our college group: what it feels like to be family.

We started to spend more time with our friends from this circle. Nick was asked to be part of Amy and Brent's wedding the following spring. Our friends

Eddie and Holly got engaged and planned for a wedding just a short time after Amy and Brent. We celebrated our first pumpkin carving contest—the winner being "Chunkin' Pumpkin," carved by Eddie and Holly. (A pumpkin with its guts, seeds and all, flowing out of the mouth all over the table). This tradition with these friends carried on for years, with a commemorative award of "Chunkin' Pumpkin" being handed out to a new winner each year.

Then our church announced that they would be starting a Saturday night service. Nick and I and our friends talked about trying it out. For several years Nick and I had struggled with the routine and schedule of our church. We loved the preaching, but we felt often there was not room left for the Holy Spirit to work in people's hearts and souls during the gatherings. It felt very scripted and scheduled down to the second. That summer we helped with worship at a church family campout, and I will never forget the sad words I heard from an elderly lady who used to be my Sunday School teacher when I was little. After we had our group song time, she asked us, "Are you all high schoolers? What type of music is that? This time was just terrible—just terrible..." It broke my heart that her perspective was not excitement seeing young people love Jesus. She had her tradition and we had, unknowingly, broken her tradition and expectation and let her down.

There was this ache in those of us who were younger to see God do something new. To reach out to the coming generations through these older generations, to be poured into and loved by them and celebrate Him. And some of those things definitely did happen and were done well at our church. But Nick and I hoped for so much more for our community. We had prayed many times that Jesus would come do something new.

I will never forget walking into our first Saturday night service. Entering into the doors that opened to the sanctuary, I remember hearing the words to "Here I am to worship,"[17] and a peace settled into my soul so unexplainable. I knew, within the depths of me, that this was home. The aching and longing for change—God had heard those prayers. He was doing something new.

After attending a few times, we knew this was our service. We were questioned about not attending Sunday mornings, asked if that was not honoring the day that the Lord had made? But we found that the rhythm of attending church on Saturday nights allowed us to continue the season of rest we needed for our marriage. We would attend, then often go have a late dinner with friends, ending up back at someone's house for games and more fellowship. On Sunday mornings Nick and I would sleep in and have a restful day for the remainder of the weekend. For us, it was very much a Sabbath rest.

We didn't jump into serving right away at these gatherings. But we heard they were starting to have prayer meetings prior to the service. Nick and I were taking our time in this, but we decided it was something we could do. We joined those meetings every Saturday night prior to the gathering.

I used to write songs all the time. Nothing that would ever amount to anything amazing in the world's eyes, but to me, they were ways I would work out my faith with the Lord, and they brought out a creative side that the Lord had instilled in me through the use of words and music. So as not to lose them, I decided to make a keepsake of these gifts that the Lord had given me and recorded them at a music studio. It was not fancy or perfect. I had a limited budget to work with, so I did one-time takes of each song, without editing or re-recording them until I hit that perfect place. It was enough that I could keep them and share them with friends and family.

I decided to get brave and leave those CDs in the worship pastor's box, as well as with the new pastor of the Saturday night service—just in case they might like one of the songs and want to use it down the road. I have always dealt with a lack of confidence in sharing things like this. One time while making announcements at a women's gathering, my friend told me I needed to not act like I was apologizing for speaking. I think that when you have written something, it's a piece of you, and the fear of what someone might say that would tear that down is a scary thought.

In a bold moment I overcame that fear, and then left the church as quickly as possible for fear they might see me leaving them in their boxes and I might actually have to talk to them about what they were.

Two weeks later, at the end of a church gathering, there was an announcement asking me and another gal to come up to the front of the stage. I had no idea what to expect. I met in person for the first time Phil Comer, the pastor over this service. He was looking for someone to help do keys, and occasionally do harmony for singing, and wanted to know if I would be up for helping out in this way.

I was very excited when I left church that night. An opportunity to serve in another small way seemed just right for the season of life I was in. At home, I was dealing with a broken dream. I so badly wanted to get pregnant and start our family together. But as each month went by, I dealt with the disappointing blow of another month without a positive pregnancy test. When I was younger, I dreamed I would grow up and pursue music and songwriting, like Amy Grant. It was truly something I loved to do. When I talked to Nick about that dream in the early years of our dating, it was not in the direction he was heading, so I released the dream of following the pursuit of music in order to follow the pursuit of another dream, marrying Nick and starting a family.

This opportunity that I had been given turned out to be a little dream that became a reality for the next several years of my life. To be part of a worship band that praised Jesus and brought other people to a place of praising God through song in their own lives each week was a big gift to me. I hadn't planned on serving in music for that season, but the Lord allowed me to be part of it while I waited for the other dream that was currently at an impasse. I never quite felt "cool" enough to be a member of the band, but in those years when I had that honor, it was as if God said to me, "You are cool enough to be in My band."

At those Saturday night services, God began to heal my heart from the hurt of dealing with infertility. He spoke to me words that brought me peace, and each week I would lay down my hopes and dreams one more time at His alter and surrender to what He was doing with today. I remember one time Luis Palau came to speak, and he gave an alter call to surrender things we were holding onto at the end of the gathering. I came up to the front of the stage with others and prayed and laid down my mama dream one more time before the Lord, as silent tears of release streamed down my face. In fact it was a rare Saturday night that I didn't cry at some point during the service.

In the meantime, the Lord was doing a work at the Saturday night service. Phil and his wife Diane started hosting monthly gatherings at their house. Nick and I attended and met so many amazing people and friends. One of those nights, at the end of our time, when we were saying our goodbyes to Phil and Diane, Phil wanted to ask us a question. I will never forget it.

"I want to ask you guys if you would pray about something. We are looking to turn this Saturday night service into a church plant, and we are trying to see how many people might be interested in being part of that. You don't need to answer now, just go home and pray about it."

I felt a stir in my heart, as if God were saying, "This is it!" Nick and I exchanged a quick glance and agreed that we would pray about it and let him know. When we got to the privacy of our car, we looked at each other and felt immediate confirmation that the Lord had spoken the same thing to both of us. We would be part of this church plant.

In the months that followed, much planning and preparation went into all the details that would need to happen to bring this church together. There was a Spirit-led unity among all involved, knitting our hearts deeply together. We spent many times praying over this church, asking the Lord to come do His work. Praying over neighborhoods, over individual people, family members. He was moving this forward—it was His work, and we were all just witnesses to His provision and faithfulness over and over again.

I will never forget the Sunday morning when our current church led a prayer send-off over us. When everyone had made their decision of whether to stay or go, our number ended up being about 150. My parents and sister attended the Saturday night service at that time, but my dad thought they were going to stay. He had gone to our church since he was a child, and it had been his family for years. I remember seeing him out in the foyer of the church right before we went in to be prayed for, reading his Bible and seeking the Lord. He looked up and smiled at me, and told me he would see us inside.

All 150 of us squeezed up on the stage as leaders of our current church laid hands over us and prayed for the work the Lord was going to do, blessing us as they prepared to send us off. Afterward, people came up to me and excitedly said, "Isn't that great about your parents?" Apparently, as my dad prayed prior to the send-off, the Lord spoke to him, and as our new church walked up to the front, he went to my mom and my sister and said, "Alright, let's go." They were coming with the church too!

One of the things I remember most about this season is the preparation of the heart that was going on in both of us. God was doing a new thing—paving the way, confirming a movement forward into an unknown—but while I was dealing with personal loss of dreams and hopes for the start of our family, it contradicted those feelings with so much life and hope. God was calling us to be part of something He wanted to do in the city. If we had children at that time of our life, we would have been distracted and unable to be as involved as we were in the beginning. It was a surrender of my dreams for a season.

It wasn't that He was forgetting my hopes for the future. He was preparing something big, so I would be able to look back on that time and see His fingerprints all over it. In Psalm 37[18] it talks about delighting yourself in the Lord and He will give you the desires of your heart. But it's not all about getting our desires. The point that I think gets missed more than anything is delighting yourself in the Lord. The more you do that, the more His desires become your desires. It is about being brought to a place of complete surrender of things out of your control, so He can start to do His work, and trust me, everything about how He eventually grew our family is all glory to Him. I would have been too unoriginal to write my story in the way He was fashioning it.

In the beginning of all of this, we had let go of something, and it didn't necessarily look like the right thing to do from the outside. Leaving our high school service to take time to rest as a couple was not a bad thing at all. It was a necessary season of rest, so we could regain His strength in our marriage and be restored to a place where we would be able to be part of what He wanted to do with us, which was to make us part of a bigger movement He was about to create from this Saturday night service. A movement where, as a new church body was being formed, we would stand back and watch the Lord move and work in ways that we could never have imagined when we said yes. The Lord was building His church. These were the words that the Lord had spoken over Phil and Diane Comer when the Lord first put the dream of planting a church on their hearts: "Make it a Jesus Church."

Dear Children,

I think of your years of schooling. Each year builds upon the last one. You learn things you need for the coming years ahead—you can't learn multiplication without learning how to add, and you can't be ready to read without having knowledge of what each letter is capable of sounding like.

The same thing is true in life. God is so gracious to prepare us for what we need each day, each year. Do you know that when we were 18, our church mentioned they might want to do a church plant someday? Both Nick and I looked at each other then, and thought that would be really cool. But at that stage in life, we weren't ready for it. The years that followed included being part of an awesome college group, getting married, helping in a high school group, and taking time to rest and mature in our marriage. God had called us to be part of this church plant. But it was over six years between when the thought entered our minds, and finding ourselves in that Saturday night service. God was already at work birthing a church plant before we were even aware of it. Next thing we knew, we were right in the middle of where God was calling us.

It was nothing we could have planned or asked for. We still stand back in awe of how God did that.

I just want to encourage you once more: don't take lightly things that God may be speaking into your lives. Pray about them, surrender them to Him. King David felt a calling to build a house for the Lord, but God told him that was for his son to do. It is always most important to remember that it's never about us, and always about Jesus. Our church when it was first started was called Solid Rock. He is the Solid Rock to build all of our dreams on. Trust Him, He has a big gospel plan He wants to accomplish, and He's taking us with Him.

Love You Guys,
Mama

2 Peter 3:8–9 (NASB)

But do not let this one fact escape your notice, beloved, that with the Lord one day is like a thousand years, and a thousand years like one day. The Lord is not slow about His promise, as some count slowness, but is patient toward you, not wishing for any to perish but for all to come to repentance.

Isaiah 30:21 (NASB)

Your ears will hear a word behind you, "This is the way, walk in it," whenever you turn to the right or to the left.

Habakkuk 2:3 (ESV)

For still the vision awaits its appointed time; it hastens to the end— it will not lie. If it seems slow, wait for it; it will surely come; it will not delay.

NICK'S STRUGGLE

After writing about the story of the birth of A Jesus Church, I am eager to get to the next part of the movement of new things He was doing, to be able to share those stories of His faithfulness. However, I have another part to share about from the early years of our marriage, one that is too important to leave out. There was much heartbreak in the early years of our marriage. The brokenness that I will share in this chapter is the reality of what happens to the dream of what married life can be like, when sin finds its way in to kill, steal, and destroy. It was a brokenness that would require me to learn to forgive and forgive and forgive and try to learn to trust and forgive once more, the man that I had committed my life to.

I want to be really careful as I write this to be sensitive to my husband. And yet I know I have his approval to share these life lessons, because the way we both feel about weaknesses is that we would rather share and have God use our hard times to help others, than keep them to ourselves. I remember a while back sitting down for dinner with some friends who were about to be married. They had the pre-wedding glow, excited for the dreams and plans for their future. And they asked us if there was any advice we could share. Nick was quick to respond to the husband. "If you struggle in the area of lust, pornography, sexual addiction of that sort, try to get it figured out now, because marriage won't fix those struggles." And it is so true.

When I met Nick, I admired him very much. He was a true gentleman, had plans for his life, was confident, and he and I shared many of the same life goals. He really was a gift from the Lord. As I mentioned in earlier chapters, several months into our relationship Nick broke down and told me about his struggle in the areas listed above. He felt terrible. He didn't even know what he was doing when he got started, and all of the sudden he was in the midst of a struggle that he didn't know how to solve. I was pretty naïve about those things and was quick to forgive. In the following years of our courtship, every so often Nick would break down and confess he had struggled once again, and then once again he would step up and start over again to try to do the right thing.

As we got closer to marriage, I figured those struggles would be taken care of once we got married—that I could meet those needs in him, and he would no longer fall into those traps. We did get married, and I don't remember exactly the first time he fell in this area, but I do remember being confused and devastated when he told me. I knew that physical intimacy was an area of struggle for us. It was and sometimes still is a hard area to communicate our needs and desires. I had started reading a few recommended books to help me, but it still wasn't easy.

Knowing that he still struggled, I would blame myself for not meeting his needs well, and I would try to figure out how to provide for him. But then he would still struggle, and I would be hurt. The hardest part about these struggles was that often I would get the feeling that maybe he had stumbled in this area, and I would ask him and he would tell me that he had not. But then an hour, or a day, or a week later, he would feel guilt ridden from lying and come back and tell me the truth, that he had struggled and that he had lied to me about it. It was this huge cycle of not trusting him after he lied, and my feelings of insecurity started to creep in more and more. This went on for several years.

I had a few friends that God richly blessed me with who I felt safe with to talk about these things, and they would encourage and pray with me. Please know that Nick knew I talked to these ladies about these things. Sometimes we as women can come together and start bashing our husbands and tearing them apart with our words—and that was not at all what was going on during that time. I felt helpless because I could not control my husband's choices. And I didn't know what I could do to make myself a better wife for him. I read books and prayed and read my Bible and did everything I could do to be the wife I was supposed to be. But still, I could not fix him. He still struggled. And it hurt so badly.

During this time, we were also struggling to figure out why I wasn't getting pregnant. I think that was one of the blessings in disguise with my infertility—it did not allow me to settle and not work at things and figure things out. God used the infertility to give me a desire to try with my husband, to spend time working on this area of our marriage, and I am grateful for that.

Almost four years into our marriage, we were in the middle of helping plant a church and just starting the adoption process. It was a very exciting time. However, Nick was still battling with this, which made me nervous about becoming parents. If Nick couldn't figure this out, would he be able to help his children with it someday?

During the middle of the summer of 2004, my friend Leah found a book that God used to change Nick's life in this area. I was sitting by the pool at our apartment with my friend, talking about these struggles. She told me she had a book, and to ask if Nick would consider reading it. It is called Every Man's Battle.[19] I gave Nick the book that night, and he was not too pleased about it at the time. I asked if he could consider reading it, and told him that Leah had bought it with us in mind. He didn't really commit to it, and that was that.

I don't remember exactly when he started to read it, but when he got halfway through the book, his eyes were opened to what needed to happen to help him change. I don't know what it was, or the exact details between him and the Lord, but I just know I began to see a huge change in my husband.

I ended up reading a few books from the same series, including one called Every Heart Restored.[20] God began to restore us in this area of hurt and pain, healing areas of brokenness and helping my husband surrender what I would call the biggest battle of his life. I can't explain it. It was just a work that the Lord did in Nick's life. What I can say is that even though it has been a long time since Nick has struggled, we recognize that it is something he could stumble in again anytime, and we try to stay on guard.

As a wife, and now as a mom to my son, I do my best to make sure the movies or shows that are viewed in our home, and even magazine articles, would not cause any stumbling. If I get magazines in the mail that I want to keep around, the first thing I do is go through them and rip out any ads that are inappropriate. I want to keep our home a protected place. But also, as Josiah continues to get older, we want to equip him as he goes out of the home to prepare him to handle the things this world will throw at him. When he was younger we had talks about how we don't look at naked pictures. We want to teach him not to defraud women.

We live in a very twisted world.

There was one time when I went into Gap Body with my kids, which in the past never had pictures that were inappropriate. But a few years ago when I went there, Josiah was about seven years old at the time, and he immediately turned his head. Watching him with his head bowed, I followed to where he had been looking, and there I saw a picture of a gal with her belly button showing, not fully dressed. I immediately apologized to Josiah, and he told Ava not to look at it, and I laid down what I had been considering purchasing and we left the store.

Another time though, I went into the store attached to Gap Body and caught Josiah trying to peek into Gap Body. That brought up a new discussion. That also brought up the realization that I need to be extra wise about where I take him in the future.

As we are coming up to entering the teenage years with our son, we are definitely not done training and preparing Josiah to be equipped to face the world in this area. But through Nick's struggles it is something extra near to our heart in raising our children.

It says in the Bible to flee sexual immorality. It's not something to leave room for any open doors. There has definitely been healing, but there are also scars that still hurt from time to time. I know that Nick and I would definitely want to put out the message to figure this out in your marriage—especially to the guys. There can be healing and forgiveness through Christ. He wants us to be able to surrender our hearts in this. And set us free.

Dear Children,

Here it is, the real us, in the midst of all our junk that we have had to walk through. The stuff that pulls us close to Jesus and reminds us of our need for Him. Yes, I will always wish, we could have experienced a completely safe place emotionally in physical intimacy, in our marriage. But that is not the story, because of sin. However, the story that God wants us to tell is of His redemption. His healing. His getting hold of Nick's heart in a big way, and piecing back together the brokenness that sin brought into our marriage. As we have drawn close to Him, He has taught us how to love each other with His love in this area of our marriage.

I want to tell you that this is one form of unfaithfulness in a marriage. I also want to take this time to share that fantasizing or daydreaming about attention from a person that is not your spouse is also a form of being unfaithful. That is an area I struggled in that I am going to write about in the next chapter. Feeling like your dad was too busy for me, and not noticing me, and instead of letting Jesus fill that void, I dreamed about attention from another man. I never acted on it, but it consumed my thoughts in a very unhealthy way for a couple of years in our marriage.

These ways are not what God wants for your marriage. He wants to take two imperfect people and knit them together as one. And what He has joined together, let no man or woman separate. Everything about this is the way He designed family to be. We have an enemy who wants to destroy what God has created. He is after our marriages and our children and anything he can do to break down the family unit. It's so important to keep a vigilant watch over your home. Put up the shield of faith over your family. Fight with the sword of the Spirit. Get help and support from people who will tell you that it doesn't have to be this way, there is a better option.

The hardest thing to do in life is forgive over and over and over, but I am so grateful God gave me the courage to when I needed it the most. If you ever find yourself in the situation of having a spouse struggle with faithfulness to you, I want you to do something that will hurt deeply. I want you to pray for them. Pray for them over and over. Fight. Fight. Fight. Take yourself out of the picture, and first think of them as a child of God who has fallen away and needs Jesus. Bring them to Jesus in prayer. There are no guarantees. We can't make people change. And sadly, not every person will.

If you are the spouse who is struggling, our strong exhortation: Find a trustworthy friend to confess to. Someone who can keep your confidence, someone who will pray for you. Someone who won't let you settle or justify or excuse your choices just to make you feel better. A real friend will love you enough to point you back to the only One who can fix you and make you whole.

My dear children, I pray God will somehow redeem brokenness from what we have walked through in your lives. That maybe, from our sharing the pain, you will get to experience intimacy with your spouse in deeper ways from the very beginning of your marriage. In hearing our story, you prepare yourselves to go into marriage not mistreating yourselves in these ways. We hope you can see yourself as a spotless creation made clean by Jesus, who does not need to follow those ways anymore.

Love You Always,
Your Mama & Dad, Kari & Nick

Hebrews 13:4 (ESV)

Let marriage be held in honor among all, and let the marriage bed be undefiled, for God will judge the sexually immoral and adulterous.

Matthew 5:27–30 (ESV)

You have heard that it was said, 'You shall not commit adultery.' But I say to you that everyone who looks at a woman with lustful intent has already committed adultery with her in his heart. If your right eye causes you to sin, tear it out and throw it away. For it is better that you lose one of your members than your whole body be thrown into hell. And if your right hand causes you to sin, cut it off and throw it away. For it is better that you lose one of your members than that your whole body go into hell.

Ephesians 6:10–18 (NASB)

Finally, be strong in the Lord and in the strength of His might. Put on the full armor of God, so that you will be able to stand firm against the schemes of the devil. For our struggle is not against flesh and blood, but against the rulers, against the powers, against the world forces of this darkness, against the spiritual forces of wickedness in the heavenly places. Therefore, take up the full armor of God, so that you will be able to resist in the evil day, and having done everything, to stand firm. Stand firm therefore, HAVING GIRDED YOUR LOINS WITH TRUTH, and HAVING PUT ON THE BREASTPLATE OF RIGHTEOUSNESS, and having shod YOUR FEET WITH THE PREPARATION OF THE GOSPEL OF PEACE; in addition to all, taking up the shield of faith with which you will be able to extinguish all the flaming arrows of the evil one. And take THE HELMET OF SALVATION, and the sword of the Spirit, which is the word of God.

With all prayer and petition pray at all times in the Spirit, and with this in view, be on the alert with all perseverance and petition for all the saints.

2 Timothy 2:21–22 (ESV)

Therefore, if anyone cleanses himself from what is dishonorable, he will be a vessel for honorable use, set apart as holy, useful to the master of the house, ready for every good work. So flee youthful passions and pursue righteousness, faith, love and peace, along with those who call on the Lord from a pure heart.

Ephesians 4:32 (ESV)

Be kind to one another, tenderhearted, forgiving one another, as God in Christ forgave you.

Acts 3:19–20 (ESV)

Repent, therefore, and turn back, that your sins may be blotted out, that times of refreshing may come from the presence of the Lord, and that He may send the Christ appointed for you, Jesus.

Proverbs 28:13 (ESV)

Whoever conceals his transgressions will not prosper, but he who confesses and forsakes them will obtain mercy.

James 5:16 (ESV)

Therefore, confess your sins to one another and pray for one another, that you may be healed. The prayer of a righteous person has great power as it is working.

⚡ MY CONFESSIONS ⚡

As I finish writing about Nick's struggle, I am compelled to take this next chapter to touch on a different struggle that many women face. It has been my struggle, and it has played its part in brokenness I have walked through in different times of my life. It is something I have to stay vigilant to not let back into my life, and continuously equip myself with the Lord to fight it when it comes. I have written about parts of it previously, but here it is, spelled out in whole form—my confessions.

So often one of the biggest terms I hear in all the romance stories out there falls under these lines: "Listen to your heart...Follow your heart...Whatever your heart tells you." I would like to say that the heart can be swayed easily and that we need to be careful of this teaching. It talks in the Bible about how we need to guard our heart, how it is a wellspring of life. When I was growing up, my parents gave me a name plaque that had my name, "Kari" listed. Below it read: "Pure One" and then it had that verse I just referenced: Proverbs 4:23 (NASB), "Watch over your heart with all diligence, for from it flow the springs of life." I always remember looking at it and desiring to be that girl.

I want to share my story about how I have failed many times in taking captive the thoughts that have settled and taken root in my heart. I am not proud of these stories or these struggles that I share. Unfortunately, this is one of the ways I have deeply hurt those around me in my life. But I think it is important to share, as it is a topic that is worth bringing to the forefront of discussion. I am guessing I am not the only one that has struggled in this way. The root of these struggles comes from a deep desire for attention—to be noticed, to be known. The truth is I am known by the One True God who matters more than any other relationship. But for whatever reason, I did not embrace that truth in the times of my life when I stumbled. I bring this before you as part of my story, so that God can bring to light the truth that it is not attention or fulfillment from anything other than Him that will satisfy.

I mentioned in earlier chapters my tendency toward being a bit boy crazy, and the longing for attention in my life from a man. I broke Nick's trust when we were just finishing high school. We struggled with waiting and Nick's means of coping through avoidance. I want to share a little more of the behind-the-scenes of that story, along with others that unfortunately followed. The neglect I felt when he would pull back and avoid me hurt deeply and made me feel unimportant to him. Around the time all of this started, a co-worker began speaking words to me, telling me he didn't picture me with Nick, but he really saw me with this other guy I had been friends with for years. I listened to these words, lies that came from a person who was very promiscuous in his own life.

After listening to those lies, I started thinking and wandering in my thoughts, not being faithful to Nick. At one point I told the other guy my feelings for him, and that's when everything fell apart. Nick broke up with me. I was heartbroken. I realized that I did care for the other guy as a great friend, but what I felt for Nick was so different, and crossing that line with my feelings while in a relationship with Nick was so hurtful to both of the guys. I ended up losing that friendship for a season, and Nick almost didn't take me back. I spent a week praying before the Lord about everything. I had to get to a place of being okay just me and God, even if Nick didn't want to pursue the relationship anymore. In the end he chose forgiveness and let me back into his life.

Can I take a moment to advise right here? There is a fine line between being a good friend with a guy and being something more, and I didn't set the best boundaries when I was in high school. I let my heart get emotionally connected to someone I was never going to have a long-term relationship with. Talking on the phone for hours with another guy was probably not the wisest choice. I know there can be good, healthy brother/sister relationships. I had plenty of experience with that when we were part of our college group. In those relationships the guys treated me like I was Nick's girl, and I treated them as brothers. I didn't make long phone calls with them, and rarely would I be alone with any of them. I kept healthy contact and thankfully never had thoughts of wondering what it would be like to be with any of them. I am so grateful for that season, because it allowed me to see and learn how I should treat guys, and what lines not to cross.

I wish I could say that was the end of my lack of loyalty in my heart to Nick, but it wasn't. While Nick was busy in college, there were two other times when I entertained thoughts of relationships with other men. Once was when a co-worker told me she thought another of our associates liked me. Once again, I longed for the attention while Nick was very busy and still avoiding me out of fear of stumbling. Another time was with a mutual friend of ours. Both of those situations thankfully dissolved because of changes in our circumstances. Nick and I drew closer to engagement and marriage, and my thoughts and desires for attention from someone outside of Nick mostly went away.

When we got married, we had very clear goals of what we hoped to accomplish in our life together. Things didn't go exactly as we had planned. But during that season, we were drawn closer together, united with the goal to start a family, to help in high school ministries for a few years, and then to help with a church plant. We had a vision which knitted our hearts together in unison.

Nine years into our marriage, when our twins arrived, we entered a life stage of parenting four children under the age of five with somewhat realistic expectations of what it was going to take. Jumping in with all I had, I put my big-girl boots on and became my own version of "supermom." After all, this is what I had signed up for in order to experience a pregnancy of my own. We also decided to sell our townhome, due to the cramped quarters for our four children—three girls and one boy sharing two bedrooms. Long term, this wasn't going to work. It took all my days to feed, bathe, and care for four children, and keep our house immaculate in case someone came by to look at it. Somewhere along the way, Nick and I became two people surviving side by side. We were just trying to make it to 7:00, when all our kids were down and we could finally breathe for a little bit before our bedtime came and we started all over again the next day.

During that season, we were focused on trying to find a new home, in case our townhome sold (it took six months in a very bad market before it finally sold—we paid $1,000 to get out of it). Nick spent much of his time on his laptop looking at houses, I think as a way to make the time pass while we waited.

I started to feel lonely again. And then I heard a lie from my hairdresser (who during the time I knew her left her husband for a new man), and I let it take root in my soul. I had shown her a picture of Nick, and she said he wasn't who she would have thought I would be married to. She pictured me with someone that was more of a GQ guy. You would think I would be more careful of what I let take root in my mind, but once again I started to listen to that lie, and to see all of Nick's imperfections. I started to dream again of attention from another person. Mind you, I never acted on any of these dreams. They were all inside my head, a secret fantasy world—a muse to help me push forward in the daily grind of life, an alternative reality of having someone admire me and appreciate and recognize all that I did. Someone who would, dare I say, put me on a pedestal...that is a scary desire for anyone to have.

Those thoughts eventually went away, but I still struggled with longing for attention. Nick wasn't the best at giving me the words of encouragement I longed for, words of admiration for all the hard work I was putting into our children. Nick is the type of person who is not intimidated by taking care of the kids, or all the work that can go with it. In his mind, it was just what I was supposed to be doing, and I felt like he didn't think the job I was doing was all that difficult.

Just months after having the twins, I was told that I appeared to have lost weight, and that I looked like I was a smaller size than what I was actually wearing. I started to become more aware of what I looked like. Hearing those words elevated my self-esteem and boosted my ego. I noticed on occasion getting looks when I was out grocery shopping. I had taken up running for the first time in my life. I started to train for a half marathon. After completing my first one and reaching the lowest weight I had been in years, I felt like I needed to keep running that distance to maintain my size. I would often run 13 to 15 miles almost every other weekend to make sure I didn't start gaining weight and lose my endurance.

Sadly, that is where a three-year period of mind struggle began for me, looking for attention from one person in particular. I remember the first glance. That's all it took—one glance. The feeling of being noticed rushed into me, and for several years I battled a desire for attention from that person. I didn't know in the beginning who his wife was, who his children were. All I knew was that he looked at me. It makes me so sad that this is part of my story, but this mind battle, this emotional affair I carried out in my head, became a way to survive each day, dreaming of attention, planning what I would wear, wondering if he would notice. It makes me sick to my stomach to think about it now.

I would like to interject again. I am grateful. Grateful that I had boundaries set up that I wouldn't cross. I didn't ever get his number. I never contacted him on Facebook. I often tried to avoid conversation with him. I know this was an attack—an open door I had allowed into my mind. God put protection on me during this time, which I am so grateful for. One day I was at a grocery store, meeting up with a friend right afterward. Nick was on a business trip for two weeks and I was single-parenting. The guy showed up at the same store, and even pulled up behind me in line and helped me put my groceries on the checkout counter, although I hadn't asked for help. I knew this was dangerous territory to be treading. Thankfully I told my friend of what happened. She and I understood each other's struggles in this, and we had developed a little accountability.

In the midst of those struggles in your mind, confess them. Don't allow them to go unspoken. When they are confessed, you can eventually—if not immediately—be set free from them. Find accountability in safe friendships. I had a few friends who knew about it, whom I found freedom to talk with in the midst of those struggles. Nick even knew I was struggling with it at times, because I told him. I know it hurt him deeply. He was committed to me, and in action I was committed to him, but in my heart I was not. One other recommendation: When those thoughts come, turn them into prayer. I have prayed many times in the midst of my struggles for that person's marriage—that God would bless and protect it. It was one of the ways I could shut down the thoughts from rabbit trailing any further. I wish I could somehow erase that battle of my mind. But if sharing this might help someone else that needs to hear it, then I will allow my sin and mistake of emotionally connecting my mind to another man who was not my husband to be shared, and to bring to light the darkness you may be in or find yourself in one day. I never planned it—I didn't premeditate it. But I found myself in the middle of it by letting a thought take root in my heart, instead of slaying it the moment it came into my mind.

I lost a lot indirectly through that struggle. Thankfully I did not lose my marriage. I'm thankful that those thoughts stayed in my mind and were never acted upon. But I was humbled in the end. I pulled out of that struggle in a way that completely removed me from the situations that would bring it to mind. And I am reminded once more that I do not ever want to go back to how it once was. To be freed from that is a place I want to stay.

My Dear Children,

The truth is, a spouse is never going to be able to give you all the attention you might long for. Your friends cannot meet those needs. Another person outside of your marriage will definitely not meet that need. The truth is, I had gotten so dried up in the midst of my laboring daily over you, my children, when you were little, and I didn't put enough effort into filling my cup to overflowing with the Holy Spirit. I looked for alternative ways to fill the empty cup that was running out of steam to give daily and sacrificially to my family. The truth is, Jesus's Spirit in me is the only thing that can fill those empty places in my heart.

I want to end with some Scriptures to help if you ever encounter a battle like this in your own life, and to encourage you. Keep the guards up. Set good boundaries around your heart. Confess your struggles in safe places, so that when a temptation does come, you are equipped to handle it.

I love you, Precious Ones.
Always, Mama Kari

Ephesians 5:6–17 (NASB)

Let no one deceive you with empty words, for because of these things the wrath of God comes upon the sons of disobedience. Therefore, do not be partakers with them; for you were formerly darkness, but now you are Light in the Lord; walk as children of Light (for the fruit of the Light consists in all goodness and righteousness and truth), trying to learn what is pleasing to the Lord. Do not participate in the unfruitful deeds of darkness, but instead even expose them; for it is disgraceful even to speak of the things which are done by them in secret. But all things become visible when they are exposed by the light, for everything that becomes visible is light. For this reason, it says "Awake, sleeper, and arise from the dead, and Christ will shine on you." Therefore, be careful how you walk, not as unwise men but as wise, making the most of your time, because the days are evil. So then do not be foolish but understand what the will of the Lord is.

James 4:6–10 (NASB)

But He gives a greater grace. Therefore it says, "God is opposed to the proud, but gives grace to the humble." Submit therefore to God. Resist the devil and he will flee from you. Draw near to God and He will draw near to you. Cleanse your hands, you sinners; and purify your hearts you double minded. Be miserable and mourn and weep; let your laughter be turned into mourning and your joy to gloom. Humble yourselves in the presence of the Lord, and He will exalt you.

2 Timothy 2:22 (NASB)

Now flee from youthful lusts and pursue righteousness, faith, love and peace, with those who call on the Lord from a pure heart.

1 Corinthians 10:13 (NASB)

No temptation has overtaken you but such as is common to man; and God is faithful, who will not allow you to be tempted beyond what you are able, but with the temptation will provide the way of escape also, so that you will be able to endure it.

Proverbs 4:23–27 (NASB)

Watch over your heart with all diligence, for from it flow the springs of life. Put away from you a deceitful mouth and put devious speech far from you. Let your eyes look directly ahead and your gaze be fixed straight in front of you. Watch the path of your feet and all your ways will be established. Do not turn to the right nor to the left; turn your foot from evil.

James 5:16 (NASB)

Therefore, confess your sins to one another, and pray for one another so that you may be healed. The effective prayer of a righteous man can accomplish much.

1 Timothy 6:11–12 (NASB)

But flee from these things, you man of God, and pursue righteousness, godliness, faith love, perseverance and gentleness. Fight the good fight of faith; take hold of the eternal life to which you were called, and you made the good confession in the presence of many witnesses.

OUR INFERTILITY STRUGGLE

I want to begin writing out the details of how each gift of a child was given to me. But to start, I am going to write the backdrop that led us to being able to have a family. I knew when I was growing up, from watching my sister Abbie be born into the world, that I wanted to grow up and be a mom someday. I loved Abbie. She was the best gift to my family. My parents weren't expecting it, but that is how the Lord gives some of the best surprises.

When I met Nick and we started our relationship, we both knew we wanted to have a family, and our plan was not to use any birth control when we got married, but to just allow the Lord to provide as many children as He wanted us to have. A few months before we got married, we were sitting around the dinner table at Nick's parents' house, and we were all joking about Nick and I getting pregnant with the honeymoon baby. Nick's dad broke into the conversation and shared, "You laugh now, but what if you don't get pregnant right away..." That sat in the back of my mind, and it didn't sit very well. Yes, that could be a possibility, but that wouldn't happen for us.

After we got married, I began to wonder if that first month we really would get pregnant. I was not working anymore, and I had no intention of finding a job because I was ready to move onto the next thing in life. It was like this checklist that I had in my mind. First comes love, then comes marriage, and then comes the baby in the baby carriage.

My period came the first month, but I was not to be discouraged. We ventured into month two, and my hopes started to build again. And once again my period came. Hmmm...I began to wonder how this getting pregnant thing really worked. Over the following months, I started to research charting my cycle on the computer. Each month I could almost pinpoint the exact time, and as I drew closer to seeing if my period would come, I would begin to do things like calculate the due date if we really were pregnant this month. I already had a name book with a boy name written in it that Nick and I had chosen when we were 18, and a list of girl name options.

When we got married God gave me a best friend that He knew I would need for this season in life. Her name was Leah. Leah had gotten married to her husband Dan three months before we had. Our husbands introduced us after meeting on a PSU Honors Society retreat. I could talk to Leah about all my struggles and I felt completely safe with her. She would pray with me and encourage me and point me to the Lord.

Leah and Dan announced in the winter of 2001 that they were pregnant. I started to get excited. Maybe God wanted me to get pregnant with her, and we could have our babies together and our families would grow up together. That was my plan anyway. But that did not happen. Leah had baby Gabriel in October of 2001. I began to wonder if something was wrong. I went in for a routine doctor appointment, and I asked my doctor what he thought. He told me that since Nick and I had never been intimate before marriage, it could take up to three years, so just give it time. When I talked to Nick about that, he said we just needed to wait. So wait we did. But I still was not getting pregnant. I kept hoping. I would even go to the dollar store and buy their pregnancy tests and take them. Every single one was negative and within a few days my period would once again begin.

In the summer of 2002, Leah was not feeling quite right, and she found out she was pregnant again. Something inside of me was screaming frustration. God was not getting it right! This was my time to be pregnant with her. Nick was at that point willing to go to the doctor and get checked out. His test results came back fine. Nick said we needed to wait and just see. I was extremely irritated at this advice. I did not want to wait anymore. I wanted action—to be able to move forward with things. I remember saying things to God like, "If I'm not pregnant by this time next year..." trying to threaten God. I had huge doubts in my faith through this season. It didn't make sense to me. Here I had "surrendered" the whole birth control thing so He could give us the family He wanted us to have and He wasn't taking advantage of that and filling our quiver full.

The Technical Side of Things

In the winter of 2003, Nick finally gave me the go-ahead to find an infertility doctor. A friend referred me to a gal she had gone to, so we went to that clinic. For the first time in three years, I felt like things were moving. We started tests right away. Our first test was this dye test that they shot in my tubes, and it made me feel super crampy. That was how we spent our Valentine's Day. Nick took me out to dinner after that appointment to our favorite Italian place. Ten minutes into our night out, I spilled my Shirley Temple all over myself, so we went home and he let me rest on the couch next to him the rest of the evening. Results came back with no blockage in the tubes. I was excited and hopeful, because they said that sometimes the dye test would clear even the smallest things up and women often would get pregnant afterwards.

But a few weeks later that period showed up on schedule.

They asked me to do temperature charting and take ovulation predictor kit tests. Those showed I ovulated, but then I would start my period 9 to 10 days afterwards, while most women start 12 to 14 days later. We did a post coital test to see how long sperm survived inside of me, and it came back with no survival. They asked us to go home and do it again, just to make sure it was done right. I was not exactly sure how we could have done it wrong, but I agreed to it. It came back negative again.

The doctor immediately started me on a basic dosage of Clomid to help me ovulate earlier in the hopes that it would increase the days after ovulation to allow more time for a conceived baby to implant in the womb. She also started us doing insemination, where they would take Nick's sperm and wash it, then put it inside of me, hoping my body would not kill it off.

We did this for three months with no positive results. Then she said she wanted to do a surgery to see if I had endometriosis. With my severe cramps, it was a possibility. That summer I went in for surgery. The result was that I had a medium case of endometriosis. The doctor lasered a lot of the sores from the endometriosis inside of me, and the hope at that time was that Nick and I would take the next few months to try on our own. We did. But it became more and more like this brick wall I could not break down. No matter what we did, I had this feeling we were not going to be getting pregnant.

The Lessons and Preparation God was Working in Me

I had a friend who was going through a similar situation. God prepared my heart, and deep down I knew that she would get pregnant, but that wasn't what He had planned for me. She did get pregnant. And He gave me such joy for her. It is definitely a hard thing to watch all of your close friends get pregnant, and long to be part of that circle, and not be able to, completely out of your control. He gave me the courage to have joy with them though. I am so glad I got to be part of all the celebrations and joys in their lives, instead of being holed up in my own hurts and aches. That was a true gift from God because it isn't easy to experience.

Another one of the best gifts He gave me were those friends including me as part of their families during the day. I would go over to their homes and hang out with them and their children. I got to watch how they were raising their kids, and Nick and I would talk a lot about the things we liked and the things we didn't like. We would pray about it, and God began to mold and prepare our thought process in how we would train our children.

For a few years, I did a Precepts Bible study. There was one lady with children in junior high and high school who I grew to love and respect. She invited me to her home, and we talked a little bit about the infertility struggle I was going through. She encouraged me, while I was waiting, to do a Bible study on what God's Word teaches about children. So that summer I met with three other friends and we did exactly that. We researched and did word studies on parenting and prayed for each other. It was once more preparing my heart for how the Lord would have us parent—and the goals He wanted us to strive for.

I remember once being very frustrated with a guy who had been part of our college group. About a year after we were married, he came up to me at church and told me he was praying that the Lord would not allow me to get pregnant right away, so that Nick and I could enjoy being married. I was so upset by that. He didn't know that I was going through infertility. However, looking back, that was something that the Lord did lay on his heart to pray for us.

Over the course of those first few years, Nick started to share that he was glad we hadn't gotten pregnant right away. I didn't understand at the time, but he had just gone along with what I was hoping for. He had wanted more time to build our marriage foundation.

So many times I wish I could go back and cherish that alone time with him a little more. Now, having been married more than 15 years and with four children, I would love to have a week with just Nick to go somewhere just the two of us. Why didn't I take advantage of that more? We have seasons in life, and we can live in joy in them, or we can live in discontent, waiting for that thing to "fulfill" us. God had to get me to a point of complete surrender to Him before He could give me the gifts He wanted me to have, which, by the way, are far better than I could ever have imagined.

In the winter of 2004, we went back to the doctor. We had not gotten pregnant on our own, so she suggested we try three more rounds of Clomid and insemination. I fought it badly. At this point I was done. Beyond done. I wanted to move on and start pursuing the adoption process. At our church our pastor's wife had been leading a women's Bible study that I had been leading the worship for. The first month of our return to treatment, I saw on my temperature chart that my temperature was dropping again, and I knew I was not pregnant. I was heartbroken and devastated, and I had Bible study that night, but I was in no shape emotionally to lead the women into worship. I stayed home that day and cried a lot in my bed and worked out my sorrow with the Lord. I was mad at Nick for making us try again, and mad at the Lord that we were having to keep trying. I did not want to have to start again and deal with two more months of disappointment.

Then the Lord gave me a song—a beautiful song from His Scripture that He had me play out on the piano. And for some reason the words comforted my heart and gave me courage. With a new resolve, I made the decision with these last few months of trying treatment to finish strong. I would trust Him.

Nick told me that he knew it was hard to keep trying these last two tries, but he knew it was what God wanted us to do. And then Nick said that maybe if we were supposed to adopt, our baby was not ready yet, and that could be why we still needed to wait. By His strength alone, I did push through those last two tries. And we did not get pregnant. And that is where the story of starting our family truly begins.

Dear Children,

This experience in life was the first time I ever walked through a broken dream. Everything else in my life had taken learning patience, but it had eventually come together. My plans that I made in life were completely taken out of my hands—I had no control. No choice in this matter. You will have times in your life when you may face situations that are completely out of your control. Situations that break your heart over and over again, and you wonder why? Why? You may not find the answers to those questions in the moment.

This is part of the process of being molded and shaped by our Creator. We can't tell our Creator, "This is what I am supposed to be, and this is what I am supposed to do," if we really want to learn surrender and trust. He sees all of it. All of it. He is not surprised by any of it. He wants us, as we wrestle with Him over these things, to learn to lay it all at His feet. Walking down the path is always so much easier when we come at it from the angle of surrender. The more we fight, the harder it is to relax and just rest and be before Him. I had to learn this lesson over and over again for several years, from multiple angles. That month when I lay in my bed so ready to be done, God came to me. With His love, He poured truth over me from His Word. He used my husband to push me to persevere a few more months.

It is easy to look back and say, "Aha, now it makes sense!" At least in my story. With some stories you may not be able to do that until the other side of eternity. But in the midst of walking through the eye of the storm, we can't see more than the few steps in front of us. That is learning to walk by faith. Committing my plans to the Lord, and letting Him take them and change them into what He had planned all along.

Surrender. Trust. Faith. Hope. Persevere. Endure. Surrender.

I love you, my children. You are the story God was working on preparing our family for. I couldn't see it, and if I had gotten my way in the beginning, I would have missed out on all of you. Just remember that.

Your Mama Always,
Kari

James 1:2–4 (NASB)

Consider it all joy, my brethren, when you encounter trials of various kind, knowing that the testing of your faith produces endurance. And let endurance have its perfect result, that you may be perfect and complete, lacking in nothing.

Psalm 37:3–7 (NASB)

Trust in the LORD and do good; Dwell in the land and cultivate faithfulness. Delight yourself in the LORD; And He will give you the desires of your heart. Commit your way to the LORD, Trust also in Him, and He will do it. He will bring forth your righteousness as the light And your judgment as the noonday. Rest in the LORD and wait patiently for Him; Do not fret because of him who prospers in his way, Because of the man who carries out wicked schemes.

Isaiah 64:8 (NASB)

But now, O LORD, You are our Father, We are the clay, and You our potter; And all of us are the work of Your hand.

My Infertility Song

To You O Lord I lift my soul, To You O God I put my trust

Make me know Your ways, Lord Teach me Your Paths

You are my God, God of my Salvation

Lead me in Your truth, For You I'd wait all day

Deliverer, Redeemer, Gracious and so kind

I shall bless Your Name

And Proclaim and Declare Your wonders, Lord

Examine me try me Lord, Test my mind, know my thoughts

My feet stand on solid ground, On the Rock I've found in You

Building my hope on nothing else, Than on Your gift of blood spilt

My heart shall see the beauty Of Your Holiness, Your Righteousness

Deliverer, Redeemer, Gracious and so kind

I shall bless Your Name

And Proclaim and Declare Your wonders Lord

↬ EVERYONE NEEDS A LOIE ↫

I was anxious. Waiting and left with no direction and no clear answers of how God wanted me to spend my time while waiting for a baby. I had swirls of dreams and ideas going around in my head of things I could do to fill the void. I wanted to be pursuing some dream, and if God wasn't going to take care of this baby dream, then I guess I needed to figure something else out. I would often get asked what I was doing these days, and I felt so stupid sometimes answering with, "Waiting to get pregnant." I wanted to have purpose in my daily life.

During this season, I started my short stint of selling Mary Kay. I actually started off really well—I had a big starter party, and a lot of parties were scheduled from it. One of those parties was an amazing group of ladies at Cedar Mill. It was three older women who had raised their families and now were spending their time mentoring young wives and new moms. A beautiful thing to watch—definitely after Titus 2. They invited me to one of their group nights to makeover all the young women and the leaders of the group as well. All three leaders invited me back to do individual makeovers for each of them.

To be able to do makeup and sit down with these beautiful older, wiser women and talk with them for an hour or two was a huge gift to me. They were encouraging and kind with their words, as they empathized with my heart of wanting to start a family but being unable to by my own efforts.

One of the ladies was named Loie.

As we picked out makeup ideas, she started asking me questions. I talked about my different thoughts and pursuits. Maybe I would go to school and get a degree, since I had the time. Although I wasn't sure which subject I would pursue, but it seemed like a good idea. Or maybe I would find work again...I rambled through my thoughts trying to make sense of the disorganized chaos going through my brain.

You know the times when God uses someone to speak into your life, just something very practical, and it ends up being so profound that it sets everything at rest? This was one of those moments.

Loie looked at me thoughtfully, and she very practically asked, "Why would you spend the money going to school if in the end, when you are all done, you still just want to be a mom?"

I know I had thought that in my own head plenty of times, but to just listen to it from someone else who had walked through more life than I had was completely different. Those words coming from Loie gave me permission that I didn't have to have things all figured out right now. That just because pieces of this dream weren't all coming together today did not mean God wanted me to pursue a different purpose or life direction. He had laid being a mom on my heart as the plan He had for me. It just wasn't the right time yet. He wanted me during this season to learn patience and to wait.

It was a relief that it was okay to just spend this time pursuing Him, to even just find rest in Him and comfort in Him when it was hard. And that was all I needed to do. I am so grateful for that small gift of time God gave me with Loie. I don't ever see her anymore, although I did receive a very special phone call from her when I was on bed rest waiting for my twins to be born.

Someday, I hope to be a Loie in someone else's life. I have struggled a lot lately with not being able to be involved in other women's lives, the way I was able to when I only had one or two children. Four children can consume time in such a way that I sometimes feel I have very little left to give at the end of the day. I thought it might change when they got older, but it is still consuming, it just looks different than when they were little. A current lesson God is teaching me is this:

Right now, I still have a lot of learning and growing up to do. When I think of Loie, or other amazing women like her who have touched my life by being those Titus 2 women who are finishing their lives strong, I have found a dream for a later date. When my children are all grown up, and I am wondering what my purpose in life should be, I pray God will allow me to be that Titus 2 woman to other younger ladies around me. That I will not grow weary of doing good, but that He will use me to bless and encourage those around me. And for now, I will keep loving the four little ones He has blessed to my care, a gift I will never stop being grateful for in this season of life.

Dear Children,

Loie was one of the gifts God gave me, along with many other women throughout my life, who poured words of life and hope into me. She is also a reminder to me of what I hope to be someday. A woman who can take the wisdom that God has shown me and allow His Spirit to use me in the people He places in front of me. Look for those in your life who can pour His truth into you. People that love Jesus the most and know His Word, who can point you to Him.

I Love You,
Mama

Titus 2:2–8 (NASB)

Older men are to be sober-minded, dignified, self-controlled, sound in faith, in love, and in steadfastness. Older women likewise are to be reverent in behavior, not slanderers or slaves to much wine. They are to teach what is good, and so train the young women to love their husbands and children, to be self-controlled, pure, workers at home, kind, and submissive to their husbands, that the word of God may not be reviled. Likewise urge the younger men to be self-controlled. Show yourself in all respects to be a model of good works, and in your teaching show integrity, dignity, and sound speech that cannot be condemned, so that an opponent may be put to shame, having nothing evil to say about us.

⚘ GRIEVING THE DREAM ⚘

When we chose the path for adoption, I was so excited! Finally, no more brick wall that I couldn't kick down. We were on a fast track that I could barely keep up with and it was so freeing.

But every once in a while, I would have a moment.

A moment when my heart ached over the loss of not being able to get pregnant on my own.

A moment of regret that I would not get to feel the baby inside me and know it intimately in that way.

An aching thought that I would not get to wear all those cute maternity clothes that I saw my other friends wearing.

Regret that I wouldn't be carrying a child in my body as a symbol of an act of love between my husband and me.

And God showed me that it was okay to grieve those losses. I would have my time to cry, to ache over the hurt, the stings of the reality that pregnancy was something that was not to be for me. And He also showed me that I was not to be consumed by the grief. When those moments came, I could tend to those heartaches with Him, but once I had, I needed to let it go and keep moving on toward the new dream God was calling me to.

If you are in a place where you are grieving the loss of a dream, or even something much deeper than that, it's okay to grieve. Just don't let it consume you to the point that you miss out on the different plans God has for your life.

This was a lesson God taught me the last summer I would spend childless.

Dear Children,

Grieving is a deep gift, even though it hurts in the moment. This very short reflection of the grief I walked through in my infertility journey doesn't even begin to touch on the depths of grief, and there are those who have walked into much more sorrowful waters, who understand the complexities of it. If we don't grieve and shut down the pain, it can cause much damage to ourselves. We can put up walls to try to protect ourselves, but in the end we are really damaging our souls. Grief is designed to allow us to work through the loss in a healthy, healing way. It is often a brokenness that is saying no to something or someone we have to let go of. It acknowledges the loss and allows us to feel it and recognize it for what we no longer have. This is a very painful process. But as we begin to let it go to the Lord, He begins to take it and restore our heart to a place of wholeness with Him, and that is a very safe place to be.

I love you, Children.

Your Mama,
Kari

Matthew 5:4 (ESV)

Blessed are those who mourn, for they shall be comforted.

Psalm 30:2–5 (NASB)

O Lord my God, I cried to You for help, and You healed me. O Lord, You have brought up my soul from Sheol; You restored life from among those who go down to the pit. Weeping may tarry for the night, but joy comes in the morning. You have kept me alive, that I would not go down to the pit. Sing praise to the LORD, you His godly ones, And give thanks to His holy name. For His anger is but for a moment, His favor is for a lifetime; Weeping may last for the night, But a shout of joy comes in the morning.

PREPARATION OF THE HEART

March 2004. My last cycle on Clomid and insemination came to an end. That night Nick was out with a friend. I was feeling pretty down about everything, when I picked up the book, A Purpose Driven Life,[21] which someone had given to me a while back. I decided for the next 40 days I was going to go through that book a chapter a day. In the back were Scripture references, so I spent each morning writing out those verses. God used that time in great ways for encouragement and poured into me exactly what I needed as He was preparing my heart for a change.

Adoption Agency Decision

Nick and I talked and at the end of March he gave me the go-ahead to start researching adoption agencies. And research I did. I talked to people, looked online, asked around for packets, figured out questions to ask, called different agencies, and asked those questions. We visited a few agency meetings, and then I talked to my friend Anastasia, who had also done some research recently, and she told me about Bethany Christian Services. We found out they had an evening meeting close by, so we went to it. Everything they said and their heart behind what they did led us to choosing them to be our agency. We felt 100 percent peace, and by the end of the evening, we left them with our first deposit. Thus began the first stage of paperwork.

The next step was to attend an all-day class in Seattle. We found out the next meeting was at the end of June, but it was on a friend's wedding day, whom I was supposed to do all the makeup for. Nick and I debated about it a bit, prayed about it, and I talked to my friend and her family. The next meeting wasn't until September, and we would not be able to start our home study until we attended this meeting, so with my friend's gracious understanding, I left them with all the makeup supplies they would need, and off we went to Seattle.

It was an interesting meeting. One term brought up that Nick and I had discussed a little was "open adoption." That idea scared me. There was an adoptive couple who spoke, along with their birth parents, acting like such good friends with each other, and I did not understand this. I knew I would not be able to handle something like that, so I made it very clear to Nick after that meeting that I would only be okay with a semi-open adoption. I was not at all open to anything like what we had just witnessed today. One thing the agency shared was that there were a lot of birth moms they were counseling through the adoption decision, and they had a shortage of adoptive families. This encouraged Nick and me, as we walked along this path, that the time was right.

I immediately got to work on more paperwork, and on four original scrapbooks about Nick and me, which we needed to submit for each Bethany office in the Northwest. We had to write autobiographies and answer specific questions about how we were raised. We started our home study and met Roxanne, our caseworker who would walk us through the process. I went online and looked at pictures and letters written by hopeful adoptive parents who were waiting to be chosen, and I started praying for them. One couple in particular stood out to me, and I prayed my little heart out for them. Then at one of our home study sessions, Roxanne shared about a couple who had been waiting for a long time and had just been placed with twins. I went back online that night and saw that the couple I had been praying for had been placed. I was so excited for them!

By the end of September, we had all our paperwork done and were approved for adoption, but we decided to wait to go on the waiting list until November. We were moving at the end of October, and I wanted to be settled in our new home and have a nursery ready before we went on the list. In the middle of November, we finally went on the list, and then we waited. During that time, my niece was born right after Thanksgiving, and I remember praying—so excited for her birth, and yet aching that my time would be soon too. I started my prayer, "Lord, I so badly want for Christmas..." and then I stopped and changed it. "Lord, you know what my heart wants for

Christmas—I don't need to tell you that. Your timing is perfect, and I would rather have that than take control of this anymore." I surrendered the dream once more and was willing to wait for His best.

Dear Children,

This was my season of "pregnancy." We had made a step forward in a new direction, and we now had many steps to take to prepare for welcoming a baby into our home. Nine months of meetings, paperwork, paperwork and more paperwork. We had people we didn't know come into our home to meet with us. Their job was to make sure we would be a good, safe couple, so that they could place a child into our care.

It was a journey filled with new hope that one day soon, we would have a child of our own. I decorated a nursery, not knowing if it would be a boy or girl. This was a dream come true for me. One I had waited years for. It felt odd to purchase a crib and changing table for a child we hadn't met. We didn't know if or when we would receive this child. It was walking by faith, preparing for something unseen.

When God calls you to do something, it takes time and effort. Laboring. All good things require it. We aren't guaranteed a fruitful harvest from the labor, but we put in effort hoping that in the end, we will obtain the fulfillment of whatever we have worked hard for.

Children, you were worth it. You're all worth our labor and time.

I Love You,
Mama

Galatians 6:9 (ESV)

And let us not grow weary of doing good, for in due season, we will reap, if we do not give up.

James 1:12 (NASB)

Blessed is the one who perseveres under trial, because having stood the test, that person will receive the crown of life that the Lord has promised to those who love Him.

Hebrews 11:1–3, 8–12 (ESV)

Now faith is the assurance of things hoped for, the conviction of things not seen. For by it the people of old received their commendation. By faith we understand that the universe was created by the word of God, so that what is seen was not made out of things that are visible.

By faith Abraham obeyed when he was called to go out to a place that he was to receive as an inheritance. And he went out, not knowing where he was going. By faith he went to live in the land of promise, as in a foreign land, living in tents with Isaac and Jacob, heirs with him of the same promise. For he was looking forward to the city that has foundations, whose designer and builder is God. By faith Sarah herself received power to conceive, even when she was past the age, since she considered Him faithful who promised. Therefore from one man, and him as good as dead, were born descendants as many as the stars of heaven and as many as innumerable grains of sand by the seashore.

❧ THE LORD'S PROVISIONS AND BLESSINGS ❧

After feeling like I kept hitting a brick wall in trying to get pregnant, the moment we started the adoption process, there was nothing I could do to stop what was going on—it was me and Nick along for the ride that God had planned for us.

One of the first things the Lord provided was a job. Solid Rock was planted on Easter of that year. During that time, we wanted to help however we could. Nick was working and in school for his Master's degree, so I was the one with more free time during that season of life. I started helping once a week in the office, and then Doug, one of the pastors, called to talk to me about working part time as a church secretary. I was beyond excited to do it. I hadn't worked since Nick and I were married. But me and my lack of tact...I wanted to make sure Doug knew that I experienced bad cramps which put me in bed once a month, just so he knew if that happened on a work day, I might need to leave in the middle of the day. Poor Doug! But he was very gracious and understanding, and I committed to working through the end of September. Thus began a very fun season of helping the pastors with a wide range of needs as our church was beginning.

I will always cherish the memory of that time and the privilege of working for three godly men. I was able to see the heart behind the church in a very real way. It was a beautiful gift from the Lord that helped us save for adoption and also allowed me to play a very small part in the huge thing He was doing.

The second thing He provided was a new home. We sold our house—the home I had dreamed of bringing my children into—and we sold it very quickly. We found an apartment to rent from my friend Jennifer for the exact amount of time we needed while we waited for our new Beaverton townhome to be built. Our house closed just a few days before we went to pick out all the features for our new place at Arbor Homes, which made it really special because it showed me God cares about the little details too—and it allowed us to choose a few extra touches on our townhome to make it special. Timing is everything. We got to move into our new townhome, and thanks to a great suggestion, I spent time painting rooms ahead of time, to really make our new place feel like home. And the money from the difference in moving was enough to help us pay for our adoption.

At the end of my time working at the church and before we moved, He even gave me the gift of a mini vacation with my friend Kathryn—one last hurrah before children. I will always be so grateful for that refreshing trip and the time spent.

The Lord showed me so much during this season. We can spend our lives discontent and unhappy because God isn't giving us what we want, or if we surrender, we can wait and follow what He calls us to. He blesses us beyond what we would ever ask or think, in very different ways, but ways that place His fingerprints all over it to confirm that it is what *He* has planned for us. We just need to go along for the ride of seeking and following and obeying His leading.

In Psalm 37²² it talks about delighting in the Lord and He will give you the desires of your heart. That is something He wanted to teach me—it wasn't about my desires, it was about how He made His desires mine. Phil Comer once asked me when I was working at the church if I would ever want to go back and change the way things were working out. I didn't have any children yet in my arms, just the hope in my heart that we were moving forward in the direction God had for us, and I was able to confidently say, "No, because I would not have learned anything that the Lord wanted me to, and I would not be who I am today if I had gotten things the way I wanted." God was so good to us.

Dear Children,

These nine months of walking through the adoption process were like walking through a breath of fresh air after the years of waiting through infertility. It was a time filled with hope and life and new dreams that God was placing inside of Nick and me. This time would not have come or been filled with the same joy if we had not walked through the years of waiting without answers.

I want to encourage you, in whatever season you walk through, to believe in what the Lord has shown you and commit those desires to Him.

I Love You So Much!
Mama Kari

This is the verse the Lord gave me during this season of waiting—a verse that a woman who walked through infertility spoke over Mary, who was expecting the birth of Jesus:

Luke 1:45 (NASB)

And blessed is she who believed that there would be fulfillment of what had been spoken to her by the Lord.

Romans 5:3–5 (ESV)

Not only that, but we rejoice in our sufferings, knowing that suffering produces endurance, and endurance produces character, and character produces hope, and hope does not put us to shame, because God's love has been poured into our hearts through the Holy Spirit who has been given to us.

The Unfolding of Our Family

Isaiah 43:18–19 (NASB)

"Do not call to mind the former things or ponder things of the past. Behold, I will do something new, now it will spring forth; will you not be aware of it? I will even make a roadway in the wilderness, rivers in the desert."

❧ CHOSEN ❧

December. It was getting close to Christmas. We were all settled in our cozy new townhome, starting to put decorations up and lights on the house. I headed to the grocery store one Monday morning, and right when I got there, Roxanne, our caseworker, was calling on my cell phone.

"Hi, Roxanne!"

"Hi, Kari. So, I am calling to let you know that there is a couple who has looked at your adoption profile." My heart began to get hopeful. Details followed.

"They actually have met with another couple, but now they aren't sure, and so they are reconsidering their options. They are expecting a little boy in January." My heart began to beat a little faster with anticipation. "The only thing is they are looking for an adoptive couple that would be willing to consider openness."

"What type of openness?"

"Well, they aren't fully sure yet, but visits once or twice a year maybe—those things could be talked about."

I can't explain it, other than God, but I had complete peace about this situation. It was almost like He had given me a glimpse of what He had planned. See, even though I thought I wanted a girl first, I felt that God wanted us to have a boy first, to be a big brother, something I never had.

Even though I didn't know if I wanted openness, with this birth couple living in Washington, I could embrace the idea because there would be space. I wouldn't risk running into them in the store and being emotionally caught off guard. God gave me peace to be willing to consider this option.

And the final thing: it was right before Christmas, and right after our first niece was born. This brought me back to when I prayed to God starting to tell

Him what I wanted for Christmas, and then stopped because He already knew and I just needed to trust Him. Peace filled my heart...

"They would like to meet you. Can you drive up to Tacoma on Wednesday?"

Yes, yes, yes! my heart cried out! "Let me talk to Nick, and we will pray about it and I will get right back to you."

After hanging up with Roxanne, I wasted no time in calling Nick. We prayed together and both felt peace to pursue this. Plans were made to go up to Tacoma in two days. I remember sitting in the car afterwards just glowing. It was a beautiful sunny amazing day in December. Even if it had been raining I think it would have been sunny to me because of hope. I was beginning to see a beautiful ray of hope after all the heartache and waiting.

We made the drive up on Wednesday, and when we got there we met our caseworker who had also driven up. She took us to a room and we waited for the birth parents to arrive. A few minutes later they did, and we were escorted into the room with them. I began to fall in love with this couple before us. I remember I was wearing a red shirt, and they both had red shirts on, and we made a comment about that. I remember seeing his red hair and thinking in my head how amazing it would be to have a redheaded baby. I remember their bright smiles and how cute she looked with her baby belly. We hit it off pretty quickly. Again, I can't explain it by anything other than God. They asked us questions to get to know us. They said they loved the pictures of our baby nursery, and then he asked if I had been hoping for a girl. I sheepishly smiled and said, "Maybe, but I would love whoever the Lord would have for us." She made a cute comment then, "I believe that the Lord has ordained for us to all go to the hospital right now and I will have this baby today."

They asked us about names. They said they would honor whatever the adoptive parents chose. They told us they had been thinking about William. We said we liked the name Josiah, that we had had that name picked out since we were dating, and that it meant "fire of the Lord." They both liked that, and we all thought it would be cool to have a redheaded baby with a name that meant that. They asked, if they chose us, to let them know what we decided so they would know what to put on the birth certificate.

We began the drive home to Portland. We didn't know if we had been chosen. Everything about the visit indicated that possibility, but it ended with, "We will let you know as soon as we decide."

It was Wednesday, and we made it home in time to go to our Wednesday night service at church that we loved. We were surrounded and prayed for by those that were walking this path with us.

The next day we didn't hear anything back until late afternoon. We had been chosen. We were going to be the adoptive parents to their baby boy. His due date was January 7.

After I received the phone call from Roxanne, I remembered my song the Lord had given me in the midst of my grief. On that day, I got to go back to the piano and with tears streaming down my face, my song became one of pure, beautiful joy. I called my friends with the news, and Leah and Jamie and Tricia announced they were taking me out to celebrate! We went to Red Robin for dessert—I even tried a sip of Jamie's Bailey's Irish cream drink, which is the only time in my life I have ever had any alcohol. To be surrounded by these friends who had walked through this season of life with me and now were all there to share in the joy with me—I was *so* grateful for this gift.

Nick and I began preparations to receive a little boy. Baby boy clothes shopping was top of the list! We had decided to choose the name Josiah

William, choosing William as a middle name to honor them (William means resolute protector, which in reflection now is very applicable to a big brother with three little sisters). We wrote them a note expressing our gratitude and letting them know the name we had chosen.

We continued with our Christmas festivities, anxiously wondering when we would receive a phone call that Josiah had been born. We waited all the way through Christmas and the New Year.

Dear Children,

God was at work in our story! We had been chosen! After years of waiting, we found ourselves in a time to celebrate. We were going to start our family. We were reaching the climax in a story of unknown in our lives, the final curtain was going to be raised, and the revealing of our first child was about to happen! As I reflect on this more, it wasn't just that we were chosen or that Josiah was chosen for us. There was and still is a bigger story going on here.

Adoption. What it symbolizes goes so much deeper. We have a God who has invited each of you to be part of His family. You are wanted and loved by a Father who wants you. Who loves you freely. Who offers everything He has and gives it to you. His child. Through Him He gives us access to His Salvation, His Son, His Holy Spirit, His Family.

I love you, Children. Always.
Your Mama Kari

Ephesians 1:3–14 (NASB)

Blessed be the God and Father of our Lord Jesus Christ, who has blessed us with every spiritual blessing in the heavenly places in Christ, just as He chose us in Him before the foundation of the world, that we would be holy and blameless before Him. In love He predestined us to adoption as sons through Jesus Christ to Himself, according to the kind intention of His will, to the praise of the glory of His grace, which He freely bestowed on us in the Beloved. In Him we have redemption through His blood, the forgiveness of our trespasses, according to the riches of His grace which He lavished on us. In all wisdom and insight He made known to us the mystery of His will, according to His kind intention which He purposed in Him with a view to an administration suitable to the fullness of the times, that is, the summing up of all things in Christ, things in the heavens and things on the earth. In Him also we have obtained an inheritance, having been predestined according to His purpose who works all things after the counsel of His will, to the end that we who were the first to hope in Christ would be to the praise of His glory. In Him, you also, after listening to the message of truth, the gospel of your salvation--having also believed, you were sealed in Him with the Holy Spirit of promise, who is given as a pledge of our inheritance, with a view to the redemption of God's own possession, to the praise of His glory.

Romans 8: 14–25 (NASB)

For all who are being led by the Spirit of God, these are the sons of God. For you have not received a spirit of slavery leading to fear again, but you have received a spirit of adoption as sons by which we cry out,

"Abba! Father!"

The Spirit Himself testifies with our spirit that we are children of God, and if children, heirs also, heirs of God and fellow heirs with Christ, if indeed we suffer with Him so that we may also be glorified with Him. For I consider that the sufferings of this present time are not worthy to be compared with the glory that is to be revealed to us. For the anxious longing of the creation waits eagerly for the revealing of the sons of God. For the creation was subjected to futility, not willingly, but because of Him who subjected it, in hope that the creation itself will also be set free from its slavery to corruption into the freedom of the glory of the children of God. For we know that the whole creation groans and suffers the pains of childbirth together until now. And not only this, but also we ourselves, having the first fruits of the Spirit, even we ourselves groan within ourselves, waiting eagerly for our adoption as sons, the redemption of our body. For in hope we have been saved, but for hope that is seen is not hope; for who hopes for what he already sees. But if we hope for what we do not see, with perseverance we wait eagerly for it.

❧ LETTING GO ❧

We were into the beginning of January and I was starting to get anxious—extremely anxious—over every type of worry you could think of. The due date was quickly coming, and we all thought she might go early. The seventh came and went and no news of a baby.

We went to church on Sunday, January 9. John Mark gave a sermon called "The Fight Against Fear." It is amazing to me how a timely sermon can speak through the Holy Spirit in us. I was in tears at the end of the sermon, and I knew that I needed prayer. Nick and I figured sometime this next week Josiah would be born and we would become parents for the first time ever. We went up and Phil and John Mark laid hands and prayed over us. One thing I remember Phil telling me afterwards is, "You do know that even though Josiah will be given to you, he won't belong to you. Josiah belongs to the Lord."

God has spoken those words over and over again as a mom of four now. My children do not belong to me. I am a steward of them for the blink of an eye, and then it will be over. To make the most of each moment. To not worry about their lives, but to trust God with them, because He is in control over everything. My worry will do nothing to protect them, to control the situations they are in. I have to trust. I have to release. I have to do my best with each day given to me and pray that they can see His love in my life.

That very night we got a phone call from Roxanne. Josiah had been born earlier in the evening and was doing well. The plan was to let his birthparents have Monday with their families, and then we would go up Tuesday to meet him, and he would be given to us. It was such a crazy thing to anticipate.

In our adoption classes, one of the things that stood out to me was that while you are in the hospital with your birth parents, it is not about you becoming new parents. It is about them and the loss they are going through as they give up this child that they carried in them for nine months and are now having to say goodbye to.

The night before, final preparations were made: Car seat was placed in the back of the car. Diaper bag loaded and ready to go. I had a cough that was not going away, and my Japanese grandma made me take some sort of gross syrup thing for it—and she gave me face masks to wear around Josiah when we were at the hospital (which I chose to leave at home).

Nick and I drove up on Tuesday morning, and we got to the hospital around 11:00. We met with our caseworker, who was in communication with the birth counselor, who came down and met with us. We talked and prayed, and when Josiah's birth parents were ready, we went up to see them and meet Josiah for the first time.

I remember the first time I held him, how solid he felt in my arms. Born at eight pounds, one ounce, he was a good, healthy weight. And his hair. He had a beautiful head of red hair. He rested peacefully and was very content as a baby.

I held back at that point, though. I knew I could not let myself get fully attached until everything was final. The words of Phil, "Josiah does not belong to you, he belongs to the Lord," echoed in my mind.

Josiah was taken to be circumcised, and we had a chance to talk with his birth parents more. His birth father shared how the nurses had put antibiotics in Josiah's eyes, and he had wiped them away because he thought they were tears. I gave them a red photo album as a thank-you gift that maybe they could use to put his pictures in...as if a photo album could really ever say thank you. Thank you for giving us your child.

How do you really ever say enough for that? There are no words that really justify the gratitude.

As the day progressed, the emotions started to get tougher. We would go in and spend time with them and Josiah, and then we would go out and they would talk. They would talk with Cindy, their birth counselor, and then they would talk with us.

"This is just a really hard thing to do."

We began to see that this could go a different direction than we had planned that morning when we left our home.

Dinner time came and went, but I barely nibbled on a bagel. We would take turns holding Josiah out in the hall while conversations in the other room were going on, but after a while there came a point when I looked at his face, and I knew I could not hold him anymore. I gave him to Roxanne and said, "I just can't do this right now."

Josiah's birth dad came out with tears, sharing that he knew it was the right thing for them to do, and he didn't understand why his birth mom would think about changing her mind. Cindy came out and told us that she was just having doubts. We went in and talked more with both of them, and let her talk through how she was feeling. We told her we wanted what was best for Josiah and prayed with them that God would show them the right decision to make.

We left them to talk again, then Cindy came out to tell us they would sign the papers. We went back into the hospital room, and I was holding Josiah again, and his precious birth mom was in tears. She said, "I feel like I am being forced to do this." When she spoke those words, a prayer went out in my heart to the Lord that said, "Please Lord, I don't want to take her baby away from her. This isn't right. Please, Lord, intervene. This is not right."

It was 8:00 at night, and the time to be discharged was quickly approaching. We left the room again, and Cindy came out and said, "I can't let her sign the papers at this point." I felt relieved in a way and said, "We would not feel comfortable with that either."

We waited a little longer, and the decision came through Cindy out to us that his birth mom would take Josiah home that night, and was asking if we could find a hotel close by to stay the night. Then she would let us know the next morning. Nick emotionally lost it at this point. He started crying, and just said, "This is just really, really hard to be sent back and forth emotionally on what we will do."

I grabbed Nick's arm with tears in my eyes, because that is what came forth when I saw my husband crying. "It's okay, Nick, it's okay," I cried.

Nick calmed down a little, and we agreed to do that, so at 9:30 we left the hospital without Josiah. We both knew in our hearts that if she was taking Josiah home with her, he would not be our son.

I made a phone call to my dear friend Leah, who had been in charge of calling everyone and asking them to pray throughout the day (we were definitely covered—in the midst of the emotional roller coaster, God's peace prevailed in our hearts). I broke down crying again and told her that we were leaving without Josiah, that they were taking him home, and that Josiah's birth parents would let us know their decision tomorrow.

As we walked out to the car empty handed, a man passed us by. Nick and I both had bloodshot eyes from tears, and he nodded to us, and all he said was, "Rough time?"

We responded with a short, "Yeah." To me somehow that was comforting. To have a perfect stranger be empathetic in such a way God used to comfort my soul.

We headed onto the road with a mission in mind to find a hotel for the night. I had surrendered in my heart that he was not ours, and I started thinking about what I would do when we got home. I didn't think I would be ready to try adoption again anytime soon. Maybe I would get a job at the mall? I really didn't know, but I needed something that would keep me busy...a new vision since the one I thought I was supposed to have hadn't worked out...

As we pulled out onto the freeway, I looked to my right, and through my watery eyes I made out the words that had purposefully been placed in front of a church, in bright red lit up letters: "JESUS CARES ABOUT YOU." Nick saw it too.

"Nick, look!" I said. "Jesus cares for us." And he smiled a little at me and said tenderly, "Yeah, He does."

We found an Extended Stay America, and Nick pulled into the parking lot at 10:00. He went inside to see if there were any rooms available. Right as he walked inside, my phone rang.

"Hello?"

"Kari, it's Roxanne."

"Hi, Roxanne."

"So, after you and Nick left, Josiah's birth parents talked some more, and his birth mom found that peace from God that she was looking for, and they signed the papers and have gone home. Josiah is yours. You need to come back to the hospital and get him."

"What? What! Hold on just a second!" I said as I flew out of our car and ran to Nick. "Here, talk to Nick," and I shoved the phone in his ear.

Wow. Really, God...Really? Really? There was no mind-changing at that point—they left, papers were signed, no going back. He had truly been given to us.

The drive back to the hospital was an amazing gift after all the emotional ups and downs of the day. My mind started thinking—we need to find out when he had his last bottle so I know when to feed him again, and we have a long drive to Vancouver where we will be staying for the next few days until courts sign off on paperwork to allow us to take him across state borders...and mom gear had totally kicked in. What had we gotten ourselves into?

My favorite memory ever of this day was when we came back to the hospital room to see our caseworker just finishing feeding him a bottle to get him ready for us.

I pulled out the going-home outfit I had picked out for him—a pastel green striped gown with mitten sleeves and a matching hat. And I got to put him in our car seat that had been given to us by friends. I gave him his cute blue hippo rattle, and I knew he was my son now.

I remember the ride to Vancouver, just beaming. He was so quiet and slept a lot of the way. I kept looking back there, as if pinching myself to tell me it was real. We really did have a baby boy in the back of our car. Nick and I had been given the gift to be parents for the first time ever by an amazing, brave, beautiful couple that loved their birth son so much and they had chosen us. Us!

To me this is a moment in life that I can only look back on and see God. GOD.

Too many fingerprints of His hands on this to ever think anything different.

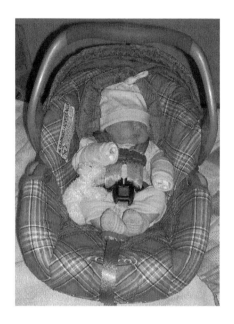

Dear Josiah,

This is your story. It can be hard to imagine being a baby, held in the middle of all of those decisions whirling around you, completely at the mercy of whatever the outcome, that was not in your control. When I watched you, held you, this first day we met you, I was amazed at how peaceful you looked. I want you to know something. You were being taken care of from the very beginning. You have to remember that. When I looked at your body at rest, it was a picture of a child who was being carried by God, covered by His peace. No awareness of anything else, other than a trust that you would be given exactly what you needed.

One of the gifts of your story that not every adoption story holds is that you had four adults who loved you deeply and had your best interest at heart. Both of your birth parents, and Daddy and I, all loved you enough to be willing to make the sacrifices necessary to help you be where God wanted you to be. Not where we all selfishly would have wanted you. Your birth parents were filled with selfless love. We all prayed for God to lead them in the hospital over the final decision of adoption. Don't ever forget that. You still have four adults that love you so much. We are all rooting for you and excited to see what God is going to do in your life as you grow up.

You are loved. You are chosen. You are wanted. This is your story.

Thank you for being our son. You are everything we never knew we always wanted and longed for in a firstborn for our family.

Love,
Your Mama, Kari

Psalm 139:13–14 (ESV)

For you formed my inward parts; you knitted me together in my mother's womb. I praise you, for I am fearfully and wonderfully made. Wonderful are your works. My soul knows it very well.

2 Chronicles 34:1–3 (NASB)

Josiah was eight years old when he began to reign, and he reigned thirty-one years in Jerusalem. And he did what was right in the eyes of the Lord, and walked in the ways of David his father; and he did not turn aside to the right hand or to the left. For in the eighth year of his reign, while he was yet a boy, he began to seek the God of David his father, and in the twelfth year he began to purge Judah and Jerusalem of the high places of the Asherim, and the carved and the metal images.

❧ TO BEGIN AGAIN ❧

It was February 2006, a year after Josiah was born. I was very exhausted from training and raising a one-year-old very hyperactive toddler who was always on the go and into everything. My sweet first little baby was becoming a little boy, and God was definitely teaching me to learn consistency in disciplining. Nick was in school a few nights a week, so I had a lot of one-on-one time with my Josiah. I was learning a lot about how to raise a little boy, and I loved it some of the time, and other times I felt like I was walking around like a half-dead mommy.

One night when I was feeling like the dead-tired mommy, Nick was home and we decided to go out to Target with Josiah. I was pushing the cart around, with barely enough energy for the remainder of the day, when I heard these words come out of Nick's mouth.

"I think it's time we start the adoption process again."

Uhh...what? Maybe we should just have our one little boy and call it good.

Looking at him with as much energy as I could muster, I responded with an unexpected fervor that shut that plan right down. I don't exactly remember my words, but they were not kind and probably involved something about him being crazy, and Josiah being only one, and Nick being busy all the time, and this was not the day to bring up such a notion! I think I was definitely in "freaking out" mode with that response.

Nick dropped the topic pretty quickly that night, and I was left feeling that my husband had a dream placed on his heart that I was not on board with yet. I needed first to get some sleep that night, and then to go before the Lord and really seek out what He had planned for us. I needed to pray and sort things through and listen to God.

On February 14, we planned a special Valentine's family date night with our friends the Jeremy and Erin. We decided to hit up Chuck E. Cheese on Valentine's night, figuring it would be pretty empty (which it was!), and let the boys (Josiah and his buddy, Preston) have a fun time playing together. That day while Josiah was taking a nap, I remember looking at the picture over the fireplace mantle. It was me and Nick with Josiah on our laps. And as I thought about it, I knew we were not complete yet. Our family was not done. And I knew what God was telling me. "It's time, Kari. Trust your husband."

When Nick came home that evening, I gave him his Valentine's card, which told him I was willing to go on the adoption waiting list again. Nick was very excited.

Erin and I with our boys, Easter Sunday, 2006.

I told Erin that night as our boys played, and she shared that they were thinking about trying to get pregnant again too. God was conceiving in both of our hearts the idea to prepare for the growth of our families. It was a special night to share our hopes and dreams together with them.

Now, mind you, even though I made a decision to follow this dream, I still had days of doubt, such as when I would hold our friend's newborn babies, and watch Josiah have a major jealousy attack.

I really wondered if we were doing the best thing for Josiah and for our family. I kept questioning the timing of all of this. And I still ached to get pregnant someday.

Then God spoke to me. In April our church held a women's retreat that I signed up to attend. The speaker was Mary Courson. She was a lady who had raised four children and had followed the Lord through many highs and lows in her life. Her children all grew up to love and serve the Lord in different, beautiful ways. Following is an excerpt from a journal I wrote during that retreat.

> I was so blessed to attend Mary Courson's last retreat. I just feel fragrant. And I'm not talking about my sweat from working out tonight. It's just when you have been around someone who loves the Lord and has loved Him as long as Mary did, you just want to hang on to that and let it overflow into other's lives.
>
> The Lord totally spoke to me this weekend. They had verse cards made, and gave one to each woman attending the retreat. I didn't realize they were not all the same until they were announced. And hearing that they had been prayed over and that each person would get a verse specifically for them, well, it totally happened. See, Nick and I are starting the adoption process again, and I've been having HUGE fears about it, and I really was hoping the Lord would speak to me to confirm it in my heart. So far it had just been a submitting to Nick's desires, and me having No Desire to do it, and tons of worries...
>
> When I first saw my verse, I thought, oh, that's a good one. It read, "You are blessed, because you believed that the Lord would do what he said." —Luke 1:45 (NLT)
>
> So, I thought, that is a great verse. Then, when I heard they were prayed over and not all the same, I realized that it was something a little more personal. And I

started to ponder that verse more, and think maybe it was my verse for this next adoption.

THEN, I went home, and this morning, I looked up Luke 1:45 in my NASB Bible, and here is what it read: "Blessed is she who believed that there would be a fulfillment of what had been spoken to her by the Lord."

That verse is the verse the Lord gave to me in the middle of our last infertility treatment, as we were coming close to winding down on pursuing getting pregnant and seriously starting to consider adoption as an option. I posted that verse on my fridge, on my mirror, on my computer monitor. (It is words Elizabeth spoke to Mary when Mary had been told she would carry Jesus and birth Him into the world). I clung to that verse, because it was spoken by a woman who had walked my path, and she had faith.

I realized, I AM BLESSED! I am so blessed. The Lord was so faithful with bringing Josiah into our lives. I don't need to worry. Period. I am jumping off this cliff into an unknown, but I have my amazing Savior who is going to carry me through it, and if He wills, bring about our second child in the best way He sees fit. So, I don't need to worry.

I just thought about this verse during worship times today and I couldn't help but praise the Lord with my whole heart. He was faithful to bring about what He had spoken to me the first time, and I know, although it is unknown of when and how and whom, He will be faithful to me once again.

Our "Sunshine Smile" boy.

Dear Children,

Someday God may ask you to do something that you don't feel ready for. This was my moment. I didn't think I was capable of taking on another child. We had a lot going on in our lives, and the idea of starting something new definitely overwhelmed me.

My advice to you is not to say yes or no. Pray about it. We should definitely seek His wisdom in making decisions. The feelings and emotions of my first response to Nick's petition were valid and needed to be considered in making the decision for our family. I love that Nick didn't push me or force me into doing this, but he allowed me room to breathe, to be able to sort it out and take time with the Lord.

God gave me peace to allow Nick to take us into the process again. But as you read, I was still not fully ready, and still carried a bit of doubt and insecurity with me. Then God in His mercy spoke to me in a way only He could. He gave me a verse that had meant so much to me, and brought it back to me once more in a fresh new way.

What a merciful God we have, to meet me like that. He was about to do something big in His gospel story. He had another child He wanted to bring into His family, and we were going to be part of that. We didn't see that at the time, we just knew that starting the process was what God was calling us into.

We may not have everything we need right up front, but He is faithful to give us what we need along the way. I love you, Children!

Your Mama,
Kari

Hebrews 11:32–34 (ESV)

And what more shall I say? For time would fail me to tell of Gideon, Barak, Samson, Jephthah, of David and Samuel and the prophets, who through faith conquered kingdoms, enforced justice, obtained promises, stopped the mouths of loins, quenched the power of fire, escaped the edge of the sword, were made strong out of weakness, became mighty in war, put foreign armies to flight.

Hebrews 12:1–3 (NASB)

Therefore, since we have so great a cloud of witnesses surrounding us, let us also lay aside every encumbrance and the sin which so easily entangles us, and let us run with endurance the race that is set before us, fixing our eyes on Jesus, the author and perfecter of faith, who for the joy set before Him endured the cross, despising the shame, and has sat down at the right hand of the throne of God. For consider Him who has endured such hostility by sinners against Himself, so that you will not grow weary and lose heart.

2 Peter 1:3–4 (ESV)

His divine power has granted to us all things that pertain to life and godliness, through the knowledge of Him who called us to His own glory and excellence, by which He has granted to us His precious and very great promises, so that through them you may become partakers of the divine nature, having escaped from the corruption that is in the world because of sinful desire.

❧ OUR FIRST ADOPTION LOSS ❧

The spring of 2006 was spent preparing paperwork and having home study appointments to get us back on the waiting list, round two. After the women's retreat, my heart was definitely on board with this plan God was leading us on. We were on the waiting list by summer. My friends Erin and Kathryn were both expecting babies around the same time in November, and I began hoping that maybe we would be, too.

We got the phone call in August that began to plant that dream inside my heart, sprinkling it with hope.

When Roxanne called, she informed us that there was a birth mom from Idaho who wanted to meet us! Her due date was November 25 for a scheduled C-section, and she was expecting a little girl. We were told we would get a call in the next week to figure out when at the end of September we would be meeting her. I had no idea what would happen in all of this, but deep down I believed God's way is perfect, and that no matter what happened, He would give us the second child He wanted for us, and He would place this baby girl exactly where she needed to be. It was exciting to think about having a baby girl. We started toying with the idea of having Jacey as our little girl name.

My dreams got away from me. Needless to say, I pretty much had it figured out—so I thought. I had already named this baby. September seemed to drag on in my head as we waited to hear confirmation of our meeting time with our potential birth mom. It seemed like the perfect fit—a baby girl in November. What more could I hope for? We were told that she wasn't going to be meeting with anyone else. Hopes just kept rising in my heart.

By the middle of September, we had a weekend planned to drive up to the Seattle office and meet with her there. It sounded like it would be a meeting just to confirm the details of her giving up this baby girl to us. Maybe it was all in my brain, but I was pretty much set on this being the next big adventure for us.

Then we got another phone call from Bethany. The birth mother had changed her mind about meeting us. She started to have some second thoughts and was leaning towards keeping this baby girl she was carrying. When I hung up, I tried to have a brave face. I held my emotions at bay as I began to walk through the motions of the weekend we were supposed to meet our next birth mom. We decided to go up to Seattle anyway, to get away for the night (secretly, I kept hoping we would get a phone call saying she had a change of heart, and we could still meet with her as planned). The next day we came back home and celebrated with our friends at a couples' baby shower I helped put together. I know people around us were concerned if it would be a hard thing for me after the loss, but honestly, there is no place I would have rather been that night.

The day after that I walked a 10K with a friend, as part of the Portland Marathon Day festivities.

When I came home, I lost it. The emotions from the loss hit me full force after setting them aside over the weekend. I went under my covers in a dark room and just laid in bed most of the afternoon. The next week I didn't want to be around anyone, I didn't want to talk to anyone, I avoided phone calls and did what I could to just stay home. I grieved the loss very hard. Why had I let my heart get so set on this dream? I hadn't even met the birth mom and I had the deal set in stone. The whole week I carried this broken heart with me.

The following Sunday I sat in the back at church. This was when our church was meeting in the cafeteria of a middle school with pizza and hamburgers painted on the walls. I remember sitting on the back windowsill of the room we met in. And then the worship band began to play a song—a song by Tim Hughes that I had not heard before called "Everything."[23]

And silent tears streamed down my cheeks. I knew that God was with me. He knows me so intimately. That He was with me in my grieving over this broken dream. And for some reason He did not have a Jacey for our family in November. I could not understand the reasons at the time, but He was there. He was in my hoping and my dreaming and my hurting, and He would be with me in my healing. After that Sunday morning at church, I was able to pick myself back up and start again. I didn't have a clue what the future would hold. But I had been reminded of Who did, and I knew He would be my *everything* while I waited on Him.

Dear Children,

Miscarriage is when a mother loses her baby that she is carrying inside of her. I have had several very close friends walk through that loss. I even watched two friends miscarry twice in a row, and I saw the fear in their eyes as they thought about trying again. When one friend was pregnant once more after the third time, she was scared, hesitant to accept that this one might take. That she wouldn't lose this child as well. Watching my friends walk through this, I could empathize with this pain. But I never could fully understand it.

I will never fully understand the physical pain that comes from a miscarriage. But the emotional heartbreak I could now understand from this adoption loss. I had let my heart get fully attached to life with this child, and I hadn't seen or held her or felt her inside of me. But I knew she was there, and I anticipated being her mama. Those dreams would never come to pass for our family.

There is a song sung by Natalie Grant called "Held,"[24] which speaks deep into the heart of loss of a little child. It was a good song to cry with, and I had once shared it with a friend who had just lost their baby. God reminded me of music and lyrics of that song and that is where God met me as I held out my disappointed heart to Him. He held me in the broken dream. The loss hit deep, and the pain was real, and He held me close.

I hate to say it, dear Children, but there may be loss like this in your life, or in the lives of those you are close to. And I am so sorry. Please know our God is a comforter. He longs to hold you tight when it hurts. He is there in the midst of all of it.

I love you.

Your Mama,
Kari

2 Corinthians 1:3–5 (ESV)

Blessed be the God and Father of our Lord Jesus Christ, the Father of mercies and God of all comfort, who comforts us in all our affliction, so that we may be able to comfort those who are in any affliction, with the comfort with which we ourselves are comforted by God. For as we share abundantly in Christ's sufferings, so through Christ we share abundantly in comfort too.

Psalm 56:8 (ESV)

You have kept count of my tossings; put all my tears in your bottle. Are they not in your book?

Psalm 9:9–10 (ESV)

The Lord is a stronghold for the oppressed, a stronghold in times of trouble. And those who know Your name put their trust in You. For You, O Lord, have not forsaken those who seek You.

⚡ HE DOES KNOW BEST ⚡

This story is just not as "picture perfect" as I feel our first one was, so it is harder to process. As I write this, I want to be sensitive to those who were involved as we walked along this journey. This part of the story is one of those situations where you can see some answers to the whys for how things went, but it doesn't always make sense. I can look back to five years ago and say, I totally understand—but in the midst of everything, I did not fully understand.

It was the middle of October. Just a few short weeks after the falling through with our Jacey baby girl, we received another phone call. As it turned out, Bethany had another birth mom for us to meet the very next Monday. She was a gal who lived in Washington, and we were potentially going to meet the birth dad as well. Excitement started to build when we found out she was working with the same birth counselor that worked with Josiah's birth parents. Cindy was just so great during the whole process, and we loved the idea of getting to do it again with her. We learned she didn't know what she was having, which would mean it would be a surprise. She was eight months along and had only found out several weeks prior that she was expecting. Her due date was around the first few weeks of November. She was a beautiful gal, a swimmer in college, and she had family support.

We also met with the birth dad, separately, that day. He had just been told that week. He was in a different relationship now and was dealing with the shock of everything. There is a lot more that was going on, but to just sum things up, it was an extremely complicated situation, where the birth parents were not talking to each other, and it just felt very messy.

After we left, I wasn't sure where we stood. The birth mom seemed pretty upbeat and ready for adoption. The birth dad was sorting things out. We waited for a few weeks, with no answers.

Then we received a letter from our birth mom letting us know that we had been chosen. We were elated and so ready to do this. The birth dad had come to peace with the adoption situation, and so we were officially the chosen parents of this little one. We followed up with our caseworker, and she informed us the due date was right around November 12 or 13, which put us less than a week away. I had a gut feeling it must be a girl. She wasn't going to find out until birth, but I just had this feeling in my heart we were supposed to have a girl next. I chose the name Ava. Our friends, Erin and Jeremy, had just given birth to a baby boy named Evan, and Ava was the feminine version of that name, meaning filled with life. They would get married and live happily ever after someday...

A week later we got the phone call sharing that our birth mom had given birth to a baby boy. He weighed in very small, less than five pounds, but he was doing well. The conversation with our caseworker left us a bit confused. The birth mom was pretty sure she still wanted to do adoption, but she just had some things she needed to talk to us about. We made plans to go up the next morning to talk with her and meet her little boy.

That night I went shopping with my friend Erin for preemie baby boy clothes, and I was excited, but holding back a little in my heart. Something didn't seem quite right, but I couldn't lay my finger on it...I had been expecting a girl, but we knew we would love a little boy just as much.

We got to the hospital up in Washington the next day, unprepared for what would come of this day. The first news we weren't prepared for was that the baby was being released from the hospital that day. We didn't have any of our baby stuff, no car seat, absolutely nothing. We started logistically trying to figure out how we would leave the hospital, go home and get everything, and then come back to get him. We knew we would need to figure things out.

The second thing was when we got there, as they introduced us to him, they had already given him a name. We were a little shocked because she hadn't asked us about naming the baby. We didn't have a solid baby boy name picked. We knew we liked the name Micah, but we wanted to avoid coming in with a forceful "this is what we want to name our baby." I started to think of what would need to be done to change legal documents for naming this little guy. And he was very little. This beautiful baby boy. After watching his mother hold him, as he was given to me, I felt very timid holding him in front of her. It didn't sit well.

We left her room and were escorted into the waiting room, where we talked with her parents and sister while the birth mother talked with her birth counselor. We waited a long while, not sure what the outcome was going to be. Cindy, the birth counselor, finally came in and told us that she had made the decision to keep the baby.

As we left the hospital, it hit me that my biggest fear of leaving the hospital without a baby had actually happened, for real this time. But in a weird way, I felt a little relieved. There were a lot of birth family dynamics that would have added a lot to our responsibilities with visits. There were unknown health issue possibilities for this little baby that would not have shown themselves right away, but could have definitely brought challenges down the road.

Nick and I had been more than willing to receive this baby into our home, into our arms. And there were definite moments of heartbreak when I returned all the baby clothes I had just purchased a few days prior. The empty arms aching, wondering what God was doing. I started to try to potty train Josiah just to take my mind off things, but having him pee all over the place and not feeling "safe" with him sitting on my lap without a diaper on, I decided not to push it, and held back a little longer on that task so I could just hold close the little boy God had given me.

I can look back on the reasons now and see God's hand in the midst of it. We needed an Ava in our family. We needed more time with just Josiah, our first child, to nurture and love just him. I wonder if this baby boy had been given to us, and had grown up having special needs, would we have considered doing the fertility treatment that brought us Mallory and Lena? But in the moment, I didn't fully know what God was doing. I would go to church on Sundays and silent tears would slide down my cheeks as they played the Tim Hughes "Everything" song that God had given me as my song of comfort during this season of an unknown plan.

Waiting...this was something I was becoming good at. Or was it something I was becoming *numb* to? I look back in reflection at the season of silence from November 2006 to April 2007, when we received only one phone call from our agency of a possibility that didn't happen.

It was a quiet time. A time when I didn't know what was going on. It was a time of internal stress. How do we handle these situations out of our control? The ways we try to cope with them. I plunged forward, trying to stay busy with Josiah. Thriving on looking for any emails from friends that might want to hang out. Looking for ways to be involved in serving.

There are some fun things I got to do during this season of waiting. I got to go on a college retreat with the church and serve tables with my friends Kristy and Becca for some amazing students. I was able to take a road trip with Amy and our two sons to California, visiting friends who had moved down there. Nick was going to be in a friend's wedding in the beginning of May. There were a lot of great things going on.

Business is something I thrived on. Looking for the next big event on the calendar. I also struggled with stress eating. I had fluctuated up and down with my weight over the last few years, but the loss of adoption number two marked a turning point when my lack of control came into play. I slowly started to put on weight and not fit into my clothes, and I felt pretty down on myself. I know I was struggling with trying to find hope and a future in all of this.

What I didn't know is that something very important happened in that month of November when we experienced our loss. We started praying hard for our second child. Friends and family prayed with us and for us as well. November marked a huge time for our family when we went before the Lord pleading with Him for His will and work to be done. We couldn't have had any idea at the time of what the Lord was preparing through all of that. He was at work creating a life that He had big plans for. And we were all about to watch and see Him do a mighty work.

Dear Children,

I would love to say by this point I had this whole waiting thing down. That I knew how to let go of broken dreams and heal through them. But the truth is I didn't. I stuffed internally during this season. I hated the phone. I never wanted to answer any call, because each ring represented one more phone call I wasn't receiving from our adoption agency. I didn't respond to friends' calls during this time, because I didn't want to talk through any of it. It hurt too much, and I was trying to be the "good girl" that had it all together.

Sadly, I didn't turn my stress towards the Lord, having Him take my anxiety and cares and lay them on Him the way I needed to. Yes, I read my Bible every day; I silently cried out to Him with my tears at church on Sundays. But when I was in my home with my very active toddler, instead of crying out to the Lord there, I turned towards food and business in my daily schedule to cover up all the stress I was feeling.

Unfortunately, this led to a heart that wasn't grieving properly. As I had watched my friends in the past with their miscarriages, thinking once again of my friend who after two miscarriages approached her third pregnancy with huge caution, I found myself in the same place. I didn't want to think about receiving another child. I wanted to swallow that dream and bury it deep. As a result, my heart wasn't preparing the way it needed to for my next child. It was holding in fear and hurts. When the time eventually came for me to take in another child, emotionally I wouldn't be as ready as I could have been, because of all of that grief buried deep.

Children, I know—trust me, I know—how hard it can be to release grief. Instead you try to tuck it all away and pretend it's not there. But all that does is allow it to be stuffed to a point that eventually it can come up in ways that can hurt you worse, and hurt others around you as well. Whatever those things are that seem scary to you—like for me answering the phone when it wasn't the agency—it's better to lay them before the Lord and ask Him to sift through it with you. He wants to take our anxieties and fears. He loves us so much. He loves you. I love you, too.

Your Mama,
Kari

1 Peter 5:6–11 (NASB)

Therefore humble yourselves under the mighty hand of God, that He may exalt you at the proper time, casting all your anxiety on Him, because He cares for you. Be of sober spirit, be on the alert. Your adversary, the devil, prowls around like a roaring lion, seeking someone to devour. But resist him, firm in your faith, knowing that the same experiences of suffering are being accomplished by your brethren who are in the world. After you have suffered for a little while, the God of all grace, who called you to His eternal glory in Christ, will Himself perfect, confirm, strengthen and establish you. To Him be dominion forever and ever. Amen.

1 John 4:16–19 (ESV)

So we have come to know and to believe the love that God has for us. God is love, and whoever abides in love abides in God, and God abides in him. By this is love perfected with us, so that we may have confidence for the day of judgment, because as He is, so also are we in this world. There is no fear in love, but perfect love casts out fear. For fear has to do with punishment, and whoever fears has not been perfected in love. We love because He first loved us.

Psalm 27:13–14 (NASB)

I would have despaired unless I had believed that I would see the goodness of the Lord In the land of the living. Wait for the Lord; Be strong and let your heart take courage; Yes, wait for the Lord.

ꙮ A MOVEMENT OF LIFE ꙮ

In April we received a phone call from our agency. A couple wanted to meet with us and another family as they were considering adoption for their baby girl who was due in May.

April. A crazy season of life for us. The last three months Nick would be finishing his Master's degree, taking two classes in his final months of school, and at work he was putting in 60 hours a week. I wasn't seeing much of him. A year prior when we had started the process, we actually planned to go off the waiting list the months of April through June of 2007, while Nick finished things up. However, after the two losses, and then not hearing much, we prayed about it and decided to stay on the list.

We met with the birth parents at the local agency office. I was really nervous and feeling really shy. I didn't know what they would think of us. She was young and beautiful; he was tall and sincere. Nick played spokesperson a lot for us. My friend watched Josiah while we talked with them, and then brought him in at the end to meet the couple. Easing my nervousness, my son burst into the room all smiles with his adorable dimples, blue eyes shining bright. There are 100 other things my very hyperactive son could have done at that moment, but somehow God knew that Josiah needed to respond like that.

In reflection, I know I was more guarded. After going through a near loss with Josiah, and with the two losses prior to this meeting, I was protecting my heart from being broken again. A part of me wishes I could go back and change how I handled my internal feelings. We thanked them for meeting with us, we prayed with them, and then we said our goodbyes. They were going to meet with another couple, so we once again waited. She was due the beginning of May.

I was planning to leave for California with my friend for our road trip, and we still had not heard anything. We called our agency, wondering if we should change our plans last minute.

We received an answer. They wanted to meet with us again. We made plans to have lunch together, and then I would leave for California right after. We met at a Chinese food restaurant in Portland. It was a little more relaxed without the counselors and case workers there, and we talked with them. Following lunch, we went to a park close by and took a walk, and then they shared how God had led them to this place of considering adoption.

This is where God's beautiful story comes into play. In the month we lost our second adoption, plans were being made for Ava. Her birth mom was in a place where she could not care for her baby. She didn't have support from family at that time. They weren't together as a couple anymore and lived in different locations. He was going to be coming to see her over the weekend, and they were making plans for an abortion during that time. But in that month of November, when we were all praying for our next child after our second failed adoption, the Lord did a work in their hearts. He showed them they were not going to be having an abortion—that this child was going to live. They didn't know what that would look like, what type of life they would choose for her, but they knew very clearly abortion was not an option. He had saved Ava's life. It is amazing to me that Ava's name means "filled with life." God had huge plans to fill her with life. I was blown away at the beauty of His hand in this.

At the end of our meeting together, they didn't give us any answers. We once again said our goodbyes, and then we waited. I left for California, not knowing how things were going to go. I think in coping, I let myself think it was not going to happen. I got to enjoy a great visit with my friend who was expecting her first baby and had just moved far away with family. It was a blessing to have something else to focus on, but I pushed all those feelings down again, instead of working through them. I got a phone call in the middle of my trip from our caseworker, but she did not have any news for us. When I returned home, we still had no answer, so we kept waiting. May came. No answer. We kept waiting. And I did not know what to think.

Dear Ava,

Please always remember how God saved you for a purpose. This is part of your story, and I know it feels hard and a bit scary at times, but Ava, it really is a beautiful piece. God had His eyes on you from the beginning. He led your birthparents into a decision to save you. To trust Him. Not knowing where the road would lead them, they chose the hard path, because they knew God had a plan for your life. And He does. Don't ever forget this, sweet girl.

You are of value and of worth to all of us, but most of all, to Him!

We love you always,
Your Mama

Psalm 139:15–18 (ESV)

My frame was not hidden from you, when I was being made in secret, intricately woven in the depths of the earth. Your eyes saw my unformed substance; in your book were written, every one of them, the days that were formed for me, when as yet there were none of them. How precious to me are your thoughts, O God! How vast the sum of them! If I would count them, they are more than the sand. I awake and I am still with You!

Isaiah 44:21–24 (ESV)

Remember these things, O Jacob, and Israel, for you are my servant; I formed you; you are my servant; O Israel, you will not be forgotten by me. I have blotted out your transgressions like a cloud and your sins like mist; return to me, for I have redeemed you. Sing, O heavens, for the Lord has done it; shout, O depths of the earth; break forth into singing, O mountains, O forest, and every tree in it! For the Lord has redeemed Jacob, and will be glorified in Israel. Thus says the Lord, your Redeemer, who formed you from the womb: "I am the Lord, who made all things, who alone stretched out the heavens, who spread out the earth by myself."

⚜ THE GIFT OF AVA ⚜

On the afternoon of May 3, 2007, Nick and I were preparing to head down to Woodburn for a wedding rehearsal. Nick was one of the groomsmen for our friend from college group, Joel, and his bride-to-be, Linda. We received a call from Roxanne, our amazing caseworker. We had been chosen. The due date was the following week. We had our answer. We were going to be parents again.

It was a crazy busy weekend, one during which we told the bride and groom of the possibility that we might be going to the hospital for our baby at a moment's notice. On Saturday morning, the day of the wedding, I went with my friend Sheri to the outlet stores while Nick was busy getting ready. We looked for baby girl clothes. Deep down inside, I felt an unsettling fear, wondering if I would have to return the clothes if they changed their mind once she was born.

I did a little more shopping that Sunday after church and hoped I had everything I needed. On Monday around 12:00, we got a phone call letting us know our birth mom had gone into labor, and that once they got to the hospital and were settled, maybe we could come visit...I took Josiah over to my parents' house just to be prepared.

I went back home to wait for any news, and then after 3:00 we got another phone call letting us know our baby girl had been born, and everything went well. We were told that maybe we could visit them that night, but they would let us know a little later. As I waited, without my busy two-year-old to keep my thoughts distracted, I went into super-cleaning mode. Nesting, if you will. I cleaned and cleaned and got my home spick and span, drawing up lots of dust into dust cloths and cleaning more. The phone call came early that evening, requesting us to come meet her and talk about names.

This was a relief in some ways, because with the last adoption that fell through, the baby boy had already been named when we arrived.

I tried to go in with an open mind. The one thing I told Nick was that the middle name I wanted to hold my ground on. I really loved the middle name "Hope." It represented all that I had anticipated in this process, what kept me going these last months of waiting without answers. We went in and there she was. This beautiful, tiny, delicate six-pound, one-ounce baby girl with these big dark brown eyes like her birth mom's, that peered right into a person's soul. The nurse had super-glued a purple bow onto her tiny bit of hair. As I held her I wondered if this was really happening.

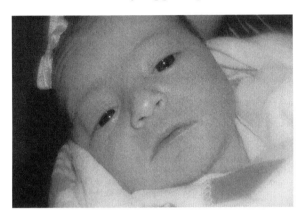

We talked about names. I originally thought about Madeline, because I loved the name Maddie. They weren't too keen on it, so I went back to my list of names that I had brought with me. When I read the name Ava, my name from the November adoption that I had laid to rest, they loved it. Ava's birth mom had a middle name she really liked as well, so we decided to give her two middle names: Ava Mae Hope.

Ava means filled with life. Mae means gift of God. Hope means to me our hope in Christ. We left the hospital. They had requested to spend the next day giving their families time to meet Ava. Plans were made for us to return Wednesday and bring her home to be our baby girl.

It was a week of Seven at our church. This was a week of fasting and praying for our city. I am terrible at fasting. I want to be good at it, but honestly it is not something that I do well at. I was determined to try and decided that I would take my Tuesday of waiting to fast. Nick took that day off, saying he would not be much use at work while waiting. I went to the early morning worship they had at church. I got to show our pastor Phil and others the picture of Ava from the hospital the night before. Then I dropped by to show my mom at the preschool she worked at. I took some time on that beautiful sunny day and sat at Summerlake Park, praying, reading my bible, thinking, and just enjoying that moment of quiet.

The night before, right after my big cleaning frenzy, I had started to feel funny. I couldn't lay my finger on it. By 2:00 on Tuesday afternoon, I was not feeling well, and Nick thought I should break my fast and eat something. I still did not feel well, and I started to develop the chills, so I took a rest. The fever would not go away, so I took some Tylenol and felt better, until it wore off again.

This continued straight into Wednesday, when we were waiting for the phone call to let us know when we could come pick up Ava and say goodbyes. I remember laying on the bed with the chills and a fever that early afternoon, thinking to myself, I can't do this, I am not feeling well, I don't know what is wrong with me. This is not how it is supposed to go. But at 2:00, we got the call to come back to the hospital. Tylenol had kicked in again, and I got myself out of bed and we headed out.

Once we arrived at the hospital, we visited with them for a little bit, then waited in another room while they said their goodbyes to Ava and signed final documents. Around 5:30, they were ready to go, and we walked out of the hospital with them. They carried Ava out in our car seat carrier, and Ava's hand was firmly wrapped around her birth mom's finger. This was not something I was prepared for at all. When Josiah was given to us, we didn't actually watch the handing over of him to us. Seeing Ava's birth parents in tears over this loss was almost unbearable, and my heart ached for them. We stood outside the hospital for a few minutes in silence, not sure of what to do as Ava continued to hold her finger. I reached out my finger as an offering, and her birth mom accepted it and transferred Ava's hand to mine. My heart ached and continued to break. We gave them hugs and they left first, pulling out in his jeep. Then Nick went and pulled our car around, and the nurse with us gave us a comforting smile and offered to take our picture with Ava.

After this long journey of waiting, we had been given a precious, beautiful gift. We loaded her up in our car and left for home.

Dear Ava Mae Hope,

When I think of your story, I am reminded of Ruth. Because Ava, you have a kinsman Redeemer, someone who loved you so deeply, who fought for you and wanted you to be in His family. And I am not talking about Daddy or me or your birth parents. We are just pieces that your Redeemer used to bring you to Him. And I know you already know who I am talking about. Jesus chose you. He wanted you. He saw the frame He was knitting together in your birth mother's womb and said, I have a plan for this girl. He gave you a name. And then He brought you into His family, and all that He has, He wants to give to you.

But it doesn't stop there. He wants you to be part of His gospel story. Ava, He wants to weave your life into what He is doing in other people's lives. You have a beautiful story to tell, and not only that, but you have the ability to love others with His love and point them to your kinsman Redeemer. Keep your eyes fixed on Him and the story He wants to continue to write in your life.

Shine for Him, Ava.

Love,
Your Mama

Isaiah 54:5 (NASB)

"For your husband is your Maker, Whose name is the LORD of hosts;
And your Redeemer is the Holy One of Israel, Who is called the God of
all the earth."

❧ LIFE AS A MOM OF TWO ❧

After we received Ava, I continued to battle this unknown sickness. I was once again in bed with fevers and chills, unsure what was wrong with me. Nick had that week off, and he took full responsibility for the children. I remember at one point lying in bed, and in the midst of my feverish sleep, he came upstairs to change his shirt and informed me that Ava had just given him a gift that Josiah had never given him. Apparently, a full squirt to his shirt. The girl had good aim at her daddy!

After a week of fevers, Tylenol, and trying to adjust to normal life, including a pizza party at our home so everyone could meet Ava, and a baby dedication on Mother's Day at our church, I remember lying on my parents' couch knowing something was not right. Nick was going back to work the next day. We decided last-minute that I needed to see a doctor, so we scheduled an appointment for first thing in the morning, and Nick took the children to my mom's for the day. I drove myself to the clinic and found out I had tonsillitis. My doctor put me on antibiotics. The next day, Nick took Ava to our friend Becca's home, who watched her for me while I waited for the antibiotics to kick in so I would not contaminate our newest little one. Josiah stayed with me and kept me company in my bed.

Ava's dedication at church

I started to feel better, and after 24 hours on antibiotics, I began my mommy job full time as a mom to two little ones. I felt like I needed to jump back into who I was again, and on a Wednesday night, I went to church with my little ones. But by the end of the night I was not feeling well. I drove the kids home and left an over-stimulated two-year-old in his room while I went to feed our little one her bottle, still not feeling quite right. I heard Josiah getting into all sorts of things, and I knew he just needed to get to bed, but I wanted to feed Ava and get her down. I was feeling very uncomfortable and needed to go to sleep myself. After holding her and trying to feed her for a little bit, I looked down at her bottle. She had not drunk one sip of her bottle. She had just been gumming it and staring at me with her big brown eyes. I was not doing well at this point, and I put her on the ground in a huff, leaving her screaming and crying while I took care of her brother. I was a frustrated mama, a sick mama, and I felt very alone, just wanting Nick to come through the doors at any moment and help me...which he didn't. I got Josiah to bed, and then I came back and worked on feeding Ava as well as I could, then I laid her down. But that night sticks out as one of the most difficult nights of my mama life.

My sickness lasted throughout the month of May. It included four different antibiotics, and getting hives from the second antibiotic as I found out for the first time I had an allergy to penicillin. I had a rash that lasted a week, starting at my head and working its way down to my toes. I remember walking one night and my legs itching terribly. I didn't want to be touched at all during this time; it was extremely uncomfortable.

I did have beautiful moments in the midst of it. I took Ava to a baby girl shower that was beautifully planned by all my friends. Ava wore her very frilly dress sent from Nick's family in Albuquerque. I was actually feeling well that day, and I received the beautiful gift of baby girl bedding that I had admired the summer before with my friend Erin. It made me cry. I did not have any time prior to Ava's birth to prepare a room for a little girl, and I left the shower with decorations to make her nursery girly and beautiful.

Receiving Baby girl gifts with tears of joy   *Ava's party dress*

Nick finished his Master's program in June, and I began to anticipate having him around more. However, that summer his work got even busier. We went through a few more months of craziness, of me not having my husband by my side and going stag with two kids to everything. In the middle of it, he came to a point when he knew things needed to change, and although I am not exactly sure what happened, they did, and he began to be home a lot more. For a little while we flipped roles. I jumped at the chance to do anything with friends to get me out of the house in the evening, while he was happy to stay home. Over that year we slowly balanced and began to figure out how to have a family life together. We could be home together and we didn't always have to be gone—we started to figure out what it meant to be a family of four.

Dear Children,

As you can tell by this last chapter, no matter how hard you might plan for it, there is no perfect time to have a child, or to have two children, in this instance. The fantasy of having babies of your own, when it meets the day-to-day taking care of them, can bring a huge reality check. Your dad and I made plenty of mistakes, and obviously you can attest to the many we still make along the way.

I would never have planned to get sick like I did when Ava came. I wish I had been healthy. If I could change anything, I would have been fully present without those shivers and chills. If I could have planned it all down to the dotted line, Nick would have been done with his Master's degree, and we would have been all ready to begin life with two children.

Life isn't perfect. There is no Disney happily ever after. At least not on this side of eternity. And that's the lesson I want to leave you with at the end of this chapter. Give yourself a higher measure of grace if you ever enter into the world of parenting. I know I put on myself huge pressure to do it all perfectly and "right." I want to tell you one thing that I want you to remember. God chose you to be the parents of the children He has given you. Not your friend's kids, or any other children you meet. Lots of people will have advice for you as you go. Take it to the Lord, and ask Him what to do with it. Some of the best well-meaning advice is not meant for your family. Other advice may be exactly what God wants you to hear. Ultimately, these children are yours to steward, gifts from the Lord. He chose you, He knows you intimately, and He knows all your successes and failures. Be intentional with the gifts the Lord has given you.

I love you. I know He has given you a great ability to be the mom/dad for your children, with Him by your side. I'm so grateful He chose you to be my children!

Your Mama Always,
Kari

Luke 1:13–16 (NASB)

But the angel said to him, "Do not be afraid, Zacharias, for your petition has been heard, and your wife Elizabeth will bear you a son, and you will give him the name John. You will have joy and gladness, and many will rejoice at his birth. For he will be great in the sight of the Lord; and he will drink no wine or liquor, and he will be filled with the Holy Spirit while yet in his mother's womb. And he will turn many of the sons of Israel back to the Lord their God."

Luke 1:30–31 (NASB)

The angel said to her, "Do not be afraid Mary; for you have found favor with God. And behold you will conceive in your womb and bear a son, and you shall name Him Jesus."

1 Samuel 1:22–23, 27–28 (NASB)

But Hannah did not go up, for she said to her husband, "I will not go up until the child is weaned; then I will bring him, that he may appear before the Lord and stay there forever." Elkanah her husband said to her, "Do what seems best to you. Remain until you have weaned him; only may the Lord confirm His word." So the woman remained and nursed her son until she weaned him. For this boy I prayed, and the Lord has given me my petition which I asked of Him. So I have also dedicated him to the Lord; as long as he lives he is dedicated to the Lord." And he worshiped the Lord there.

Deuteronomy 6:6–9 (ESV)

And these words that I command you today shall be on your heart. You shall teach them diligently to your children, and shall talk of them when you sit in your house, and when you walk by the way, and when you lie down and when you rise. You shall bind them on your hands and they shall be as frontlets between your eyes. You shall write them on the doorposts of your house and on your gates.

Adjusting to life with two was proving to be a very difficult and exhausting transition for me. Josiah and Ava's temperaments were as opposite as could be. Josiah was a go-getter. As soon as that kid learned to crawl and lift himself up onto things, he was into *everything*. Diane Comer, our pastor's wife, has talked in the past in her child training study about children who are boundary pushers and constantly testing the box. This was Josiah. I always had to be on my toes, because he was 10 steps ahead of me physically and mentally. One of our friends who is a social worker said he wasn't ADHD, but she labeled him "H," standing for Hyper. He had an amazing attention span, but constantly needed to be busy.

When Ava was a baby, I decided to start training for walking a marathon. I had a sit-and-stand stroller, and I would place Ava in the front. Josiah had easy access to hop in and out of the back seat whenever he needed. He took full advantage of that stroller. We have memories of him on a two-mile walk, running as he pushed Ava in the stroller the whole way. Or the one time I took a walk with him and Ava to a restaurant four miles away. With his bright blue Buzz Lightyear helmet securely fastened to his head, he hopped on his Kettler tricycle, and I had to walk quickly to keep up with his pace the entire time. He impressed us with his speed and ability, and I needed to keep two steps ahead of him at all times. He needed to be going, moving, exploring, busy, busy, busy.

Then there was Ava. As a baby, she was very whiny and emotional. She slept a ton. I carried her around in a sling right next to me, until she no longer fit. She was Josiah's exact opposite. Laid back, she did not like to be challenged. She was content to make everyone work for her and dote over her. My life consisted of keeping up with Josiah while trying to pull Ava along to catch up. This was very exhausting at times.

I remember once, we were late getting out the door to hop on the MAX train to go downtown. We were going to meet with friends at Jamison Square in Portland to let the kids play in the park fountains. I was scrambling to get everything together, and I asked Josiah if he could "please get a water bottle for Ava." In my mind, I meant for making Ava's bottle later. In his mind, that meant take the cap off the water bottle and hand it to his sister who was not a year old. That water bottle of course spilled all over the floors, and cleaning up added an extra 10 minutes to get out the door. I was none too pleased with Josiah, until I reflected on my words later and realized he had been following my exact directions. Oh, sometimes as moms if we could just slow down!

Another trip to Jamison Square included Josiah having to go pee and stripping off his swimsuit bottoms in downtown Portland, running frantically across the park. The only place to take them to the bathroom was this coffee shop called Sip and Kranz. As moms we always planned on taking our kids for a bathroom break and purchasing a drink and maybe a few pastries, for the free service of using their bathroom. But with my son's trunks off, there was no way I could even try to put them back on with the impending release due at any moment. However, my quick-thinking friend Becca did what I couldn't do as I stood mortified and stuck. She escorted him to a tree and told him to pee on a tree in downtown Portland. Oh, boy!

The other "fond" memory I have in this department is being at a "Moms in the Park" event—a weekly summer gathering where moms from our church would gather together for fellowship time. My son had just gone on a fishing trip with Dad, Papa and Uncle. He learned how men relieve themselves in the wilderness. As all the moms were gathering to have lunch on their picnic blankets, he stood up, faced everyone, pulled his shorts down and let loose. Apparently he had been holding it for a while, because I felt like it lasted a good 30 seconds at least to get it all out. His aim couldn't have been better; it was within a few inches of hitting everyone's blankets.

I will give all credit to the precision in that life skill to my husband.

I was in the middle of crazytown with two kids, but believe it or not, we still wanted to grow our family. My number had always been four or five children. Nick wasn't done at two, either. The big struggle, of course, came down to the fact that we were eight years into our marriage, had never taken birth control, and had never gotten pregnant. Nothing had changed in that department. We also had two open adoptions that we were vested in, and I didn't think I could take on another open adoption. Openness is a responsibility, a commitment, and we felt that adding another open adoption situation for our family would be a bigger commitment than we were prepared to handle. We prayed and didn't feel a strong calling to international adoption either.

At that point we had also looked into something called snowflake adoptions, with the same agency we had used in Josiah and Ava's adoptions. Embryo adoption would give me the opportunity to carry a child inside of me for the first time. We didn't have a peace about pursuing that. We decided to keep that thought on the back burner of our minds as we continued to pray.

We took all of these dreams and desires to the Lord once more and asked Him to show us what He had for us next.

Dear Children,

I want to pause and encourage you to do something with where you are today. Take a moment to stop and thank God for a few of the details in your life that are to be celebrated right now. When I look back at this chapter, I know I was so exhausted at times. Going from one to two children was the most difficult transition in my life as a mom. As a parent, when you start with one, a little bit of the person you have been all these years has to die. Or at least be put on hold. Your time is taken into the world of feeding, diapers, and schedules revolving around bedtimes and naps. But it is easy enough with one to cart that child around with you wherever you go, with the exception of when they want to run off all the time because they are a busy child!

Josiah and Ava, when I became a mom of you two children, so much more of the things I enjoyed doing had to be let go. This was the season I started releasing being able to help on the worship band at church. I had to divide myself between the two of you, requiring attention in very different ways. I still found ways to do some of the things I loved, but it was a fight for my personal time. Nothing really is ever personal time after you have children.

This is where I pause and remember how much joy I found in doing things with both of you. I loved taking our MAX transit adventure rides into downtown Portland, exploring the zoo, children's museum, quesadillas at Cha Cha Cha's, walks around the river, and meeting friends at Sip and Kranz and Jamison Square. This was a time in life when I got to share a little bit of my love for the city with the two of you. You may not ever remember it, but I will fondly remember those times with my Josiah and Ava.

Take those times to always remember the details of your life worth celebrating right now. I know you will find them.

Love You Always,
Mama

Ecclesiastes 3:9–13 (ESV)

What gain has the worker from his toil? I have seen the business that God has given to the children of man to be busy with. He has made everything beautiful in its time. Also He has put eternity into man's heart, yet so that he cannot find out what God has done from the beginning to the end. I perceived that there is nothing better for them than to be joyful and to do good as long as they live; also that everyone should eat and drink and take pleasure in all his toil—this is God's gift to man.

❧ THE BEGINNING OF OUR LENA AND MALLORY STORY ❧

In my heart, there was an unspoken dream that would not go away. I remember talking to another adoptive mom about it, about my desire to experience pregnancy firsthand. She said she didn't have that desire, and she was very content with the children she had. In the hospital, Ava's birth parents shared that they talked about how I might never experience what it was like to carry a life inside of me and give birth. They were sensitive towards me in their thoughts about that as they prepared to give Ava to us. Deep down I longed and ached to understand what most of my other friends who were moms had experienced. I also wanted to understand deeper what it took for my children's birth moms to have the courage to do what they did when they released their babies into Nick's and my arms. I wanted to know how to pray for other women in a deeper way when they longed for a child, or pray for friends with true empathy through their pregnancies.

But I had surrendered that dream long ago. I had grieved the loss of not carrying a child inside of me. Not wearing the maternity clothes. Not feeling a flutter inside of me, or a kick, or seeing an ultrasound, or taking a pregnancy test that was actually positive. To not be pregnant with my friends...that was a huge dream I had to let go of. Now I was content. I knew the reality that came after giving birth. Raising children is not an easy task. It takes hard work and time and learning self-sacrifice on whole new levels.

Then during the summer of 2008, we found out his insurance benefits had changed. They were going to start covering infertility treatments. My heart began to dream a little. We had been through infertility treatment before the kids, with no success. We had hit that point without huge cost to our bank account with no guarantees. We let the dream go for a different dream God was preparing for us to walk, the path that led us to receiving the gifts of Josiah and Ava.

Nick and I took a trip to Denver for our anniversary that fall. On this trip we talked much about the idea of finding a new doctor and seeing what our options might be. We weighed the pros and cons, and when we returned home from our trip, Nick started researching infertility clinics and doctors in our area who were covered by our insurance. He read reviews and ratings online, and we found a doctor that we wanted to meet. Nick scheduled an appointment, which ended up being in the last week of his sabbatical. I started to get excited at the possibility. I felt amazingly peaceful as well. I knew this time around all pressure was off. I had my family. I was content with the way things were. I knew that no matter the outcome of all this, I would be okay. God had proven Himself faithful through times of grieving and times of joy and times of blessing, and I was so blessed. I can't explain it. It was just a peace from the Lord that surpassed all comprehension and guarded my heart and my mind.

In dealing with infertility treatment, there are a lot of moral questions to consider. Nick and I saw every life that could be created with the help of treatment as a creation of God, so as we proceeded, that was how we went about making each decision. We sat down with Dr. Hesla, who had taken time to review our medical history prior to the appointment. He was gentle, patient, respectful of our beliefs, and took all of that into consideration as he shared what our options were. There was no beating around the bush or encouragement to try other procedures. He took us straight to the final option of treatment and shared that in vitro was our best choice. As I was just 30, he gave us a 75% success rate. We then began to draw out a plan.

He wanted to give me medication for three months that would stop my period. The purpose was to put my endometriosis into remission. Endometriosis thrives on the monthly cycle, and he felt that for optimal results, it would be a good way to start the treatment. Our plan would take full effect in February, when the treatment for in vitro would commence. He gave us a handful of paperwork to read over that covered a lot of things to consider as we proceeded in making decisions. We scheduled my first appointment for getting a shot to suppress my period.

We left our appointment with all the information he gave us, and we prayed. Finding peace from God, we made the decision to quietly try one more time, to go forward with Dr. Hesla and see what would happen. I say quietly, because we didn't tell very many people—just a few of our friends and our family who we asked to be praying for us as we started treatment. I remember even being in awe of the peace God gave me about having to do the shot process for the endometriosis, instead of just jumping right into in vitro the next month, which I had hoped to do. I had to remind myself of the truth God had shown me through adoption. He already had Josiah and Ava chosen for our family from the beginning. If He had any more children for us, they would be worth the wait to follow the direction and wisdom from the doctor and not push, but trust and see who else God might have chosen for us. Once again that unexplainable peace filled my heart while we waited and I began treatment for suppressing my period.

I remember walking around downtown Portland with Nick after our appointment. As we talked through things, we asked ourselves this question: Ten years down the road, would we regret it if we didn't take the opportunity to try one more time? And the answer was yes. God knew my unspoken dream laid to rest years ago, and He was beginning to work. I was privileged enough to be able to witness what He was going to do. No matter what.

Dear Children,

I was 30 years old when we walked into the infertility clinic this second time around. I had no idea how this would unfold for our family. Still walking a path of surrender. Yet this deep-rooted hope that had been buried deep in the soil of my heart was starting to spread its roots. On the edge of the unknown, we approached the dream of pregnancy one more time, cautiously, but with an eagerness of heart.

I want you to know that we have a God that cares about those dreams. But He wants us to love Him more than the dreams. Our dreams can become idols if we let them. Don't let them. Allow Him to do His big gospel plan and see how He wants to use the dreams in you, as part of His work.

Below I have listed a line-up of women, all playing a part one way or another in the genealogy leading up to the birth of Jesus. Most of these women walked through infertility or deep loss in some way. God used their infertility over and over, showing His mighty works. Children, He used my infertility to show His mighty work to our family.

I Love You,
Mama

Genesis 18:14 (ESV)

"Is anything too hard for the Lord? At the appointed time I will return to you, about this time next year, and Sarah shall have a son."

Genesis 25:21 (ESV)

And Isaac prayed to the Lord for his wife, because she was barren. And the Lord granted his prayer, and Rebekah his wife conceived.

Genesis 30:22–23 (ESV)

Then God remembered Rachel, and God listened to her and opened her womb. She conceived and bore a son and said, "God has taken away my reproach."

Ruth 4:14–15 (ESV)

Then the women said to Naomi, "Blessed be the Lord, who has not left you this day without a redeemer, and may his name be renowned in Israel! He shall be to you a restorer of life and a nourisher of your old age, for your daughter in law, who loves you, who is more to you than seven sons, has given birth to him."

1 Samuel 1:19–20 (NASB)

Then they arose early in the morning and worshiped before the LORD, and returned again to their house in Ramah. And Elkanah had relations with Hannah his wife, and the LORD remembered her. It came about in due time, after Hannah had conceived, that she gave birth to a son; and she named him Samuel, saying, "Because I have asked him of the LORD."

Luke 1:13–15 (ESV)

But the angel said to him, "Do not be afraid, Zechariah, for your prayer has been heard, and your wife Elizabeth will bear you a son, and you shall call his name John. And you will have joy and gladness, and many will rejoice at his birth, for he will be great before the Lord. And he must not drink wine or strong drink, and he will be filled with the Holy Spirit, even from his mother's womb.

Luke 1:31–33 (NASB)

And behold, you will conceive in your womb and bear a son, and you shall name Him Jesus. He will be great and will be called the Son of the Most High; and the Lord God will give Him the throne of His father David; and He will reign over the house of Jacob forever, and His kingdom will have no end."

The next few months kept me pretty busy. With Nick back at work, I was in full swing being mama of two kids at home. I spent time preparing for Christmas, decorating, wrapping purchased gifts. Life was filled with play dates, as well as doing a little bit of homeschool with Josiah. I started potty training Ava, which she picked up very quickly, like a champ. I knew I did not want to be dealing with that if I did get pregnant, so I worked hard to be diligent with her while I was not.

We took a Sunriver trip with friends, which ended up taking almost eight hours because snow fell on the Portland area and in the mountains on the day we left. I held my breath, hoping Ava wouldn't have an accident. When we got to the other side of the mountain, I exhaled a sigh of relief when we reached the gas station bathroom and found she had held it the whole time. We grabbed pizza before we got to our vacation rental. When we arrived, it didn't have the water turned on. After a call to the rental company, we were moved to a bigger, nicer resort home, which fit our group even better than the first one. We spent the next few days by a warm fire, looking out at the beautiful snow, making cookies, taking the kids tubing, ice skating, and getting ice cream bars at Goodys. I remember my friend Emily's husband reading Ava a book many times called <u>What's Wrong Little Pookie</u>,[25] in his rich Hispanic accent. We stayed up late playing cards, and the ladies went shopping and looked at clothes, while I wondered if in a few months I would not be able to fit into them. It was great to have that beautiful time of fellowship with our friends.

On the drive back, there was more snow. The weather report said Portland would be due for freezing rain the next day, a typical thing when Portland transitions from snow back to the winter rain. I was scheduled to go in for my third suppression shot when that was predicted to take place, so we called the clinic when we were an hour outside of Portland and asked if we could swing by on our way through, to save us the trip out the next day. They willingly complied. I ran in, got my shot, and then we drove the rest of the way home to celebrate Christmas with our family.

Our church holds an annual Night of Prayer from midnight to 6:00 in the morning. My friends Becca, Emily, April, and I decided to get a hotel one night and have our own night of prayer that would end at midnight instead of beginning at midnight. With me being on hormones, and April being pregnant, and really none of us super excited about the idea of not getting sleep all night long and having to pay for it later with our children, we decided that we would follow the pattern of how the church prayed and what they prayed for, and do it together. We had so much fun, it was a beautiful time of lifting up the plans God had for us and our children and any children to come. I am so grateful for the time we had together to do that.

I also planned a trip to see some of our extended family in Albuquerque at the very beginning of February. It would be without my two children, and a chance to just be a friend, sister, and auntie to my niece and nephews. I am so grateful for that time and those memories. Sometimes making sure we take the opportunity to do something God lays on our heart is important.

On that flight I had a layover and decided to get frozen yogurt for my lunch. Not the best decision. I felt nauseous on the second leg to Albuquerque. But I will never forget what God did on that flight. I sat next to a man who was probably about 20 years older than me, named Paul. I remember he had a very musky cologne on, which was not a help to feeling better. But we started talking basics. I had two children that we had adopted, and we had struggled with not getting pregnant on our own. I was visiting family in Albuquerque. He wanted to show me pictures of his daughters. As he pulled them out, they seemed a bit dated to me. They reminded me of pictures taken of my family when I was a child, and the hair styles were ones that were from the late 80s early 90s era.

As I wondered about the pictures, he began to share his story. He had a wife and three daughters. They were beautiful daughters—they all had blonde hair and gorgeous smiles. Then he shared that they were all killed by a drunk driver. This man sitting next to me gained all my respect in the world as he shared his heart—the loss, but also his desire to let the man who did it know that he was forgiven. He was a man who would have given anything to have them back in his arms, but chose in his life to embrace what God had placed in front of him and desired to show God's love and kindness and forgiveness to others. Towards the end of the flight, he took my hands in his, and he prayed for my time with my family. He prayed for my husband and I, and for the plans God had for my life.

I had never felt so covered or blessed in my life by a stranger, who was a brother in the Lord. I think I share these things just as a reminder to myself. I could have been pushy at the doctor's office and not wanted to follow the advice to make my endometriosis go into remission for three months before we tried in vitro. We could have tried to get pregnant in December instead of February.

But I would have missed out on so many things God wanted to do in my life during that time. I literally felt carried through February. No rushing to the finish line, just living each day at a time, enjoying each moment He placed in front of me, no matter the outcome of the treatment. I would have missed out on so much if I had chosen to go that other route.

Some of the memories I am grateful for during the time I waited for in vitro:

Potty training Ava

Josiah's birthday

Going to Sunriver with friends

Running in the snow

Prayer Retreat with April, Becca and Emily

Spending time with family in Albuquerque

Meeting Paul and being prayed over by him

Ava at Josiah's swimming lessons. King Josiah at his Burger King birthday.

My beautiful friends on our night of prayer.

The crazy snow in Portland.

Taking Josiah ice skating for the first time in Sunriver.

Ava watches the big kids play from inside

Josiah eating snow with friends.

Dear Children,

God's timing is a journey. I know I could have rushed through this. I kept thinking about how Nick had told me several years back that he wanted us to try infertility treatment the last two times. If we were supposed to adopt, maybe the child God wanted us to have was not ready for us. Thinking of the eggs my body would be preparing to create in February, I couldn't help but wonder the same thing. If God had children for us through in vitro, He had already chosen the eggs He was going to create to be part of our family. That set my mind at peace while we waited.

It was a safe place to rest in His Way, His Will, His Timing. The gifts He laid in front of us along the way were some of the most beautiful I had experienced, especially my encounter with Paul on the plane. If we had rushed and told the infertility doctor we didn't want to follow his advice to suppress my cycle for three months, but pushed for urgency to start right away, I would have missed out on the little gifts He had along the way, and also would not have the children that I have now.

I am humbled and in awe of that fact. It was like sitting in a pocket of God's grace, knowing we would be preparing for something and that we were in the beginning stages, but other things needed to take place. I didn't need to be anxious about any of it, but just sit in God's grace, knowing He was at work.

Remember these truths. I know you will have times when you want to rush things, and you are advised otherwise in your own lives. There are times when we need to push for urgency, and other times when resting and waiting is an act of trust. This was the time for us to rest and wait.

I love you, Children. You all were worth the wait.

Your Mama,
Kari

Psalm 8:1–4 (NASB)

O LORD, our Lord, How majestic is Your name in all the earth, Who have displayed Your splendor above the heavens! From the mouth of infants and nursing babes You have established strength Because of Your adversaries, To make the enemy and the revengeful cease. When I consider Your heavens, the work of Your fingers, The moon and the stars, which You have ordained; What is man that You take thought of him, And the son of man that You care for him?

Psalm 103:17–19 (NASB)

But the lovingkindness of the LORD is from everlasting to everlasting on those who fear Him, And His righteousness to children's children, To those who keep His covenant And remember His precepts to do them. The LORD has established His throne in the heavens, And His sovereignty rules over all.

Ephesians 2:10 (NASB)

For we are His workmanship, created in Christ Jesus for good works, which God prepared beforehand that we should walk in them.

Psalm 19:1–6 (ESV)

The heavens declare the glory of God, and the sky above proclaims his handiwork. Day to day pours out speech and night to night reveals knowledge. There is no speech, nor are there words, whose voice is not heard. Their voice goes out through all the earth, and their words to the end of the world. In them he has set a tent for the sun, which comes out like a bridegroom leaving his chamber, and like a strong man, runs its course with joy. Its rising is from the end of the heavens and its circuit to the end of them, and there is nothing hidden from its heat.

THE MONTH OF FEBRUARY

Our goal month was quickly approaching. I would begin the official treatment process at the end of January, all leading up to the month of February. Large shots that I had to learn to give myself whenever Nick couldn't be around, and a wide variety of pills spread out on a very detailed calendar from the clinic for me. Some days I could not stand the idea of another treatment. I was put on birth control the one and only time I ever took it, to get my body synced up for egg releasing. I decided I did not like being on birth control and found myself very grateful for the decision we made before we got married not to take it. I was not a nice person that week.

Sometimes I would start having little doubts of whether we were doing the right thing in all of this. Every time those doubts would rise to the surface, the Lord would give me a song. I would have the radio on, many different times, wrestling in my mind about the decision...when I would hear Aaron Shust's song, "My Savior, My God"[26] start to play on the radio.

It spoke deep into me truth. His truth. I didn't know how this was going to go. But it would be what He had willed and planned, and I would be okay no matter what, because I have the One who is my Savior.

Nick and I attended a few group meetings with other couples going through in vitro treatment around the same time as us. There were people all across the spectrum, but I will never forget one woman giving her opinion on selective birth reduction. Oh, I cringed at that terminology. I couldn't fathom someone who had walked through the pain of infertility being okay with the idea of aborting one baby too many inside of her. It broke my heart.

As Nick and I prayed through each decision we had to make as a couple, we checked our motives every time before the Lord, making sure we were always choosing life. Our first decisions revolved around how many eggs we would have fertilized, and would we use ICSI (ICSI is a procedure where they insert the sperm directly into the egg) versus eggs in a dish with sperm (think free range). We decided several things through those questions. First, the Lord led us to use all of the eggs and to go with both options of fertilization. My medical issues made it unclear if my eggs were impenetrable, so we didn't want to take the risk of none fertilizing because of that. Second, we felt that we were leaving the decision up to the Lord on how many would fertilize, and let Him choose life for them. Third, we decided that when we were done growing our family, we would give the remaining embryos up for adoption to a family going through the snowflake program, so they might be able to have their own family with whatever remained. It took me back to Phil Comer's words to us about Josiah: "He doesn't belong to you, he belongs to the Lord." As that was true then, it rang true to us now in this situation. I called them our Eggy Babies, and every one of them belonged to the Lord.

Dear Children,

As you walk through life, I want to encourage you to take all of your decisions to the Lord. Walk with integrity spread into all the deep corners of your being. Integrity is being honest and having strong moral principles, walking in moral uprightness. These choices we made with our infertility clinic required the strongest integrity in every aspect of consideration. We prayed about everything that came our way.

Value life. There are many lies spread out into the world, given by the deceiver who wants to destroy God's creation. Lies that include those that are created with special needs should be "spared" from being born. Lies that it is okay to eliminate a life if it puts the mother and other babies at risk. Lies that if it's inconvenient for your family, it's okay to end life before it starts. Or lies that if you are done living your life, it is your choice to end it. Who are we to tell God, the Creator of Life, that He does not know what He has done? That we know better?

We don't. We aren't. We are not skilled to understand the things that God wills and plans.

All we need to rest in through life decisions, is that at the Father's right hand, we have One who is our Savior. He is Creator God. The One who breaths life into existence.

I love you, Children. Always look to make choices with integrity. And always choose life.

Your Mama,
Kari

Hebrews 2:6–8 (NASB)

But one has testified somewhere, saying,

"WHAT IS MAN, THAT YOU REMEMBER HIM? OR THE SON OF MAN, THAT YOU ARE CONCERNED ABOUT HIM? 7"YOU HAVE MADE HIM FOR A LITTLE WHILE LOWER THAN THE ANGELS; YOU HAVE CROWNED HIM WITH GLORY AND HONOR, AND

HAVE APPOINTED HIM OVER THE WORKS OF YOUR HANDS; YOU HAVE PUT ALL THINGS IN SUBJECTION UNDER HIS FEET."

For in subjecting all things to him, He left nothing that is not subject to him. But now we do not yet see all things subjected to him.

John 8:44 (NASB)

You are of your father the devil, and you want to do the desires of your father. He was a murderer from the beginning, and does not stand in the truth because there is no truth in him. Whenever he speaks a lie, he speaks from his own nature, for he is a liar and father of lies.

Proverbs 11:3 (NASB)

The integrity of the upright will guide them, but the crookedness of the treacherous will destroy them.

Proverbs 2:7 (NASB)

He stores up sound wisdom for the upright; He is a shield to those who walk in integrity.

Romans 9:20-24 (NASB)

On the contrary, who are you, O man, who answers back to God? The thing molded will not say to the molder, "Why did you make me like this," will it? Or does not the potter have a right over the clay, to make from the same lump one vessel for honorable use and another for common use? What if God, although willing to demonstrate His wrath and to make His power known, endured with much patience vessels of wrath prepared for destruction? And He did so to make known the riches of His glory upon vessels of mercy, which He prepared beforehand for glory, even us, whom He also called, not from among Jews only, but also from among Gentiles.

❧ LIFE AS WE KNOW IT ☙

We were coming up on harvesting time. The eggs were almost ready to be drawn out. And all along, the focus of life continued. We told the clinic we wanted to make sure that if something happened to us while the eggs were being fertilized in their lab for five days, they would not be given to scientific research, but be given for adoption, for life. Right before the big procedure was about to take place, we learned they needed us to have physicals done to allow that choice to happen. For extra care, we went in last minute to our doctors and had physicals, blood draws, everything that was requested. We took all the forms back to our clinic, with instructions that if something happened to us during the five days they were not inside me, they would be given for adoption.

Egg Day had arrived. I felt very full and bloated, ready to do this. Dr. Hesla was very impressed with the quality of my eggs. He ended up retrieving 26 of them. I went home that day, and over the course of the next few days they would call us with updates. We found out that we had eggs fertilized both through ICSI and in the dish without help, which answered the mystery of our infertility that we had suspected all along. My body doesn't like Nick's sperm, and it does not survive in me. But our egg and sperm are compatible.

Five days later when we got to Implantation Day, there were 10 baby embryos filled with life that had survived to this point in their progression— 10! They took two, which is what Nick and I had agreed upon in the beginning, and the remaining eight were frozen in pairs to be saved for a later date. Again we were choosing life, and choosing to entrust them to the Lord, that He had plans for each one of them.

As I laid on the operating bed with a full bladder as instructed prior to coming in, my doctor showed me a picture of the two baby embryos they were going to be placing inside of me. I felt such love and hope for both of them. Then they transferred me to a bed on wheels and moved me to a room with a curtain for privacy. I was given strict instructions not to pee for half an hour, for optimal results. Nick played a CD for me that I had made of my favorite worship songs, and finally after 40 minutes had passed, Nick hunted down a nurse and I was given a bed pan to relieve myself. Shortly after that, we were sent home and I was put on bed rest for the next 24 hours.

Then we were to wait once more. Normally it's a 14-day wait from when you ovulate; however, I was already five days in, so I only had nine days remaining until I would go back to the clinic for a blood draw to find out the results. As each day passed, I wondered if my two eggy babies had made it inside of me. I was told not to read much into how my body was feeling, because since I was on hormone treatment, my body had all sorts of wackiness going on. The Sunday afternoon before my test, I had made a loaf of French bread. Within 20 minutes of pulling it out of the oven, I had demolished over a third of the loaf with butter. Afterwards I thought to myself, "I had better be pregnant, otherwise I am going to have to do a ton of exercising when all of this is done."

The day came for me to be tested. I drove in early that morning. They drew a quick sample of my blood, then I returned home. Nick headed off to work and I took over kid duty. I tried not to think of the phone call that I was waiting for. I told myself I probably wouldn't hear anything until the end of the day. As I went about preparing lunch for Josiah and Ava, the phone rang. I talked to Roxanne, the gal who worked with Dr. Hesla overseeing the care of his patients. (I love that her name was Roxanne, just like our case worker at Bethany who had cared for us during our adoption season.) She shared with me the numbers that came back for my hormone levels. I asked her what that meant. It meant I was pregnant.

Roxanne requested that I come back in a few more days to make sure the hormone levels continued to rise. I hung up the phone in a bit of a shock. Then I told Josiah and Ava the news. Mommy was going to have a baby (or two)! I avoided Nick's call and email because I wanted to tell him in person. The kids and I took a trip to Target to celebrate. We picked out a card for Nick congratulating him on becoming a dad again, and then two Easter eggs filled with his favorite Reese's Peanut Butter Cup candies. When he got home from work that night, I had Ava and Josiah greet him at the front door, each carrying an egg, sharing the news with him. We were so excited. We decided to keep the news among our family and close friends until we could confirm at our six-week ultrasound appointment.

At about five weeks, we went to my parents' house after our dinner. I felt funny. I didn't want to eat what I had made. When we arrived at my parents' house, I started raiding their cabinets and pantry and picking at food, trying to find something that sounded good to eat. As it turned out, I was having my first experience of "morning sickness," which really translated for me into night sickness that continued a miserable consistent pattern for the following few months. I would try to eat anything nutritious by 3:00 each afternoon. After that I could not handle much other than basic carbs for the rest of the evening. Little by little more food started sounding gross to me. I could not stand the smell of rotisserie chicken. Broccoli, my favorite vegetable, was off the list. I learned that if I had a craving for Chinese food at 2:30 in the afternoon, I could not eat it at 5:30. I could smell PF Chang's several blocks away when driving by, and for the remainder of my pregnancy, even three months after I had the twins I did not want to go near that place. I invented the spinach-salmon-cheese omelet and would have that almost every morning. It was the only way I could get any meat and vegetables inside of me each day.

There were many evenings I felt miserable. My body also required a ton of sleep. Nap time would often come two times a day. I knew this was all part of everything I had hoped for. And although it really didn't feel awesome at times, God was fulfilling this dream to give life to a child inside of me, which I had carried for almost nine years at that point. When I had worked at the church and we were just starting the adoption process, one of the pastors asked me if I would change what I had gone through with infertility. At this point I didn't have a child in my arms, I was still waiting, still not knowing how all of this would turn out in the end. The Spirit confidently answered through me, "No, because I wouldn't have learned all that the Lord has shown me through this time."

I knew that if I had been given the honeymoon baby I always hoped for, I probably would not have appreciated that gift. I can be pretty selfish with my time, and as I have learned over the years, children love to take all of that selfishness away. Instead, God chose for me to wait, and He molded me and shaped me into who He wanted me to be. He drew me close to His word and into prayer before Him, being vulnerable in the deep places of my soul. In His mercy, He brought me to a place where I could be truly grateful for the gifts He had given to me, in Josiah and Ava, and now the gift of life I was carrying inside of me. Not taking anything for granted, I was grateful for every part of my pregnancy, because it meant I was pregnant!

Dear Children,

I want to let you know that being pregnant isn't easy. There, now there will be no culture shock for you, if you or someone around you is expecting. It's uncomfortable and you feel miserable, and all the dreams I had of finally being able to eat chocolate and ice cream free of guilt were replaced with the fact that, "while I am pregnant right now, I don't like how chocolate or ice cream make me feel. So instead I will eat a Tillamook strawberry yogurt."

There is much about pregnancy that dictates and rules over your body, and that you have no control over. If you need to sleep, you sleep. It's just that simple.

You know what the funny thing is? For something that made me so miserable, I would do it again in a heartbeat if I could. The ability to know that your body is doing something really important, supporting and sustaining life inside of it, is honestly just mind-blowing to me. After all the years I waited to be pregnant, I finally was. I was also left with the reminder of what a blessing it was to be pregnant when so many of the people I knew who struggled with infertility didn't get to experience the same outcome. So even though I felt terrible in those first few months, the awe that I felt over carrying babies inside of me sent waves over me of this sense of gratefulness and overwhelming joy.

My one word to you from this letter to carry with you is gratitude. Take it with you. No matter what the circumstances.

I Love You,
Mama

1 Thessalonians 5:16–18 (NASB)

Rejoice always; pray without ceasing; in everything give thanks; for this is God's will for you in Christ Jesus.

Hebrews 13:15 (NASB)

Through Him then, let us continually offer up a sacrifice of praise to God, that is, the fruit of lips that give thanks to His name.

Psalm 100 (NASB)

Shout joyfully to the Lord, all the earth. Serve the Lord with gladness; Come before Him with joyful singing. Know that the Lord Himself is God; It is He who has made us, and not we ourselves; We are His people and the sheep of His pasture. Enter His gates with thanksgiving and His courts with praise. Give thanks to Him, bless His name. For the Lord is good; His lovingkindness is everlasting and His faithfulness to all generations.

❧ THE GIFT OF SHARING THE SEASON WITH FRIENDS ❧

One of the hardest things of not getting pregnant before we adopted was seeing all my friends get pregnant, and not getting to share in the experience with them. This was a little dream tucked away inside that I didn't even remember I longed for, until God gave it to me in a huge way. There was the phone call from my friend Joy. In January, she found out she was pregnant. I began to hope a little bit that maybe, just maybe, God might let us be pregnant at the same time together.

I got a phone call from my friend Lee at the very beginning of February. She was expecting! She wanted to make sure to tell me before I went on my trip to Albuquerque to visit family.

My friend April was pregnant. In our house church community group, we had prayed for a fourth child for Alissa, who was now pregnant with a child God had the timing all worked out for. Carissa was expecting. Tanya, Breanna, and even Tricia—my dear infertility buddy—was expecting her third child. Ladies from church were finding out left and right they were expecting. And I silently hoped and prayed that this time around, I might be part of it too.

Then when I found out I was expecting, a few weeks later my friend Sheri told me on a walk that she was pregnant too. And then at a Chuck E. Cheese birthday party, my friend Erin told me she was pregnant.

And my friend Monica...she felt that God had told her we would be pregnant at the same time, and around the time of my baby shower, she shared the news that she was going to be having a baby too. At this baby shower, she also gave me a verse that God had put upon her heart. Guess which one it was? *Luke 1:45 And blessed is she who believed there would be a fulfillment of what was spoken to her from the Lord.* It was truly God's own gift to me at the baby shower. His reminder that He was fulfilling what had been spoken to me by the Lord.

There was my friend Amy...after some painful losses in her life from miscarriages, we had prayed together on the beach and watched a beautiful sunset, and hoped for a future of more children. She was in the process of adoption, and I was in the process of preparing to try to achieve pregnancy. As I was getting ready to leave my baby shower with the few remaining friends, she burst back into the house with tears of joy streaming down her face. They had been chosen for a baby! She was going to get to be a mama to a beautiful Ethiopian baby girl. God had seen her heart and deep hopes and needed to give her that gift on that day. We all cried tears of joy and surrounded her with hugs. Then we circled around her and prayed prayers of deep thankfulness for His faithfulness once more.

I got to be part of the pregnancy club. For one time in my life, God had given me not only the beautiful gift of pregnancy, but the beautiful gift of sharing in it with so many other beautiful mamas and mamas to be. He had given me that dream and fulfilled it when I didn't expect it. And some of these beautiful mamas had to go through some loss before they got to be pregnant, and that made my heart's joy so much greater. I remember praying that no one around me would miscarry or lose a baby while I was pregnant, because I couldn't bear the thought of a friend going through that, and I wanted us all to make it to the finish line holding our precious little ones.

God was so faithful in that request. Every child was born in that circle of friends, without one miscarriage. In that season He chose to breathe out the gift of creation to each of our families. One of my friends had a son who was born just barely over four pounds. Another friend had a son born with a severe disability. God was not limited in those areas. In the whole journey, He kept every baby alive inside their mama's tummies, and when those babies were birthed into the world, He breathed His life into them.

Those are some of the best gifts, when He takes those really hard times from our past and brings them back as a beautiful, fulfilled gift. I was so blown away and amazed at His faithfulness and goodness in giving all of us something like that. The littlest details of our hearts really are important to Him.

A baby boom prior, my friends Joy and Erin were both pregnant around the same time as each other. Erin bought this beautiful dress to wear at a wedding. And then she passed it on to Joy to wear. I loved this dress and thought it was so cute. Erin promised me that if I ever got pregnant, she would

save it for me to wear. When she said that, I smiled, but I figured that wasn't happening. But the heart behind it meant a lot.

They saved that dress for me. As we passed clothes around among all of us who were pregnant, it was our sisterhood of the traveling maternity dress, and this time I got to be part of it. Granted, being pregnant with twins, when it was my turn to wear it, I only got a few times in it before I outgrew it, but it really was another awesome blessing.

With those dreams and heart's desires, I had to commit those plans to the Lord. He knew my heart. His love runs deep. He took that dream I had buried for so long and brought life into it again. I had learned the importance of making the most of today and trusting Him to take care of the details. Regardless of the outcome, I knew He had my best in mind, even when I didn't see it in the moments.

Some of the beautiful pregnant women around me, shortly before I became pregnant, and some of the cute babies:

Dear Children,

When I was first married, I had my sweet friends around me—my Jaime, Kathryn, Leah and Tricia. They were friends I wanted to have my babies alongside, to start our families together. While I was in the middle of it, I didn't understand why that wasn't part of my story. Then God called us into church planting. When our church started, He put me in a place of being a new mom to Josiah and meeting a lot of other new moms who needed to get connected. I often wonder, had I been so connected to my sweet young married friends, all having our babies together, if I would have been willing to take off and do a church plant and let go of those friendships. Instead, it naturally happened, because of things like our children being on different nap schedules, or not going to girls' nights because I needed to stay home with Josiah while Nick was at an evening class.

Those important relationships that God had used in my life in the beginning became difficult to figure out with the age gap of our children. I see now that God had a different plan for me at the new church. I had to be at a point where I was free to connect with new friendships and relationships, in order to do that. It was hard at times—I grieved the drastic change in those friendships for quite a while. I will always love those gals that walked with me through my infertility journey. Over the course of a few years, God gave me new friendships to walk alongside of, ladies to love and care for. And He built a community through our church plant.

What I love about God is that He saw my broken dream of not getting to be pregnant with friends, and He did not forget it. He gave it back to me in a way I will always cherish. He knew how much that would mean to me. It was His congratulations bouquet to me. The card read like this: "Congratulations, Kari! You are pregnant. Enclosed is my gift. I am going to surround you with friends who are also going to get to share in the gift of having their own baby at the same time as you. Love, God." It was one of my favorite parts of being pregnant, and I will always be grateful.

I love you, Children. May God surround you with beautiful gifts like this that show up unexpectedly to bless your souls richly.

Your Mama,
Kari

Psalm 9:1–2 (NASB)

I will give thanks to the LORD with all my heart; I will tell of all Your wonders. I will be glad and exult in You; I will sing praise to Your name, O Most High.

Matthew 7:11 (NASB)

If you then, being evil, know how to give good gifts to your children, how much more will your Father who is in heaven give what is good to those who ask Him!

❧ AND GOD CHOSE FOR US TWO ❧

At six weeks, we were scheduled for that first ultrasound. Nick and I wondered, would we have one or two littles inside of me? With my hormone levels spiking high at the second blood draw, we both had a small inkling that there might be two. Our suspicions were confirmed as we saw two tinies, firmly in place inside of my womb. Nick and I were excited, with a little bit of, "What did we just get ourselves into?"

I told my grandparents the news at Easter. My little Japanese grandma was so surprised and happy. We went viral on a big Facebook announcement after our ultrasound. Everyone around us was celebrating in the joy of the news. I was thrilled, but these babies were also making me feel pretty miserable every evening. My body started requiring a lot of sleep.

By thirteen weeks my appetite slowly started to come back. Unfortunately, foods that had made my stomach turn during my worst weeks of nausea remained on the "no thank you" list for the duration of my pregnancy. I continued to enjoy a steady diet of bagels and yogurt in the evening, bran pear muffins in the morning, and spinach-salmon-cheese omelets. Oh yes, and peaches! My mouth still salivates at the thought of that delicious juicy fruit.

Carrying twins, it is amazing how fast your body grows. A need for maternity clothes became evident early on. I had dreamed of wearing maternity clothes for years. This dream was met with the reality of feeling miserable when trying them on. As I wore them over the next few months, I would remember the foods I had eaten that made me sick while I was wearing them. Then I would feel gross all over again. When I grew out of my maternity clothes and needed to go up a size, I was happy to pick out new clothes that were not associated with the morning sickness of the first trimester.

At fifteen weeks, I felt a flutter inside me for the first time. It was the strangest sensation, and I doubted if I was actually feeling our babies. But then they began to come more frequently. The bigger the twins grew inside of me, the more visible their movement would become. Having twins, which is considered a high-risk pregnancy, afforded me frequent ultrasounds of our babies, which I loved. On the screen I would see Twin "A." This baby stayed in the same spot throughout the whole pregnancy. Head down, first position. The screen would show little fingers and hands waving and wiggling at us, as if to say hi. Twin "B," on the other hand, was a non-stop mover. This baby constantly spread all over the place and danced a storm inside me. The more I felt them, the more I could distinguish the difference between the two of them. I would feel Twin A's hands softly move at the bottom of my belly. And I would see Twin B's heels move softly across the top of my belly, close to my rib cage.

As these two little ones began to grow inside of my belly, we reassessed our car situation. I began to accept the fact that my cute SUV holding a family of six was starting to look very unrealistic. Nick said the "M" word. I cringed at the words. A minivan? Please, anything but that! Can we say soccer mom? Yikes!

The SUV we bought when Josiah was our only baby was my dream "mom" car. I picked the color, it had a moon roof, and the heated seats were an unexpected bonus. I loved it. But deep down I knew I needed to give it up for the benefit of our family. But not without a fight! I wanted the right colors if I was going to get a minivan. I had a list of colors I would not accept for the exterior and the interior. And if it didn't meet my standards, well, forget it! I was giving up a lot to drive a minivan, and colors played a huge part in what type of car I would drive, at least in my mind.

Over the course of a week, we received many emails from dealers with listings for the kind of car we were looking for, but they were always in one of my none-negotiable colors. One came through on Saturday: gold with tan interior. It was exactly the same car on the inside as my SUV, and it even had heated seats. It had 8,000 fewer miles than our current car, it would include a warranty, and it would probably cost about the same as what we could sell our car for. I told the dealer thanks, but no thanks, it is not my color.

Then we got to church on Sunday. I was sitting in church enjoying an awesome time of worship, getting into our pastor's message, when all of the sudden the words of the pastor entered my ears: "...a car does not define who you are..."

I looked over at Nick, and my eye caught a couple sitting next to us with their baby. That baby looked right at Nick and gave him the cutest smile ever. Then my friend Alissa, who was very pregnant and due in two weeks, leaned over to me and said, "That will be you guys in a few months, just with two babies!" And it hit me to the core. My car, the one I was giving up and the one we would be getting, did not define me. It did not make me an individual. I am definitely that girl who would go home and change if I went to a party and saw that someone was wearing the same shirt as me. I don't like to be copied, I like to be different...

However, God's purpose for my life—His calling to raise my children, to teach them about Jesus and show them His love every day—that is what makes me who God wants me to be, fulfilling His purpose and calling for my life right now. I knew I needed to give up the color thing to the Lord. Getting a minivan really was a blessing, because it meant He had given us two more beautiful gifts of life. I told Nick after the sermon what God called me to do. We decided to go look at that gold minivan. We brought our kids with us so we would have an excuse to leave at any time and not feel pressured into a decision.

God provided us a gold minivan with tan interior, with a basic trade across the board for our SUV. It was a huge provision for our growing family, and it became a reminder to me of God's word to me every time I looked at it.

When we arrived at 20 weeks, we had the "big reveal" ultrasound appointment. I was not interested in the element of surprise, being a planner through and through. For practicality's sake, I did not want to deal with clothes shopping right after giving birth, for two brand-new babies, taking my four children in tow as I tried to hunt for deals. I had been anticipating the news this ultrasound would bring. I had a feeling we had at least one little girl, and I thought it would be cool to have a boy as well. Nick and I talked about names, and a week before our appointment, we had two girl names picked out, but we could not figure out boy names. I remember Nick starting to think we were having two girls, and he said maybe we didn't need to figure out those boy names. I wasn't 100% sure, but I was almost positive we would see at least one little girl.

We brought my sister Abbie to be part of the day, while my mom stayed home with Josiah and Ava. This was to be a very extensive ultrasound that would take almost an hour. The ultrasound technician went about her job. She checked measurements to confirm healthy development. When we got about halfway through, she asked if we were ready to find out the genders. First she rolled the scanner over Twin A, which clearly showed that this was a little girl. When she focused on Twin B next, Nick was not surprised at all to find out that she was also a little girl. We were delighted, and Nick half rolled his eyes in the way only Nick can do, to show his happiness mixed with the thought, "By the time our three girls are in middle school, and my wife is pre-menopausal, I need to find a man cave in the house. Non-negotiable." With our beloved girl names, we decided to let Josiah select which twin belonged to the names we had chosen. He named Twin A "Lena Grace," and Twin B was to be our "Mallory Joy."

We loved those names. In choosing them, Nick decided that no member of our immediate family could have the same first initial, so N, K, J and A were already taken. We both loved the name Mallory. Every Mallory we had ever met, we liked. Nick wanted an MJ, so choosing Joy with that first name made perfect sense. We posted our announcement on social media of twin girls along with their names. One comment on Lena's name was, "Lena, is that like Lena from the movie 'Sisterhood of the Traveling Pants'?"[27] Nick's face when he read that post was priceless. He looked at me and said, "Really Kari? That's where Lena came from?" Busted! I sheepishly smiled back at him. There was no going back on the name, it was already publicly announced. Lena was here to stay!

Our twins now had names. Our hearts were full of love for these girls. We were now entering the second half of my pregnancy. They looked very healthy and were progressing well. This was nothing to take for granted. We couldn't have been more full of gratitude to God for the gifts He was continuing to grow inside of me. And continue to grow, they did.

Dear Children,

I always knew the Bible said God designed and created our inward parts, the tiny details of each new baby preparing to make its entrance into the world. But to feel it happening on the inside of me was indescribable. Between the ultrasounds and knowing the positions of each of the two babies inside of me, I started to get to know Lena and Mallory and become intimate with their ways. Their personalities did not change when they came out of me.

Lena as a toddler did not need anything other than a solid lap to sit on. She wasn't a wiggler, she just wanted to have arms wrapped around her, keeping her steady, giving her the feeling of being secure. She won't ask for love, but her big blue eyes express how much she needs it. To find out what she is thinking takes time, because she is a girl who tries to always do the right thing, but with that comes this struggle not to show anything she feels might not be okay.

Mallory was the non-stop mover inside me. One time she told me the reason she moved so much inside of me was because she was giving me lots of kisses. She has a lot of love to give, is passionate, and is happy if someone is rubbing her back, stroking her hair, or touching her in any affectionate way. She has wild spasms of joy that continually burst through her body at unexpected times. She is a lover and is very hurt if someone does not reciprocate her love. She feels very deeply and lets everyone around her know exactly what she is thinking.

I have said it before and I will say it again: Babies inside the womb are filled with life. I could see it from the time of their second ultrasound at eight weeks, the way they moved differently. Anyone who would tell you differently is feeding you a lie to justify a choice that would be devastating, not only for the life that is inside, but also for themselves. Be fighters for and celebrators of life, Children.

I Love You,
Mama

Jeremiah 1:5a (NASB)

Before I formed you in the womb I knew you, and before you were born I consecrated you.

Psalm 127:3–5 (NASB)

Behold, children are a gift of the Lord, the fruit of the womb is a reward.
Like arrows in the hand of a warrior, So are the children of one's youth.
How blessed is the man whose quiver is full of them; They will not be
ashamed when they speak with their enemies at the gate.

Luke 1:44 (NASB)

For behold, when the sound of your greeting reached my ears, the baby
leaped in my womb for joy.

❧ NOT THE WAY I PLANNED ❧

A month later I was at the doctor's office once again for my 24-week appointment. I loved getting to see the girls on the ultrasound machine. Everything was continuing to grow well. After my ultrasound, I was brought in for my check-up with the doctor. My doctor was an older man, near retirement. I chose him when I was given one of two options from the clinic. The other doctor, I'm sure, would have been just fine. But one of our pastors had shared a story once of his wife at the same clinic, pregnant with their first. A young, "hot-looking" doctor came in to check on her, who was their age and looked like he could have been on a TV show like "ER" or "Grey's Anatomy." And our pastor said no way will this be the guy caring for my wife through her pregnancy!

That story stuck with me. When I called to see who my options were, I had the clinic's website up on my laptop and quickly scanned the pictures as they shared the doctor's names. The first doctor looked like he could have been close to my parents' age. As the scheduler gave me the second name, I flipped to his profile. When I saw his picture, I immediately knew this was the doctor our pastor had been referring to. I said no to "hot, young, made-for-TV doctor" and chose one that our pastor would have approved for his wife.

My doctor would always ask me how many kids I had, and then he would comment with a follow up, "Four kids, eh? He, he, he... You are going to be busy! He, he, he..." He had three children of his own who were mostly grown up, so I knew he was speaking from some experience. He seemed to take delight and humor in telling me how busy my life would be. Apparently he felt I needed to be prepared and educated by him on this matter at every appointment.

At this particular appointment, though, I received news that any independent, hands-on control freak like myself would hate to hear. My doctor told me that at 28 weeks he was going to place me on an eight-week preventative bed rest. I immediately began negotiating with him. I had two children at home that I needed to care for. Josiah would be starting preschool in September—I had to be able to take him. I needed to cook meals for my family and keep my house clean. I tried to find any possible loopholes, but he was not budging. He was old school. I would be allowed one trip up and down my stairs each day. And then my rule for getting up off the couch was 90/10: 90% rest, 10% up for bathroom breaks. No going anywhere except to doctor appointments.

I was mad. I was devastated. How could I do this? I released my fears and concerns to my friend Joy, who lived out of state. She couldn't do anything hands-on herself, but she started letting my church community up here in Oregon know, and the next thing I knew, my friend Holly called me. Holly told me this would be okay. Holly went to work setting up a website for our family, inviting people to sign up for meals, for cleaning our home every other week, and for taking our son to and from preschool.

When 28 weeks came, I still felt sad about some things. I did not get to be the one to take Josiah to his first day of preschool, or to go on his pumpkin patch field trip. I often went stir crazy as days would slowly pass into weeks. I longed to be at church. Each Sunday the family was gone and I would play the sermon from the week prior and sing worship songs, just me and the twins inside of me, in the solitude of my own home. I didn't like to be a burden to people, and I found myself at the mercy of others freely giving to our family. Every once in a while, I would get up for 15 minutes and vacuum downstairs, because I just couldn't handle being on the couch feeling unproductive for one more minute.

But honestly, it ended up bringing some of the best gifts. Although it was humbling for me, one caring friend after another brought us a meal. Our house was kept clean. Josiah was taken back and forth to preschool every time. Nick even took a swing at cooking one evening and devoted two hours on a Sunday evening to make a few meals for the week. Everything I couldn't do was taken care of.

My husband had led a house church at our friends' home. At the last one I was able to attend prior to bed rest, I was sitting with a few gal friends. I asked one of them, Tanya Johnson, what her plans were for serving and ministry in the fall. She looked at me with her big smile and bright eyes and said, "You!" She was true to her word. Tanya brought me a few meals each month, picked up Josiah every so often from preschool, and cleaned my home several times. But my favorite part was when she was done, and she would sit right next to me and talk with me. She would bring me books on pregnancy with twins. She even included a fun book that her mother-in-law had taken part in writing. It was a collection of women that shared their personal stories of pregnancy with twins, who all happened to live in the same neighborhood.

Tanya became so much more than someone I knew from church. She turned into one of my closest friends who has been with me through some deep waters of life. If you think of Pilgrim's Progress,[28] Christian's companion, Faithful, would be a great description of what it has been like to have her in my life, a gift I would have possibly missed out on had I not been put on bed rest. It was a season I had dreaded and wished I could avoid. But then God humbled me in it, put me in a place of complete dependence on everyone around me, and gave me the gift of so many great people in our lives being His hands and feet to us. He was our Provider, and He took care of us.

At about 33-and-a-half weeks, I started having very minor contractions—more like Braxton Hicks. They were happening five minutes apart. We called the clinic and they asked us to check into the hospital so they could put me under surveillance. The conclusion after several hours was that nothing was progressing and it was fine for me to go home and continue on bed rest. Prior to that, I had still been struggling with an attitude of rebelliousness. But the day after going in, I found out that another gal who shared my due date of November 18 for her singleton pregnancy was admitted to the hospital. She gave birth early to her son, who had to be in the ICU for several weeks. That was all I needed to remind myself that bed rest was serious business. From that point on I obeyed and stayed put until I hit 36 weeks. At that point I took myself off restrictive bed rest, being told by the doctors that anytime from here on out, they would let me go into full labor without stopping it. However, at 36 weeks I was huge and uncomfortable, and I did not feel like doing much more than I had been permitted to do on bed rest.

In the month of October 2009, an epidemic of swine flu spread through the country. There were huge concerns of babies coming down with this illness. I started to panic a bit when I saw on social media that families from church were being hit with it. I asked Nick to have the kids avoid the snack tables at church on future Sundays. The medical world had just come out with a vaccine, but it was super limited, so at my clinic they put women on a call waitlist. I received a call one afternoon, 12 days before my scheduled induction at 38 weeks. They informed me more vaccines were available. I called my friend Erin, and she willingly loaded up her children and my children into her minivan and drove me down for my shot. There was a possibility being investigated that if your baby was inside the womb for 10–14 days after receiving the vaccination, it could transfer into their bloodstream as well, helping them build immunity to it. That was what I was hoping and praying for, and the Lord had been so faithful to meet me even in the midst of my fear and provide the vaccination. Not only that, but after the twins were born, our children's clinic had a few extra vaccinations, and they gave them to our family, which was such a gift to us.

Now that I was off bed rest, I got to go on a few short outings. My friend Leanne and her two kids took me and Ava out for breakfast at Biscuits Café close to my home. I was also excited to return to church after missing out on eight weeks of it, and receiving hugs and encouragement for what the next chapter would bring. We were coming down to the final count. November was just a few days away. My bed rest had successfully done the job of keeping Lena and Mallory growing healthy and strong inside of me, with no complications to be seen. They were both head down in first position, getting ready to make their grand entrance. We were very eager to meet them. Final plans started to come together, all leading up to our scheduled inducement. We were ready to do this!

Dear Children,

I am a very independent person. I don't like to be a burden to anyone. I hate to be an inconvenience. If I think I might be causing a problem, I do what I can to get out of that spot. When I was told bed rest, it sent me into a panic. The last thing I wanted was to impose my needs on other people, let alone my two older children's needs. You guys are my job. Yet I was at an impasse. In order to take care of my two younger children inside of me, I had to release my two older children and my home into the care of others.

Once I got over being mad and let go, what I witnessed was something I had never seen or experienced in my life. It was humbling and full of more surrender. I watched our church family act out the body of Christ in our own home, each using the gifts and abilities, the talents and resources, the time they had been given, to pour into our family. With the love of Christ, they joyfully served us without complaining about the sacrifice of their time.

Children, keep your eyes open for ways you can be the body of Christ to those around you. It may be as simple as being a listening ear, praying for a friend, or interceding for someone with a need. It could be a labor of work, like helping someone move, watching friends' children to give them a date night, or a sacrifice of your time. You each have things to offer that can fit into the flow of the life you are living. Be on the watch for it, be sensitive to the nudges the Holy Spirit may give you, and be willing to be a servant.

I Love You, Children,
Mama

Romans 12:10–13 (NASB)

Be devoted to one another in brotherly love; give preference to one another in honor; not lagging behind in diligence, fervent in spirit, serving the Lord; rejoicing in hope, persevering in tribulation, devoted to prayer, contributing to the needs of the saints, practicing hospitality.

2 Corinthians 9:6-15 (NASB)

Now this I say, he who sows sparingly will also reap sparingly, and he who sows bountifully will also reap bountifully. Each one must do just as he has purposed in his heart, not grudgingly or under compulsion, for God loves a cheerful giver. And God is able to make all grace abound to you, so that always having all sufficiency in everything, you may have an abundance for every good deed; as it is written,

"HE SCATTERED ABROAD, HE GAVE TO THE POOR, HIS RIGHTEOUSNESS ENDURES FOREVER."

Now He who supplies seed to the sower and bread for food will supply and multiply your seed for sowing and increase the harvest of your righteousness; you will be enriched in everything for all liberality, which through us is producing thanksgiving to God. For the ministry of this service is not only fully supplying the needs of the saints, but is also overflowing through many thanksgivings to God. Because of the proof given by this ministry, they will glorify God for your obedience to your confession of the gospel of Christ and for the liberality of your contribution to them and to all, while they also, by prayer on your behalf, yearn for you because of the surpassing grace of God in you. Thanks be to God for His indescribable gift.

❧ INTRODUCING LENA AND MALLORY ❧

During the week of November 5, 2009, Nick and I went out for our last date night prior to becoming a family of six. We enjoyed a meal at the Cheesecake Factory. Then we took a short walk down to Pottery Barn Kids in the mall, which was about five stores away from our restaurant. It was about as far as I could manage before hitting the tired and out-of-breath button. In spite of getting worn out quickly, I was so grateful to have that time with Nick for just a bit, one last time.

We dropped Josiah and Ava off with my family in the early evening of November 4, and just after midnight I checked into the hospital to be admitted. With the swine flu being of particular concern that fall, the hospital would not be permitting children in the infant wing, taking huge precautionary measures. I also would only be allowed two guests at a time. For my labor and delivery, Nick and Abbie would be the only ones allowed in the hospital room with me. Josiah and Ava were going to spend part of the time with my parents, and the other part with our friends Chris & Kristy, from church.

Once checked in at the hospital, I was put on a medication called Cervidil to soften my cervix, and they would monitor the twins through the rest of the night. With two heart rate monitors and a contraction monitor strapped to my belly, and having to use the bathroom every hour, I did not get much sleep that night. At 6:00 a.m., I got up, freshened up for the day, and did my makeup. I know—silly—but I knew there would be lots of pictures, so I wanted to be prepared. The next part of the plan was to induce labor by giving me Pitocin.

Being 38 weeks along, I had been given the choice to be induced or continue carrying them. At that point, the decision was easy for me. I had 50 pounds of extra weight sticking straight out in front of me, and no decent sleep for over a month. The choice was an obvious one. Time to get it done!

The Pitocin did not progress things the way they had hoped, and it raised the girls' heart rates just a bit, so instead of increasing my dosage, our doctor decided it was time to break my water.

Compared to every description I had ever heard of what contractions were like, mine were nothing like I expected. I don't recall pain, just a tightness and being unable to focus on much other than breathing through them. In between contractions, as they were growing stronger, I heard two voices. Nick and Abbie had brought their laptops, and while I worked through the beginning of labor, they talked.

"Hey Nick, are you playing Farmville?"

"Yup, it's my first time!"

"Hey, me too!"

In my head, I thought, "Oh brother, so glad you guys are here to help! Just in labor over here on my own, but no worries, I've got this!"

Part of the requirement when having twins was that I needed to deliver in the operating room. It was higher risk, so they needed me to be ready for anything. I was not into the idea of intense pain and doing it au natural. I believed this was a time pain medication would be my friend. When I was dilated to about four centimeters, I decided it was time for the epidural. I was feeling very exhausted from the lack of sleep, and I wanted to save as much energy as possible for labor. The epidural went in without a hitch. My body began to relax, and I ended up falling asleep. In fact, I slept for about three hours. My doctor woke me up and checked me at 1:30 p.m., and he informed me that I was at nine-and-a-half centimeters, so they began to make preparations to move me to the operating room. I was allowed only one person with me. I begged them to make an exception for my sister, but they would not budge. We left Abbie in the hospital room, and letting go of the disappointment of not having her there when the twins were born, we said our goodbyes for now and they carted me away.

At 2:00 p.m. I was fully dilated and the time for pushing began. For three hours I worked at pushing, with a half hour break to rest in the middle. The sleep I had gotten in the morning was so helpful, but at the end, I was running low on energy and my doctor mentioned the C-section word. I had been open to considering this, but in the moment, after working so hard at pushing, it was not what I wanted to hear. I felt hot tears streaming down my cheeks. In the end we made the decision to go forward with the Cesarean, while the girls were still doing well inside of me and not having complications.

By 5:30 p.m. they were ready to go. Lena Grace entered the world at 5:31, with Mallory Joy following at 5:32. Both at healthy weights, Lena was seven pounds ten ounces. Our doctor informed us she was the second-biggest twin he had ever delivered. Mallory was a healthy six pounds six ounces.

At that point I started having the shakes uncontrollably, and I felt very cold. Nick brought me Lena, and she had these big poochy lips that I just had to kiss. Next he brought me Mallory, and she was this tiny creature with delicate features. I was not physically able to hold them. I felt some tugging as the doctor stitched me up, and after they finished cleaning me up, we were moved to a recovery room. Once they cleaned the girls up and wrapped them in warm swaddling blankets, they laid both of them next to me, and I was able to have them close to me for the first time.

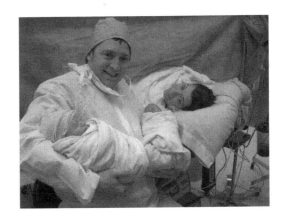

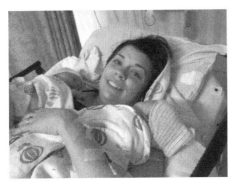

I wanted someone to get word to my sister of the news. I wanted to get back to our hospital room so she could meet them. It seemed like forever, but they finally carted me and our newborn baby girls, with my husband behind us, back to the room. I had slowly recovered from the shakes and was getting to a point where I could hold them in my arms, as the numb feeling from the epidural began to dissipate.

Abbie got to meet her nieces for the first time. I felt awful that she had to wait so long for us to come back to the room. I so badly wished she could have been there for the birth.

As we stared at these brand-new-to-the-world lives that lay before us, I started to observe their unique characteristics. I had expected our biological children to come out with full heads of hair like their Aunt Abbie had when she was born. Lena had a light layer of blonde spikes, showing early evidence of cowlicks that later both sides of the family would claim as their genetic fault. Once again I noticed her big poochy lips, and she had a fascination with her tongue. When we could see her eyes, they were a beautiful blue, shaped just like her daddy's, with a mouth that had the potential to be as big as her mama's. I remember glancing at her stats the next day, written on a hospital card posted next to her crib, and doing a double take when I read that her length was 14-and-a-half inches and her head was 20 inches. Yikes! No wonder she wouldn't come out naturally! Or maybe the nurse had mixed up the numbers. Either way I was glad I had not pushed out a 20-inch head!

Mallory was very delicate to the touch, and seemed small and fragile compared to her sister, probably because she weighed over a pound less than Lena. Her hair color was darker than Lena's, but nowhere close to mine or Nick's dark brown. It was also very fine, not thick and long the way I remembered my sister's hair to be. She had smaller eyes, closer to a hazel color. They would definitely not be baby blue. They both had this beady-eyed look about them.

As I lay in my hospital bed, I bundled them up next to me like two baby burritos while they slept. I stared at them, in awe and amazement over the gift of each one. One thing I had prayed in the beginning of my twin pregnancy was that I would not play favorites, but that I would be able to love them both fully and completely. I remember during our stay at the hospital, thinking about that desire and making a very clear choice to spend time cuddling each one separately, so that I could bond with both of them.

That night and the two nights following, while nurses monitored my recovery and the health of the girls, we decided to put them in the nursery at bedtime. I had been exhausted the month prior to their birth, so being offered some decent sleep as I recovered sounded like a wise decision to start off in the best shape possible when we returned home. I had made the decision to bottle feed the girls. Never having experienced breastfeeding, already having two young ones at home to care for, and hearing numerous stories of other moms of multiples that had tried a variety of different ways to feed their babies, I felt that bottle feeding would be the best option for our family. So at 10:00 each night, I would give my babies goodnight kisses and leave them in the safe care of the doting hospital nurses while Nick and I slept.

The very first night I felt awful pain from my incision stitches and the thought of never wanting to do this again crossed my mind. The next day, after the pain had subsided to almost nothing, the nurse asked me how I was doing on pain meds. She checked my chart and saw that I had not received anything other than a two-hour pain medication shortly after birth, which explained the severity of the pain from the night before. I had no medicine running through me by the time she asked and I felt just fine, so we decided I didn't need anything else.

When I first woke up the next morning, the room was blurred and spinning. There was concern I might need a blood transfusion at one point, but thankfully my body kicked into healing gear and I improved throughout the morning. It's amazing how God created our bodies to restore like that.

We had friends and family eager to meet our little ones. Many visits took place, from grandparents to friends, from people who had prayed over us all of these years to those who dreamed and hoped with us while God did what only He could to create the family He had planned for us. It was the family of His dreams, and one we could never have envisioned when we first got married. We were surrounded by a crowd of witnesses of His faithfulness in our lives. It was truly a celebration of life.

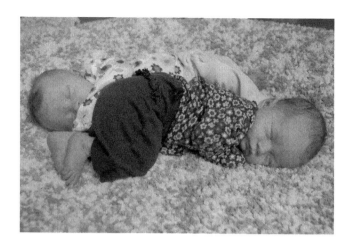

Dear Lena,

You looked nothing like I expected when you made your entrance into the world. I never thought your daddy and I could produce a blonde-haired, blue-eyed baby. God took all our recessive genes and gave us you, a baby that physically matched her big brother in so many of her features. Freckles that sprinkled across your face. God knew we needed you, Lena. Lena, I love the way you keep track of time, and how you figure out directions and when we need to leave to get somewhere on time. It's fun to watch you do math problems in your head that Dad gives you.

You bring solid consistency to our family, not only in having two blonde-haired, blue-eyed children now, but also with your solid stature, your kindness, and how you are always trying to do the right thing. You even make sure everyone else is doing what they are supposed to as well. You always want to live righteously. Lena, use this gift of doing the right thing with the attitude of helping others, and never let this gift convince you that you are better than everyone else. You don't want to land there. When these gifts are applied in love and filled with grace, they can do great things.

Thank you for being our daughter. God knew we needed you in our family. I love you, baby girl.

Your Mama,
Kari

James 4:6 (NASB)

But He gives a greater grace. Therefore, it says, "GOD IS OPPOSED TO
THE PROUD, BUT GIVES GRACE TO THE HUMBLE."

Psalm 37:29–31 (NASB)

The righteous will inherit the land and dwell in it forever. The mouth of
the righteous utters wisdom, and his tongue speaks justice. The law of
his God is in his heart; His steps do not slip.

Dear Mallory,

You know the key to your mama's heart. You truly are the baby of our family. I have never experienced love from a child the way you offer it. You love everyone around you. When you release a laugh or share excitement, joy flies out of you and lands on all those that surround you. You are passionate in all you put effort into. In the things you feel confident, you excel and shine brilliantly. I have never seen a child's eyes shine as bright as yours when you are excited or in love. You just glow.

Mallory, sometimes the sensitivity of your heart can go the opposite direction, when your heart is broken over something. Whether it is an injustice that has been done, or a disappointment in something you were looking forward to, it hurts very deeply—that is something that can be so hard for passionate people like you. Learn to love as Christ would love, sweet Mallory. It is a love impossible without Him. This type of love can still love, even when wronged, and be joyful even in the midst of sadness. Mallory, if you learn to love like that, I know God will do some amazing things with this gift of yours.

Thank you for being a child who loves. I love you, sweet girl.

Your Mama Always,
Kari

John 15:12 (NASB)

This is My commandment, that you love one another, just as I have loved you.

Philippians 4:4–5 (NASB)

Rejoice in the Lord always; again I will say, rejoice! Let your gentle spirit be known to all men, the Lord is near.

❧ COMING HOME ❧

Our stay at the hospital came to an end and we were being sent home. I was eager to get home and see our family of six together for the first time. But I was also nervous to take on all the tasks that would be laid in front of me. As we bundled the girls in their car seats, for the first time the reality started to sift through me and anxiety hit full force. By the time we got home, I needed to feed the twins, I needed to feed myself, and I just wanted to take care of those things before having the older kids come to meet the girls. But my kids arrived back at our townhome the same time we did, so it was a bit of a chaotic entrance into the world of being mama of four. But it was reality.

Having had a C-section, I was not allowed to drive for a few weeks, so Nick took the first week off work. My sister helped me the next week on the days Josiah had preschool, providing a way to get him to and from school. The following week was Thanksgiving, and Nick took a few more days off. But the first week of December was approaching and staring me in the face. It would be my first time out, driving my four children around, and I was scared. Terrified. How would I get the girls fed before we left for preschool? What about getting all four children up the stairs to take Josiah to his class three days a week? Every part of me wanted to run and hide under the covers of my cozy bed and never have to leave the house again.

The day arrived for my first solo run. As I woke early, read my Bible, and prayed for the day, I knew I wasn't running this alone. God went before me, helping me pull my big girl boots on, and somehow by His mercy and strength we got out the door, clothes on, fed, and we made it through the day. Then He took us through the next day, and the next. He helped me find a new rhythm to this life with four kids. The years to come promised to be chaotic, messy, and sure to teach me a whole new level of flexibility. But I would learn that only with His strength and love could I do what He had placed before me.

We were in the thick of it all. We decided to try to sell our small townhome right after the twins were born, to find a home we could grow into.

It took six months of keeping our home constantly clean, with four children. We prayed and the Lord provided a way out.

We went through a year of sickness from the time the twins turned 10 months old until that following summer. We walked through a scare on Mallory's neck. After tests and scans and MRI's, and being sent to an oncologist/hematologist, we discovered thankfully that it was a treatable infection that could be removed by surgery. She was anemic and required intensive iron treatments, but praise God she fully recovered. Next was what I would call the "six-week cough" that started with me and circled through our entire family. In January the ear infections started to hit. Ava had one, Mallory had three, and Lena had five, which eventually led her to a surgery in May to have tubes put in her ears. In February Josiah got a rash and a fever, which turned out to be Scarlet Fever. All the kids got the stomach bug in February. I got strep throat in March. Josiah got it again that summer.

Dreams and plans of things we could do together as a family would fall apart over and over again. There were so many times I felt discouraged in that season, yet it was filled with joy through all of it. My doctor had been right: My life was busy. Most of the time, I tried to celebrate the little moments filled with joy. The twin cuteness factor Mallory and Lena brought to our home. There were fun moments of watching my twins follow each other down the hall, train style, when they first learned how to crawl. Once Lena had tubes put in her ears, it was amazing how quickly her vocabulary picked up. She started saying all sorts of cute words. Mallory followed Lena verbally about three months later.

Sometimes, as I go through my morning ritual, I find that the monthly gift of a period has graced itself once again in my life. Every so often I wonder if by some miracle of God, I might experience the joy of unexpected pregnancy. One that no one else would know about, a secret I could spill to my husband in some form of surprise, watch his jaw drop to the ground, then help him pick it back up. I could teach Ava, Mallory, and Lena how to be little mommies to a real baby instead of their toy ones. Just an unplanned gift from the Lord.

I know a lot of women go through that as they come to the end of "starting their family" and enter into the building stages with any of the gifts God has given. They wonder what it would be like to have just one more. As our children get older, we clear out our baby stuff little by little. My heart and quiver is full. But I do sometimes wonder...what if? It has been 16 years and Nick and I have never gotten pregnant on our own. Not once. And I am at peace about it, but I think it will be a question that will always linger somewhere in the back of my mind.

I look at the four beautiful gifts God has given me. Life got busy. It has gone by in a blink. It's hard, but I still fight to find those moments to cuddle my growing littles and bigs. To shower them with hugs and kisses, pray over them, teach them His word, and be a reflection of Christ in the midst of the chaos they bring.

I remember years ago, when I was 16, my dad brought me out on the back deck of our home, and he had me look up at the stars. He said, "Kari, snap your fingers." So I did. Then he paused for a moment and said, "Kari, snap your fingers again." Once again I did. "Kari, your life may seem like it is just getting started right now, you have all these things you long for, want to have happening in your life. But it is going to go by fast. And you will look back and see how fast it goes. Take time to appreciate each moment now."

It is crazy to think as I write this, and all my children are off at full-time school, how fast the time has gone. I want to say it once more: Cherish the moments worth celebrating, grieve the moments that hurt, wait patiently on Him. Learn to be at home and content in the here and now.

Dear Children,

When I think back to that first day of stepping into the role of full-time mama of four, I know the fear I felt leading up to that day. I just wished for one more week, one more day, when I did not have to rush around to accomplish all that needed to get done. I was not naïve to what four children would be. After we had Josiah and Ava, I knew full well what being a mom of two more would add to my life. It was this image of having to put on my big girl boots and just do it.

I wrote on that day about how I knew I couldn't do it without God. But I have to confess, after I jumped into the daily chaotic life, I sometimes stumbled with pride. I felt like I could do it all, that maybe I was Super Mom. When people asked how I did it, I didn't always give glory to the One who was carrying me through. If I think about it, was it all with Him? Or sometimes was I doing it from the strength found in making myself the ideal mom, one that people looked at and admired, and elevating myself beyond where I should have been?

This is not how parenting should ever be. And I am sorry for those times that I did that, when I didn't recognize that maybe I couldn't do it all and that it was okay to fail on occasion. I know I did fail. You all may know better than anyone of those moments that I failed.

I want you to know that the truth is, I could not have made it through the craziness without the God we serve. Ultimately, the love for you guys had to come from Him. Love to daily dress, feed, change you, take you to school, potty train you, read to you, clean our home, bathe you, and the list goes on and on. Sometimes I would do it with His love, and other times I tried it on my own.

I wish there were a button that could have put some of my favorite moments in slow motion. I wish I could go back and hold all of you, my babies, in my arms one more time. To see all of you singing in the back of our gold minivan the song "Strong Enough" on days I didn't feel like I could do it on my own. I miss those days. I always will. And yet, I am loving watching you now, seeing you grow and learn in so many new ways. It is such a gift to be a witness to your lives!

We love you, kids. Thank you for letting us be your parents.

Love,
Mama

Philippians 3:3–4, 7 (NASB)

For we are the circumcision, who worship by the Spirit of God and the glory in Christ Jesus and put no confidence in the flesh—though I myself have reason for confidence in the flesh also, If anyone else thinks he has reason for confidence in the flesh I have more. But whatever gain I had, I counted loss for the sake of Christ.

Philippians 4:13 (NASB)

I can do all things through Him who strengthens me.

Joshua 1:9 (NASB)

Have I not commanded you? Be strong and courageous! Do not tremble or be dismayed, for the Lord your God is with you wherever you go."

Ecclesiastes 3:11 (NASB)

He has made everything appropriate in its time. He has also set eternity in their heart, yet so that man will not find out the work which God has done from the beginning even to the end.

❧ A BEAUTIFUL THING TO WITNESS ❧

Ava. My dear, sweet Ava whose name means "gift from God." She is a child I don't always understand. I march to a world of checklists and multi-tasking and getting things accomplished. She floats along in life, patient and kind, always looking out for others. Living in a world of timeframes does not come naturally to her.

She is a child that potty trained at 18 months, but who I had to remind twice a day until she was four that she needed to go poop. A daughter who needed to be reminded to eat her food, otherwise she would sit and stare off into lala land. A baby who after a half hour of sucking on her bottle, I would find had not drank one sip, but had spent the whole time staring at me with her big brown eyes.

I have not always parented her well. I was conditioned to having a firstborn named Josiah, his name meaning "fire of the Lord," whose lightning speed capabilities trained me to always think 10 steps ahead, and still I would find him passing me up. A son who rode his tricycle on a three-and-a-half mile ride from our townhouse to Pastini Pastaria for dinner when he was only three years old. I often felt stuck in the middle of these two, with one arm trying to catch up to my son while the other reached back to help my daughter keep up. They are extremely different and God created them so special and unique. I can't wait to see what they do in life.

I have often thought about how my children would come to Jesus and make it their own choice. As a mom, I have never wanted them to make that decision just to please Nick and I, but to teach them about it and have it be a decision they could stand on, knowing it was their choice. A few years back I asked Josiah when he was in bed if he had ever thought about asking Jesus to be his Savior and to forgive his sins. Josiah went into an in-depth conversation explaining everything that he believed to be true, and told me he had already asked Jesus to be His Savior, several times actually. In response, I confirmed that choice and knew he understood it—he had it.

With Ava, I just assumed that maybe she had made that decision at church. She talked about it. She knew about it. But then I began to wonder, had she ever personally before the Lord made that decision? He impressed upon me that I needed to ask her about it. But I forgot about it and the thought was laid to the side for the next few weeks.

One particular day I was having a hormone-filled morning, and I became that mama I don't recognize. (Think Mother Gothel from "Rapunzel"[29] times five!) I was very poorly going through my responsibilities with Josiah and Ava, doing our Thursday homeschool. I became overwhelmed with one of Josiah's assignments that I didn't know how to do, and I flew off the handle with much drama. After I cried and apologized and calmed down a little, Josiah figured out what he needed to do without my help and we sat down for Bible time.

Then I got the nudge. God reminded me, "You need to ask her." As we wrapped up our Bible time, I looked at Ava and asked her, "Ava, do you know what it means to have Jesus be your Savior and Lord of your life and to follow Him?" She explained very sweetly what she knew. Then I asked her, "Ava, have you asked Him?" Her face changed and she replied, "No I haven't." We talked a little more, and told her that when you make the decision to follow Christ, God sends His Spirit into your life to help you make choices and seek God with your life. And then I asked her, "Ava is that something you want to do?" She very seriously responded, "Yes I do." Then I told her it was her choice, and she needed to do it—I couldn't do it for her.

That's when it happened. I saw her bow her head and begin to pray for Jesus to come into her life and forgive her sins, and that she wanted to follow Him. And as she prayed, tears started streaming down her cheeks. It was one of the most beautiful moments I have ever witnessed.

When she was done praying and still crying, I asked her what the tears were for. She told me that they were tears over her sins. That's when we started celebrating, because we got to tell her that her sins were now washed whiter than snow. And I saw my beautiful daughter's face light up in a way I have never seen before. She began to understand the decision she had made.

We celebrated at lunch with pretty donuts and a headband crown that our new princess of the King got to wear, and a few gifts that Josiah and I had picked out for her. We sang happy birthday to her for her new birth.

I texted Nick, telling him to call when he could because Ava needed to tell him something. She got to talk to her daddy and tell him, and Nick texted me after and told me, "You know what is funny? I already knew before she called."

It was such a beautiful gift to see! God answered my prayer for Ava, that it would be her own choice, which she could stand on. And watching her talk to her Savior, I could see that she understood completely the choice she was making.

I am happy to announce that on November 8, 2012, I was given a new sister in the Lord, and her name is Ava Mae Hope Adams.

Dear Children,

I don't want any of you to ever forget you are washed whiter than snow, no matter what you do. It doesn't mean we have a pass to just walk in sin all the time, but each of you is a child of the one true king. He loves you with an everlasting love. No matter what you do, He loves you.

You will make mistakes in life. I know it can be heartbreaking, but don't forget that that's what Jesus came for. He doesn't want you to hide the sin. Jesus wants you to bring them all to Him. This is what He died for. Choosing to hide it takes away the one thing He wants more than anything else in the world: to take you in His arms and remind you once more that you are His child, and He loves you. You are forgiven.

It's easy to find yourself filled with regret and unsure how to start over. Please listen and hear this: Go back to Him. Every single time. That is how you begin again.

Satan wants you to believe the lie that you are a failure—to think that your sins are too big for Jesus to carry. Don't let him win in his attempts to diminish the power of the cross. Those words are not from God. God delights in each of you. He has big things in store for your lives!

My beautiful children, be filled with His life, and don't ever forget the hope we have in Christ from your personal decisions to follow Him. Be the gift that He has created each one of you to be to all those around you.

We Love You,
Mom and Dad

Isaiah 1:18 (ESV)

"Come now, let us reason together," says the Lord: "Though your sins are like scarlet, they shall be as white as snow; though they are red like crimson, they shall become like wool."

Galatians 3:26 (NASB)

For you are all sons of God through faith in Christ Jesus.

Psalm 51:1–13 (NASB)

Be gracious to me, O God, according to Your lovingkindness; According to the greatness of Your compassion blot out my transgressions. Wash me thoroughly from my iniquity and cleanse me from my sin. For I know my transgressions, and my sin is ever before me. Against You, You only I have sinned and done what is evil in Your sight, So that You are justified when You speak and blameless when You judge. Behold I was brought forth in iniquity, and in sin my mother conceived me. Behold, You desire truth in the innermost being, and in the hidden part You will make me know wisdom. Purify me with hyssop, and I shall be clean; wash me and I shall be whiter than snow. Make me to hear joy and gladness, Let the bones which You have broken rejoice. Hide your face from my sins and blot out all of my iniquities. Create in me a clean heart, O God, and renew a steadfast spirit within me. Do not cast me away from Your presence, and do not take Your Holy Spirit from me. Restore to me the joy of Your salvation. And sustain me with a willing spirit. Then I will teach transgressors Your ways, and sinners will be converted to You.

Romans 8:38–39 (NASB)

For I am convinced that neither death, nor life, nor angels, nor principalities, nor things present nor things to come, nor powers, nor height, nor depth, nor any other created thing, shall be able to separate us, from the love of God. Which is in Christ Jesus our Lord.

❧ BUILDING COMMUNITY IN OUR NEIGHBORHOOD ❧

I want to share how God taught us to build friendships in our neighborhood community. When we moved our family of six people plus two kitties to our home on the hill after the twins were born, the first few years were pure chaos at times, as we lived with our children hitting so many milestones in those early years of their lives.

During that season, our church started encouraging us through the sermons to start building relationships with our neighbors. As an adult, I sometimes still feel like an awkward homeschool kid, and often can operate in a way that is more of a people watcher instead of a people participator. I still notice times when I meet someone's eyes and my tendency is to duck my eyes down, almost as if I am apologizing for being myself, ashamed of myself. I am not sure where these responses come from, but I have been recognizing that they may give people the impression that I am not interested in them. This is not the case at all, so my shyness will always be something I have to continue to overcome for all of my life.

As we heard these messages on Sundays, I felt very inspired. But the fear of letting people in would always win, and not wanting to be pushed outside of my comfort zone, I did nothing. I saw from the protective windows of my world a neighbor who had a new baby. And another home went vacant for a while, until someone purchased it and moved in, although I did nothing to reach out to those new neighbors. I saw the cute, young married couple with no children that lived at the corner of our street, and I often wondered what their story was. Did they struggle with infertility like we once had? I would often go on runs, and as I passed by the homes, I prayed for the lives inside them. On occasion when I was feeling bold, I would give a neighborly wave and a smile from my car as I drove by.

One spring day, my seven-year-old son Josiah asked me a question. A question that sent this idea of building community into a direction I was too scared to take on my own accord.

"Hey, Mom?" Josiah asked. "Do you mind if I go over and ask the neighbor boy across the street if he wants to ride bikes?"

Everything inside of me—my natural introverted instincts—wanted to say no. Was my son old enough to ride bikes around our neighborhood loop with a boy I hadn't met? That would mean we would have to cross the street and say hi. I was terrified. Nick wasn't around, and he was so much better at talking with people. But I knew what God wanted my answer to be. He made it very clear to me—He had been speaking this message for a while now, and this was the time to act in obedience and not hide in fear.

"Ummm..." I stammered and stumbled through my answer. "Sure..."

"Great, thanks, Mom!" As he ran out the door, I gathered up all of his little sisters and followed him outside to see what would happen. He crossed the road with his bike and helmet on, and with huge confidence and a big grin, went over and said hi to the neighbor boy. Within a minute, they both had their bikes and were making little laps up and down the neighborhood street.

I knew it was my turn to be bold and say hi to my neighbors. Three of the guys, including the dad of the neighbor boy, were talking in one of the driveways. I decided it was now or never. I walked over, held out my hand to shake, and introduced myself. An hour went by and I was no longer afraid. The bridge to meeting my neighbors had been built. I found out basic details about these guys and their wives and children. I was wondering in my head why it took me so long to say hello in the first place, and why this required my son to be brave for me, but at that point I was just grateful to be meeting people we lived next to.

Over the following few years, we built relationships and did life with our neighbors. The mother with the new baby ended up becoming a walking buddy with me. We would take walks several times a week together and have some really nice talks together. The family next to them was the one with the son Josiah asked to go bike riding. Quite often we would all end up at their driveway, the kids playing together, throwing a ball around or kicking a soccer ball, drawing sidewalk chalk, blowing bubbles, riding scooters. During the school year and rainy season, we would all migrate into our own homes, but the second the sun started showing itself, I would plop my kids in the front yard, and the other kids would come out and we would all be community together.

There was our sweet next-door neighbor, who had the most beautiful and creative garden I had ever seen, who became like an extra grandma to my kids, especially my girls. She would teach them how to deadhead plants and eat strawberries with the stems, because stems are vegetables. She would occasionally go to Burgerville and bring them home a picnic to eat in her yard. The girls would devour all her organic fruit she purchased from the grocery store. My girls would bring home beautiful flower-filled vases from her home to fill our home. And then I would send back to her doorstep extra home-baked goods that we wanted to share.

On May Day we would leave flowers on our neighbors' doorsteps. In July we would fill jars with blueberries to share from the overflow of our pickings. At Christmas we would make cookies and treats for little gifts, although the one year we had Norovirus in our home, those treats were not quite so desirable and perhaps shared a little more than we wanted to with a few of our neighbors.

On the Fourth of July our driveway had the perfect view of the neighborhood below us lighting off a bunch of sky-high, illegal fireworks. We opened up our driveway to watch the show with all of our neighbors. One year two of the dads got Trager grills and camped out on their driveways on July third, preparing some of the best meat I have ever tasted and sharing it with all who came to their Fourth of July potluck that afternoon.

Then there was our Josh and Maddy. Or as my girls would call Josh, "Our Joshie." They were the young married couple I often wondered about and prayed for when I went on my runs. That life-changing day my son asked the neighbor boy to ride a bike with him, I met Josh, and later on in the month I was able to meet his wife, Maddy.

Josh and Maddy went to church where all of my kids went to preschool. They became part of our family. At one point we invited a family in need to come live with us, and Josh and Maddy were right there with us in that season, helping out with our kids when we needed it, supporting us and praying for us. Once we had to make an emergency hospital trip, and Josh came over at 11:00 at night and stayed there while our kids slept. We would have them over for game nights, or Nick would go over to their house to play a game and Maddy would come over to hang out with me, eat banana soft-serve ice cream, and watch a movie. They loved us, and they loved our children well.

This, this is what I had been so afraid of? Fearful of letting people in to do life with us?

For the remainder of the time we lived in our home on the hill, I cannot imagine what our life would have been like if we had kept our doors closed and not gotten to know and love the people that lived in that neighborhood. So often trying to protect ourselves, we choose to operate in fear, instead of God's love, and we miss out on some great things God wants to do in our lives. I will always be so grateful for the boldness of my seven-year-old boy, who made a decision based on wanting to reach out and make a friend, when his mama would have stayed hidden on her own accord. That season will always be filled with sweet reminders of what it looked like to have fellowship and community in our own front yard.

Dear Children,

I love watching each one of you. So often I see how brave you are, and you encourage me by example to not be afraid to step out in boldness, to be a friend to someone else, to take my eyes off of my own shortcomings and fears that I might not be likeable. Thank you, my dear son Josiah, for being inspired to reach out to our neighbor boy across the street, and for asking me.

I think this is one of those places in life where, had I acted in fear or on my own desires of not wanting to go outside with all four of my children to keep watch of them, we could have missed out on several great years of being in community with some pretty great people. Deep inside of me I wanted to say no, out of selfishness and wanting to protect myself. At least that is what I thought I would be doing. But the reality was that the protection piece was a big lie. Instead of protecting my heart, I would have been sabotaging a great thing God wanted to do in our lives.

We need to be attentive and alert in those moments. Don't let those little lies that speak into inconveniencing your time, or protecting your soul, dictate your decisions. Instead, filter them through the lens of Christ, and ask Him to help you act in obedience. He doesn't promise it will be easy all the time, but it will be walking with Him, and He will continually meet you in it.

I want to encourage you when the times come for you to build your own neighborhoods and communities to be part of, keep your eyes up and looking to see ways that you can say hi and make friends and build fellowship with people that need the love of Christ poured into their lives.

Thank you for being my bold and brave children, for never hesitating to take gifts to the neighbors' doors and share big smiles with all of those that surround our family.

I Love You,
Mama

Matthew 22:37–39 (NASB)

And He said to him, "'YOU SHALL LOVE THE LORD YOUR GOD WITH ALL YOUR HEART, AND WITH ALL YOUR SOUL, AND WITH ALL YOUR MIND.' This is the great and foremost commandment. The second is like it, 'YOU SHALL LOVE YOUR NEIGHBOR AS YOURSELF.'"

Matthew 14:13–20 (NASB)

Now when Jesus heard about John, He withdrew from there in a boat to a secluded place by Himself; and when the people heard of this, they followed Him on foot from the cities. When He went ashore, He saw a large crowd, and felt compassion for them and healed their sick. When it was evening, the disciples came to Him and said, "This place is desolate and the hour is already late; so send the crowds away, that they may go into the villages and buy food for themselves." But Jesus said to them, "They do not need to go away; you give them something to eat!" They said to Him, "We have here only five loaves and two fish." And He said, "Bring them here to Me." Ordering the people to sit down on the grass, He took the five loaves and the two fish, and looking up toward heaven, He blessed the food, and breaking the loaves He gave them to the disciples, and the disciples gave them to the crowds, and they all ate and were satisfied. They picked up what was left over of the broken pieces, twelve full baskets.

Romans 15:5–7 (ESV)

May the God of endurance and encouragement grant you to live in harmony with one another, in accord with Christ Jesus, that together you may with one voice glorify the God and Father of our Lord Jesus Christ. Therefore welcome one another as Christ has welcomed you, for the glory of God.

Galatians 5:13–17 (ESV)

For you were called to freedom brothers. Only do not use your freedom as an opportunity for the flesh, but through love serve one another. For the whole law is fulfilled in one word, "You shall love your neighbor as yourself." But if you bite and devour one another, watch out that you are not consumed by one another. But I say, walk by the Spirit, and you will not gratify the desires of the flesh. For the desires of the flesh are against the Spirit and the desires of the Spirit are against the flesh, for these are opposed to each other, to keep you from doing the things you want to do.

God's Gift Continues

❧ CHOOSING SNOWFLAKES ❧

I want to share one more extension of our family that the Lord orchestrated into our story.

When Nick and I found out we were having twins, and as they began to grow healthy inside of me, reaching each milestone along the way with no signs of danger, we started having conversations in regards to the remaining eight baby embryos under the care of our infertility clinic and the plans God might have for them. Nick and I had it in our minds to pursue embryo adoption for them, to give a couple that couldn't have their own children a chance to have a family, and to give these little ones the best shot possible by not holding onto them for a long period of time in the clinic.

We made the decision to contact Bethany and began conversations with a case worker who handled their "Snowflake" adoptions. She set up a time to talk with us while I was on bed rest. We gathered together the basic information she needed, and she began to put a file together for us to start. At that time, I was ready to jump in and begin the process. I knew that with the twins on the way, we were going to be very busy, so I was ready to cross the t's and dot the i's. She advised us to wait for six months after we had our twins, and then start the process again. The OCD part of me that wanted everything neat and orderly was a little frustrated to not have the ball rolling as quickly as planned, but we heeded her wisdom and agreed to contact her once our life had settled down with the twins.

The summer after they were born, we had moved out of our crowded townhouse into a new home. Our frantic pace slowed down, and we decided to reach out to Bethany once more. There was a new gal in charge of the Snowflake process, so we were put in touch with her. As we started to email back and forth, I began to sort through some emotions I was having about all of this.

Three months after I had the twins, I couldn't shake the desire to have one more baby. Four or five was the number in my head, and five was more desirable to me. I figured one more in the mix would be fun. The problem with this dream was that Nick was done having children. I should say, he would have been fine if we had miraculously without any help from agencies or clinics had another child, but he was not going to purposefully try again. He wanted to be able to provide for the children we had. I completely understood this. I just didn't have peace about being done, so we were not fully unified. What I did know is that we couldn't have eight more children. Our clinic had frozen them in pairs, so it would have meant committing to another set of twins, and we knew we were not ready to take that on for at least four or five years, when our twins were school age. My pregnancy had been a huge sacrifice on everyone around me. We also didn't want to thaw two and refreeze one. I didn't feel right about that at all.

When it came down to it, we wanted the best for all eight of them. We knew God had a plan for each one, and that some might not make it, but we wanted to give them all the best chance possible. I was grieving through the process of releasing them completely. I had to get to a place of coming under the authority of Nick's leading with complete peace. God had put on our hearts embryo adoption at the very beginning of the in vitro process, so we knew we were headed in the right direction. I debated wanting to keep at least one pair. The most difficult part was releasing all eight of them over to the Lord. But I knew there was no guarantee that four or five years down the road, Nick and I would want to try one more time.

We had a phone call with our caseworker discussing these struggles. I went on a women's retreat following that conversation. I had some good talks with other mamas who were supporting me and encouraging me to surrender, to trust Nick, to come alongside of him. One woman shared a story of a gal she knew who pushed for one more child when her husband said no. They ended up getting pregnant and their marriage was really in a rocky place because of it. That resonated with me.

God ministered to my heart that weekend, when I was given a chance to take a moment to step away from my busy life with four children. It had been a crazy year, and I hadn't found time to fully process everything. He showed me that He had a plan for these eight baby embryos He had created. He wanted me to surrender under the leadership of my husband. Nick would never force me to do something he knew I didn't have peace about. But I knew Nick was done, happy with our four children, and he hadn't ever been like that the other times we made decisions to stop or pursue having children. This is what God had laid on our hearts to do all along. I was so grateful for the time He allowed me to work through it.

Although I knew it would be hard in some ways, I couldn't help but think of how cool it would be to see whomever He would bring forth to give these little ones to. We made the decision to continue the process with Bethany. I contacted our clinic to find out what they would need from us on their side, and we started to move things forward. Our desire was that we would find a couple that loved Jesus with all their hearts, and would show His love to these babies and to each other.

Dear Children,

I am going to write to you on a topic that can come across as pretty controversial. It's called submitting to your husband. For a man to talk about it, submission can sound sexist. For a woman to say it, she can sound like a pushover. That's society's opinion. And there are valid concerns, especially in marriages where the husband abuses his wife's submission in a way that is unhealthy for his wife and family. I always like to take worldviews back to the Bible, so at the end of this letter, I will leave you with a few Scriptures for you to consider.

I want to share what I have found with submission. I was raised by a firm father—you did what he said. Period. Submitting was very clear. If you weren't doing what he told you, you weren't submitting. But I married a man who often "leads" me into submission by having me make decisions for myself, meaning he wants me to think for myself and not have him make all the decisions. I can get so frustrated by this. In the beginning, I used to say he wasn't being a leader, that he was escaping the role by having me make the decision. But the truth is, he just leads very differently than my father. His leading wants me to have my own mind and thoughts and make decisions for myself. That is how he leads.

Nick would never push or force me to do something I wasn't okay with. He leaves me room to sort it out. However, when he is sure of a decision that we have to make together, there is very little budging room, and honestly, I don't ever want to push him the other way and force him into something he isn't okay with. He is the leader of our home. In a tie, his decision would be the final call. But he would prefer that I come alongside of him once that decision is made.

He laid it out pretty clearly that he didn't want to take on another child by choice. He believed those eight were not for us. You want to know something? Deep down, I knew the remaining eight were not ours. But I had to process it. Even today I still would love just one more child. However, I needed to let it go and be thankful for the four I had been given. God in His grace provided me the time away I needed to sort it out with Him and surrender once more.

Obedience to God isn't always an easy decision, but once it has been done, it's definitely the best one. So I encourage you from the passages below: Husbands, love your wives deeply. Wives, submit to your husbands. Pray for each other. If one isn't walking with the Lord, give them over to the Lord.

I Love You,
Mama

Ephesians 5:22–28 (NASB)

Wives, be subject to your own husbands, as to the Lord. For the husband is the head of the wife, as Christ also is the head of the church, He Himself being the Savior of the body. But as the church is subject to Christ, so also the wives ought to be to their husbands in everything. Husbands, love your wives, just as Christ also loved the church and gave Himself up for her, so that He might sanctify her, having cleansed her by the washing of water with the word, that He might present to Himself the church in all her glory, having no spot or wrinkle or any such thing; but that she would be holy and blameless. So husbands ought also to love their own wives as their own bodies. He who loves his own wife loves himself.

1 Peter 3:1–2,7 (NASB)

In the same way, you wives, be submissive to your own husbands so that even if any of them are disobedient to the word, they may be won without a word by the behavior of their wives, as they observe your chaste and respectful behavior. You husbands in the same way, live with your wives in an understanding way, as with someone weaker, since she is a woman; and show her honor as a fellow heir of the grace of life, so that your prayers will not be hindered.

❧ THE PARENTS GOD HAD CHOSEN ❧

It was right around Thanksgiving. Nick and I had finished everything we needed to on our end, and now our caseworker was keeping her eye out and looking for a couple that would be a good match for us. We covered this couple in prayer and waited with expectancy, knowing the Lord was working things out. I sent an email to our caseworker just to touch base, and she emailed back right away.

She had some exciting news! There was a couple that she thought would be a great fit, and she asked if she could send us the letter they were preparing for the Snowflake adoption waiting list. She said she was impressed with them and their devotion to each other and to growing their family. We eagerly anticipated receiving the email that would contain their information.

That week, Nick had a business trip to Arizona, and we decided to leave all four children with my parents for the first time, allowing me to fly down and meet Nick so we could spend that time together. A few weeks prior to the trip, I started to hear all around me this cough that sounded awful. I heard it from friends, at the grocery store, during church, sitting on the airplane, on a shuttle train to the hotel where I was meeting Nick... The next morning when I woke up in the hotel, I started to feel sick. Instead of all the plans I had to explore the area where we were staying, I buried myself under the covers of the comfortable hotel bed and pulled my laptop out. My body found freedom in the midst of this rest to release all that sickness, with no children around to care for.

Rest and a quiet day ended up being exactly what I needed. That morning while Nick was at work, we received the profile letter from the agency. I stared at the pictures of this couple in front of me. I read their letter over and over. God was so good to me, in His grace and mercy, to give me exactly what I needed to process that decision. I would have taken away being sick, but He brought me out of the chaos of my family into the peace of a quiet hotel room by myself, where I could receive the news.

Earlier in the week, when I had first heard about the possibility of finding a couple, I was at a friend's house for book club night; she had Hillsong United music playing in the background. The song "None But Jesus"[30] came on and caught my spirit that evening as I processed. I found myself playing that song over and over on my laptop as I laid in bed that day, in His presence. The Lord poured peace over my soul and met me that day quietly singing the song over me.

As I read the details shared in their letter, I began to fall in love with them. Their names were Paul and Rachel, they had been married four years, were living in Los Angeles, and were unable to have children on their own. They had first looked into international adoption, but then the husband found out about embryo adoptions and shared the idea with his wife. They knew this is what God had for them, and they were so excited to get to be a family through this method. They were very involved with their local church. He helped out with the media ministry, and she was involved on the worship team and taking pictures for church events. Their friends and family were all very supportive of them and praying for God's plan in all of this. They were excited to see how the Lord was going to provide. And they had a cat!

Nick and I talked and prayed about it that evening. The words of the song continued to wash over my soul. He was calling us to do this. He was giving us the grace to do His will. This couple was part of the plans He had for our family. It was time to answer this call He had given us since the very beginning of the in vitro process. They were His gift, He had created Mallory and Lena for our family, and now it was time to see what He had designed for this other family. Delight filled my soul. My hope was in Him. This story was *His*, and we were going to get to stand back and watch and bring Him praise.

Dear Children,

He is enough for us. He is all that we need. We have our plans, and He directs our steps. I went to Arizona with the hopes of a few days away with your daddy. God knew what I really needed during that time was a few days of quietness, to be away with Him, to prepare my heart for what was next as we looked to adopt out our baby embryos.

He asks of us big things sometimes, and He is faithful to be there when we need Him the most. Keep your hope in Him. He is all that we need.

I Love You,

Mama

Proverbs 16:1 (NASB)

The plans of the heart belong to man, but the answer of the tongue is from the Lord.

Psalm 40:8 (NASB)

I delight to do Your will, O my God; Your law is within my heart.

Psalm 62:5–8 (NASB)

For God alone, O my soul, wait in silence, for my hope is from Him. He only is my rock and my salvation, my fortress; I shall not be shaken. On God rests my salvation and my glory; my mighty rock, my refuge is my God. Trust in Him at all times, O people; pour out your heart before Him; God is a refuge for us. Selah.

❧ COMING TO A PLACE OF OPENNESS ❧

We had come to an agreement between our families to continue pursuing the path of adopting our embryos to this beautiful couple. We began to exchange emails back and forth, slowly getting to know each other better. We began to discuss what type of openness they would be comfortable with. Nick and I hoped that maybe we could get letters and pictures every so often just to hear how things were going for their family, but we really wanted to respect their space. The Lord had shown us through the experience of both good and trying situations in open adoptions that we needed to be sensitive to them in this. Here is a little of what I shared with them:

We want you to know right off the bat that we would like to completely respect whatever you are comfortable with, in talking and being open, or needing your space with us. I know when we were in the adoption process, I was nervous about openness, because I wanted to feel like the parents. I also know that when we started the in vitro process, I was in denial and heart protection mode, surrounding the dream that I could possibly get pregnant. I was shocked when I found out that I was. There is a certain amount of guarding your heart that is good to be sensitive to, and we know that God will show you guys as you walk down this new journey exactly what is right for you and your family.

Our communication continued through email as we worked with clinics to figure out the next steps. As details started to come together, the decision was made that for the safest and most effective chance in thawing the babies, she would come up to our clinic to do a mock trial transfer, and then begin preparation to return with her husband for an official transfer of two baby embryos.

When we found out she was coming up, we offered her the opportunity to meet us. We very carefully expressed that if she felt it would make her nervous and she was not ready, we completely understood. She bravely agreed to it.

We made plans to meet at Pepino's in downtown Portland. I told her over and over that she could cancel on us last minute if she needed to. But she didn't. Nick and I arrived early. I was excited and nervous and jittery. It was typical rainy Oregon wintertime. We stood with our rain jackets on under the streetlight waiting for her arrival.

When we saw her walking toward us, we greeted each other—I gave her a big hug. After ordering, I am pretty sure I chatted her ear off most of the night from being nervous, and she graciously listened and responded to the questions we had for her. At the end of our visit, we offered to drive her back through the dark rainy streets of Portland to where she was staying. We said our goodbyes and drove home. I know my smile was so big. I was so excited for Rachel and Paul, and to be able to stand back and witness what God was going to do with them as He started to make plans for their family.

Two months later, as planned, they came back to Oregon together as a couple. Rachel had her scheduled procedure and they let her know that the transfer of two thawed embryos had been successful. Afterward, she went to the hotel with her husband for the required bed rest. They agreed to meet our family for lunch on the day they were flying out. We met at Red Robin by the airport and introduced them to all of our children. That was such a fun visit. The stress of the procedure was done, and the kids made it a very lively lunch with them.

Now the waiting period for their family had begun. Nick and I were excited and hopeful for them. I eagerly awaited any email, phone call, or text that might share more information about how things were progressing. After nine days, Rachel let us know that she and Paul were officially expecting. We were over-the-moon excited for them.

At their first ultrasound, their doctor informed them that there was only one heartbeat. But then a month later, he informed them that actually two babies were living and growing inside of her! When she texted that update to me, I had been on a run and could not finish it due to laughing and being excited for them, filled with so much joy. I knew what it meant for her—twins are not an easy task—but she and Paul were up for the challenge, and we eagerly waited to find out if she would be having boys or girls or a mix.

That summer, they found out they were expecting twin boys! Twin *boys!* This news was crazy to me. God had created these boys inside of Rachel to be their family. I love how intimately He knows all of us—from the moment He creates us in our mother's womb. He was knitting together two boys for their family. I want to share a little piece from my journal blog that I wrote in processing through all of this.

> *Paul and Rachel. They are our adoptive embryo couple from California that flew up tonight, and tomorrow at 2:45 p.m., will have two baby embryos implanted inside of Rachel.*

> *Then she will be on bed rest for two days in her hotel room, and they will leave Thursday evening. It takes me back 2+ years ago, to when I was about to go in to have baby embryos implanted in me. Mallory and Lena. I saw pictures of the five-day-old fertilized eggs on a screen, as they carefully placed them through a tube inside of me. It happened so fast, and nine days later I found out through a blood test I was pregnant.*

> *I so badly want Paul and Rachel to have an amazing success story through this treatment. I don't want them to be the couple that receives the call to let them know Rachel is not pregnant, and that she will have to try again. I don't want to hear that two of the little baby embryos of the eight remaining didn't make it. I would be heartbroken for them, and for the little lives that didn't survive.*

> *You know, I can go back and forth on the whole moral dilemma that wraps around in vitro, and wonder did we handle things right? Maybe we shouldn't have done it this way, or should have done it this way. But when we started the process, we knew that if there were any remaining, that when we decided we were done growing our family, we would give the rest up for adoption through Bethany's snowflake program. That is something we have 100% peace on. And knowing how hard this can be for a couple aching for a family, to trust God with the hopes of having a baby(ies) and waiting to see what will happen...*

> *I just never realized to the fullest extent how much each of these little ones has a face, has a name, until I met my little girls. God let us have two, named Mallory and Lena. I just wonder if the rest of them will make it when it comes time for their thawing, and I'm hoping and praying for the greatest success for each one.*

Praying for the lives that the surviving ones will lead, praying that they will grow up to be beautiful women and strong men of God—men and women that love Jesus and want to serve Him with their lives. I know I won't be part of shaping them and training them hands-on, but I will pray for them, and I am excited to continue to live my life and see what He does...

I just keep thinking of the song by Aaron Shust "My Savior, My God," that played on the radio every time I questioned the in vitro process as Nick and I went through it over a three-month period...

I don't know how this will all turn out—I could drive myself crazy with the what-ifs or should-haves, but what I do know is that I have a Savior, and He loves us, and He loves Paul and Rachel, and I am just praying that we through our embryos get to play a small part in His big plan of providing them with a family to love and to raise up, teaching their children about Jesus through their words and actions and love. My prayer and heart's desire is that by this time next year Rachel will be able to celebrate Mother's Day with a baby or two in her arms.

So grateful for a Savior who sits at the right hand of our Father.

Dear Children,

Our story with the Paul and Rachel is something only God could have done. I love how He took our two families and brought us together, through a journey we both had walked through separately—the path of infertility. It was a passing of a baton; we were at the end of our journey of starting our family, and they were just beginning.

The experiences I had through our first two adoptions, with open adoptions and birth parent relationships, helped me to figure out how to be on the other side of the adoption process. To know how to respect this couple we were placed with, and to treat them the way they needed to be treated—as parents expecting their first children. Nick and I understood the loss a couple feels when the ability to have children the "normal" way doesn't pan out the way you planned. My goal was to help Rachel and Paul have as much of a normal experience as possible, at least when it came to their relationship with us.

God taught us how to navigate through our communication and build trust between us. I have been asked if when I see pictures of their boys, I feel like they are mine. The truth is, I don't. When I look at my Josiah, my Ava, my Lena, and my Mallory—you are the faces of the children God has given to your daddy and me. Taylor, Aiden, Lucas, and Lily are the faces of Paul and Rachel's sons and daughter. And the biggest truth is, all of you belong to the Lord. Not to me and Nick, or Paul and Rachel. We just get to have you under our care for the season of parenting.

This is the true miracle in all of this: God could take all of these broken stories and create family from them. He is amazing in all of His work! He is faithful!

We Love All of You!
Mama Kari

Psalm 40:1–5 (NASB)

I waited patiently for the LORD; And He inclined to me and heard my cry. He brought me up out of the pit of destruction, out of the miry clay, And He set my feet upon a rock making my footsteps firm. He put a new song in my mouth, a song of praise to our God; Many will see and fear And will trust in the LORD. How blessed is the man who has made the LORD his trust, And has not turned to the proud, nor to those who lapse into falsehood. Many, O LORD my God, are the wonders which You have done, And Your thoughts toward us; There is none to compare with You. If I would declare and speak of them, They would be too numerous to count.

Psalm 71:14–19 (NASB)

But as for me, I will hope continually, and will praise You yet more and more. My mouth shall tell of Your righteousness and of Your salvation all day long; for I do not know the sum of them. I will come with the mighty deeds of the Lord God; I will make mention of Your righteousness, Yours alone. O God, you have taught me from my youth, and I still declare Your wondrous deeds. And even when I am old and gray, O God, do not forsake me, Until I declare Your strength to this generation, Your power to all who are to come. For Your righteousness, O God, reaches to the heavens, You who have done great things; O God who is like You?

ᴥ AN INVITATION BEYOND MY COMPREHENSION ᴥ

Rachel was coming to the end of her third trimester. She was due in January, just days from Josiah's birthdate. God had kept the boys growing strong and healthy inside of her. In the meantime, I was making plans for a trip to California. It had been before Mallory and Lena were born that I had been given a chance to do something without the kids, and Nick was allowing me to go to a conference in California called Mom Heart Conference. I was ecstatic for the chance to get away, see some sunshine, and get refreshed.

Rachel happened to catch on social media that I was going to be down in California. And what she offered me was beyond generous and beautiful. She invited me to come visit the twins while I was there. They were about 40 minutes away from where I was staying. I told her that she could change her mind last minute if she was feeling overwhelmed after giving birth to the boys. I wanted to make sure she was feeling well, and just be sensitive to how things were going, but the blessing that she was offering that possibility to me...well, no words could describe what it meant to me and how grateful I was.

On January 6, Rachel gave birth to their twin boys. The labor had been intense, but she was a trooper through the whole thing. I felt so proud of her. When we saw pictures of the boys, I just sat in awe, examining their faces, seeing how unique God had created both of them.

As I continued to plan for the trip, one evening I received a text from my beautiful friend Monica. She had just bought her ticket to accompany me to the Sally Clarkson conference in February. The Lord had given me a companion to come along with me, so that I could glean wisdom from another mama who has walked before me in raising her children. A faithful friend to be there with me to meet Paul and Rachel's baby boys.

Then, as if meeting them weren't enough, Rachel and Paul extended their invitation for me and Monica to come to church with them that Sunday. The morning I was going to be coming, their boys were going to be dedicated to the

Lord, and they were going to share a little bit of their testimony. The timing of all of this was a gift from the Lord. I had no idea when He had impressed upon my heart back in October to make plans to attend this conference, what He had in store for me. But He did. He planned all of it. My heart was swelling with joy. I will share once more from my journal blog about the time He gave me. It felt like a weekend of opening up beautiful gifts that He had placed for me to find.

I am sitting at the airport waiting to board a plane to start my journey home. My heart is brimming full of joy and awe over this weekend. The best way to describe the experience: It was like unwrapping a bunch of beautiful gifts that the Lord had planned out in advance for me. I am so undeserving and beyond grateful for what an awesome Creator God we serve.

This weekend started with arriving Friday morning to the beautiful sunshine in California. After we checked into our hotel, Monica and I took a walk and had us some In and Out (we justified splitting a chocolate shake because we did walk there). We arrived back at the hotel and got our packets for the weekend. Seats had already been saved for us by my dear friend Hannah. At our table sat five moms from Oregon and five moms from California. We shared the common bond of wanting to raise our children to love the Lord, and we knew our inadequacies without Jesus. And for the next 24 hours, we got to glean and be the Titus 2 young women soaking up words of wisdom and encouragement from moms that have walked these steps before us.

We had the chance to share a little bit about ourselves at the tables. One of the gals from California started sharing how she has four children, her oldest son was named Josiah and that she has another son and then twin boys to finish her four. Later her sister leaned over after a time of worship and said that I harmonized just like Amanda. As we talked more throughout the weekend we discovered we both had our children enrolled in part-time private, part-time homeschool education. Then she shared that she was running a half marathon the next day, which is again another common bond. By the end of the conference her friends told me they were glad I lived in Oregon or else they would never see her anymore. To which I laughed and said that I would just join their group and hang out with all of them. I noticed that we even had opposite initials. Mine are K.A. and hers are A.K. As we hugged goodbye, she smiled and said, "Goodbye, sister from another mother!" Truth be told, I found a lot of sisters from another mother this weekend. I have sorely missed this type of fellowship and was so grateful for it this weekend.

I know some have asked me to share about what I learned at the conference. I'm not sure exactly what to share, other than these two things: We need to find those Titus 2 "older women." And we also need to be them. We need to remember that unless we are filling ourselves daily in the Word, we cannot be pouring into our children and husbands the love that they need. We cannot do things on our own strength.

Find creative ways to make memories in our homes, and know that God gave us the children we have to parent. He chose me to be a mom to Josiah and Ava and Lena and Mallory. Parenting will look different in each family, so don't judge one another, but support one another in love. Follow Jesus and pray we can reflect Christ onto our kids.

Dream again, and dream with my children. I want to start finding out what Josiah and Ava dream and hope for and think about. I love to travel; I hope to someday plan trips for our family to explore new places. Most importantly, commit my dreams and hopes to the Lord, asking Him what His dreams for me are, and then see what He does. I am excited to start seeking God on the "what next" for our family.

Last night when the conference was over, Monica and I got a rental car (a fun green Kia Soul), and drove to Huntington Beach. I bought a frivolous pair of red Toms wedges that I love. We meandered through beach clothing shops. Then I faced my fear of the ocean ever since the tsunamis in Japan happened, and we walked out on the dock and ate at Ruby's Diner

These little adventures fill my soul with so much delight.

This morning I woke up once again to beautiful sunshine and enjoyed a run. Then I came back to the hotel and got ready to go to church. Monica and I stopped for breakfast at Corner Bakery, then we hopped in our green, boxy, fun car and headed up the freeway to Paul and Rachel's church.

Words can't explain how I felt when I saw them. But I will try anyway.

I was nervous. I wore my beautiful snowflake necklace they purchased for me for Christmas (it only seemed fitting).

Paul and Rachel took the boys up front and shared the story of how God brought them their boys. I cried. We prayed for them as a church congregation. I know they are well loved and supported.

We went out to King's Hawaiian Grill for lunch. The boys are beautiful. Paul and Rachel shared how Taylor is wigglier and the mover. How Aiden snores and how

Taylor snorts. They are all so unique. Aiden does have similar features to Mallory, but when he opens his eyes, they look very blue. Taylor and Lena have similar cute poochy lips.

Meeting Paul's parents was another gift. These little boys are well loved, and Paul and Rachel are more than we ever could have dreamed of when we were praying for the right couple to receive these embryos. To play a part in God's big plan on the other end of adoption is truly an honor, and to have a couple so willing to embrace us and call us their family in front of their church congregation is... Indescribable.

Rachel and Paul's parents, Aiden and Taylor's Papa and Mema.

The start of a new family.

Dear Taylor, Aiden, Lucas & Liliana -

I wanted to write the four of you a letter to tell you we love all of you very much. We enjoy seeing the pictures from your mom and hearing updates from your parents, watching you grow from babies into little children, and someday into young adults.

I want to tell you that we know with all of our hearts that you belong in the family He has given you, and we all are family together because of God's love for all of us. He planned from the beginning of time that you would be raised up by your mama Rachel and your daddy Paul, to always love Jesus the most. God chose you and breathed His life into each one of you. I stand in awe of God when I think about how He orchestrated your family. He did it all—we just played a small part and followed in obedience to Him.

Thank you for letting us be part of your lives in this way. We will always love you from afar.

Paul and Rachel,

Thank you for being the parents that God chose for these children. For loving them with His love, for being willing to give them life. For letting me witness and be part of Taylor and Aiden's dedication to the Lord, and allowing us to be a part of the continuing journey that brought you first Lucas & then Liliana. We are forever grateful for the choice of obedience you made in searching out the snowflakes program. You guys are incredible, and we love you with all of our hearts.

Love,
The Adams Family

Romans 8:28 (NASB)

And we know that God causes all things to work together for good to those who love God, to those who are called according to His purpose.

Broken Places

❧ OPENING OUR HOME ❧

Our home on the hill was the biggest place we had ever lived. After living in a tiny townhome for several years, I was excited to have a place to invite people over. I was determined to make it a place where all would be welcome and feel like family whenever they were inside. Nick and I wanted to make sure, after being entrusted with such a place, that we would always stay open to using it however God led us.

A few years into it, God made it very clear He had a need that He wanted us to fill. We had a family very close to us walk through some very difficult circumstances that put them in need of a home for an indefinite amount of time. We loved their family so much. I got along so well with the mom, we parented similarly, and our children were close in age. When they were together, the dynamics of the kids worked really well. We prayed about it and brought them into our home to live with us.

In a perfect world, this would have gone really well and ended really well.

But the reality is that life is messy, the world is messy, and there is brokenness. When we opened our home, we also opened ourselves to walking through brokenness with them. We did not understand the depths or the rawness of the situation. If we had known ahead of time, I don't know if we would have chosen to place ourselves in that position. But God knew that their family needed a home, a safe place to be, and for the five months they lived with us, that is what He used it for.

I witnessed God being a Provider of everything we needed each day. Somehow our grocery budget came through each month. When we needed money for certain unexpected expenses, He met us there. He truly is Father to the Fatherless and Husband to the Widow, and He moves in ways that are beyond our explanation. For example, several months prior to their moving in with us, one day God put it on my heart to buy cheese for their family. When I used their house key to put it in the fridge, and I realized the cupboards and fridge were almost empty, the twins and I went back to the grocery store for an emergency shopping trip. That whole time, the twins sat in the cart singing their hearts to Jesus. As I walked down each aisle, they rocked back and forth and sang beautiful two-year-old music to the Lord. I can't explain it any other way than that even at their age, they knew they were doing a job that was for Jesus. It was one of the most beautiful things I have seen.

When they came to live in our home, I got to spend many hours with their three children. One of our friends commented when he came into our home, filled with the sounds of seven children, that there was a constant background noise—almost like the ebb and flow of the ocean waves. It was loud, and it was filled with good memories for seven children who loved each other well, while the outside world and the circumstances surrounding that family were filled with darkness. I will always cherish the memories of them sitting around the dinner table together and doing Bible time with Nick leading the way. He would often play "Jesus Freak"[31] by D.C. Talk on his phone, which delighted all of the kids. They would jump and dance their way around the living room, singing at the top of their lungs.

I had thought life when we added the twins to our family wore me out, but seven kids in the home took me to a new level of non-stop work throughout my days. I am not sure how I was operating at that point; somehow, I was making it day to day on whatever adrenaline I could find. Nick also had to have shoulder surgery in the midst of everything, so as he recovered I worked at caring for him, too. Little by little my bucket was getting drained and not being filled back up.

One of the lessons I learned through this time is that there is a difference between being Jesus's love, and being Jesus. I think I walked a very fine line that crossed over at times in how I made my decisions, based on the thought that I wanted to be Jesus for them. Whenever a need arose, I made sure it got taken care of, whether it was clothing or school, groceries or money for gas. I'm not saying I shouldn't have done that, but I was off just a bit. Being Jesus's love also means sometimes not getting in the way of what He is trying to do and teach through some of those hard circumstances.

I had put myself on a pedestal and found my identity in fixing it all, when it really wasn't my job. I found myself thriving on the moments when I met a need, and I found my purpose in that, even if it was at the expense of my own family. It didn't matter to me in those moments, because I was "being like Jesus."

In retrospect, if I could go back and change how things went during those months, I would operate differently. Instead of walking the line of trying to be a "Perfect Savior," which is a role never meant for me, I would have pressed into my Perfect Savior more each day, asked Him how He wanted me to take each day to Him, and watched what He did with it. I would not have been so afraid to let some of the little things fall apart so that He could come in and fix them. It really was such a gray line that was crossed sometimes more than it should have been.

When they were able to move out at the end of November, I found myself coming to the end of all I had to give. Once during their stay with us, I had a panic attack and went up to my room and cried and cried—I had no words to speak, I opened my mouth and nothing came out. There was so much brokenness happening outside our home that would crash like waves against my soul, and I began to find myself slowly sinking.

I did not know at the time that I was heading into a deep, dark battle with depression that would take me down for several years. We had made it through providing a home for a season to a family that needed it...and then I started to fall, and at the time I didn't know if I would ever make it up again.

Dear Children,

I love you so much. I know that so much of what happened in the months we had this family live with us will forever be imprinted on your minds. Your dad and I hope that the lesson you will take with you in life from that experience is that what God gives us is not ours, it belongs to Him. We wanted you to see our home as a gift to share, not to keep to ourselves.

When we asked you to give up your own space in your rooms, we loved watching how you did it with whole hearts, not selfishly, but freely, with care, getting to love each other well through that season. I loved watching you with their children, seeing how you interacted and treated each other like brothers and sisters. I cherished seeing all seven of your beautiful faces around the dinner table and kitchen island, breaking bread together.

I will never regret the time we had them in our home. I would make that same decision over again in a heartbeat. Just remember this truth that I learned the hard way in the midst of this time, and take it with you in your own lives: Always be Jesus's love, and let Jesus be Jesus. Don't be something you were never made to be. It is easy to want to be the answer to a person's every prayer. But that can be a dangerous line to walk, so remember the importance of always keeping Jesus on the throne and falling at His feet when serving Him. He can meet the needs and care for His people far better than we may think in the moment of our serving and giving. He wants us to be generous, to be His hands and feet. But let Jesus be Jesus.

Love You Always,
Mama

John 15:5 (NASB)

I am the vine, you are the branches; he who abides in Me and I in him, he bears much fruit, for apart from Me you can do nothing.

1 Timothy 6:17–18 (NASB)

Instruct those who are rich in this present world not to be conceited or to fix their hope on the uncertainty of riches, but on God, who richly supplies us with all things to enjoy. Instruct them to do good, to be rich in good works, to be generous and ready to share.

Psalms 68:4–5 (NASB)

Sing to God, sing praises to His name; Lift up a song for Him who rides through the deserts, Whose name is the Lord, and exult before Him. A father of the fatherless and a judge for the widows, Is God in His holy habitation.

In December, I knew God wanted me to take the time to start pouring into my husband and children once more. I was scheduled to have a foot surgery two weeks before Christmas, so right before that time, I took my kids out for a little mommy-kid date. We had spent so much time pouring out our time and resources in different ways, so I wanted to make sure they knew how loved and important they were. I took them out to the mall and got them all hot chocolate and cake pops from Starbucks. Then I let them each pick one thing from the mall to take home with them.

The next day I went in for foot surgery and came out determined to make a strong recovery and get back to normal as soon as possible. But normal was the furthest thing that would be taking place. I was told I would not be able to run long distances anymore. Running had become a lifeline for me when the twins were babies, a chance to have an hour or two for myself to just listen to praise and worship music, to think and process and pray and sort things out with the Lord. But it had also become an identity that needed to be stripped.

Running had become part of an obsession to keep a physically healthy body and fit into a size smaller than I had ever been as an adult. I loved being that size, loved how I felt about myself, and I was afraid if I gave up running I would no longer be that size. Sadly, I had also twisted into this the desire for attention from someone other than my husband, an emotional struggle that I battled for a few years. Although I never acted on the thought, it definitely skewed my perspective and warped the gift that running was meant to be in my life. There was so much vanity mixed in with all the good things that came from my runs. I needed to have those pieces that were twisted together pulled apart and separated. God was asking me to lay all of that at the altar before Him.

As I recovered from foot surgery, some things were brought up to our church leadership about how we handled and communicated needs when we opened up our home to the family living with us for several months. When it was first brought up, it felt like an attack on our integrity, and it added to more brokenness—just one more thing that weighed heavy over us. However, when we met with the church leadership and sorted through all the things that had happened, they gave us their full support in what we had done. That was a relief, yet at the same time, their involvement brought deeper pain to the situation.

During our meeting with church leadership, we were asked to make some changes in our approach to the situation, which we did. Sadly, in response to those changes, over the next few months, we were slowly cut out of that family's life. It was confusing and hurtful on so many levels. We had hoped to continue the relationship, to surround them with support as a community and family through the changes suggested by our church leadership, but they wanted nothing to do with it.

I had a tight bond to the mom of that family. She had been my closest friend during the season of having all four of my littles at home. We had spent the last few years watching each other's kids, helping each other out in a pinch, taking kids to school, grabbing extra groceries for each other. While Nick had been busy working hard for our family, we helped each other out in very real, tangible, and practical ways. We talked through things, prayed for each other, cried together...but now I was no longer welcome into that relationship. There was nothing I could do to mend it or fix it. What had once been one of the safest places for me to share my deepest thoughts and struggles was no longer available. It was a deep severing of relationship that broke my heart, like a divorce. The friendship we shared that had helped me through my years with four littles was broken. I found myself feeling very alone.

In reflection, I see what I had done wrong on my side. When I was in my twenties, I had walked through a tough situation with someone else that I was very close with. That person went through some stuff that was difficult in their life. I know that I made some mistakes in how I handled that situation. I tried to reconcile, but after a time they came to a decision that it was not helpful for me to be part of their life, and they cut me out. It broke my heart and I struggled for years to somehow fix the cut, to be able to find relationship once more. Nothing I could do would mend it. As a result of that, in many ways I had been making my decisions based on of fear of losing this friend, too. I realized I had compromised in some areas, when it came to what I said or did not say to her. I was afraid of losing the relationship. I never wanted to scare her away, so I acted on that fear and kept things to myself that should have been said throughout our friendship. In the end, I could no longer stay silent; God was calling me to act in His love. I cared too much not to speak.

But she didn't like what I had to say, and she no longer wanted me as part of her life. Just like the situation from when I was younger, I was once more being cut out, no longer wanted or needed. And just like the brokenness I felt over the loss of what happened years prior, I felt like somehow this was all my fault.

I started doubting all the times I had prayed with her, prayed for her. I wondered if it really had been God that was leading me. She communicated in a way that made me believe she could no longer have a relationship with me because God told her not to. That was so complicated and confusing. If God was telling her not to have a relationship with me, then did that mean I was not close to God? That I was the one that was off on things? It shook the foundation of who I had known God to be and the things I had seen Him do in my life.

I struggled with insomnia; if my phone buzzed in the middle of the night I would wake up terrified of the unknown it might bring. After six months of this, I figured out how to turn the vibration off so I would sleep better. I was always afraid it was going to be a late-night text telling me that one more thing was falling apart.

I started shutting down in new relationships. I would make a new friend, then I would try to make that new friend her replacement. If it started to get close, I would shut down and pull away. I just couldn't do new friendships. I hurt people along the way with that. I didn't mean to, I just was so weighed down from the fear of being rejected one more time that I would do it first in self-protective mode.

I was able to maintain the friendships I had prior to the disconnect with her. I desperately clung to those relationships. Then in crazy moments I would try and push away, yet they still remained faithful to me through those times. Those became "closer than a sister" relationships.

And then God. Then God. His faithfulness through a husband who stuck by my side, through all of my healing, and His Provisions in those coming days to restore me to a place of being whole once more.

I want to take some pages to write about those moments, because even in those dark places, God is faithful.

Dear Children,

I have struggled for years with allowing my friendships to dictate how I respond and act in certain situations. Stemming from the early rejection I felt when I was in elementary school, I fought to be the friend that people would want around them. Yet so many times, I felt like the second-string friend. In response, often my actions in relationship were to try to ensure not being rejected or pushed away. But that was not being a friend—it was acting in a way to protect my heart from being broken by a person; in truth, it was being selfish.

It's good to be a friend that loves at all times. But being a friend who compromises on His truth so she won't lose that friendship is not being a friend at all. Sometimes in life, you may be required to love enough to speak His truth in love. And in those moments, it may not be welcomed or accepted. You can't control how people respond, and you can't make a person love you—they have free will just like you in how they live their life and how they choose to act and love.

In those situations, pray for truth, discernment, and wisdom, and ask God to help His word and His truth come forth with love and grace. And remember, it's not your job to be a person's Holy Spirit. It is your job to love with His love and let God do the work.

I want to close with a few verses on friendship and relationships.

Love You So Much,
Mama

Romans 12:18 (ESV)

If possible, so far as it depends on you, live peaceably with all.

Proverbs 27:5–6 (ESV)

Better is open rebuke than hidden love. Faithful are the wounds of a friend; profuse are the kisses of an enemy.

Ephesians 4:25,32 (ESV)

Therefore, having put away falsehood, let each one of you speak the truth with his neighbor, for we are members of one another. Be kind to one another, tenderhearted, forgiving one another, as God in Christ forgave you.

Although my season of brokenness and dark depression took place after this family moved out of our home, there were some things that had been building up in my life that added fuel to the fire.

Being part of a church plant many years back was amazing and incredible, watching what God was doing in people's lives. But at the same time, it became a constant cycle of meeting new people. Nick led a house church small group for a while, and we had to encourage people to break off and start new house churches several times. People kept coming to the church who needed relationship and connection, but over time I hit a wall over continually making new friendships. I felt so overwhelmed by new people. And then having four children, the days of having extra time when I could squeeze in a play date here or there were gone. My days were filled with constant care for my four children and maintaining a clean house and feeding my family. It was a rare occasion when I got a night out with gal friends. And even when I did, after caring for my needy children all day, I found myself wanting to be alone rather than going out for the night to be around more people.

The last time the group that Nick was leading split, we had 85 people show up at a park potluck, and we looked at the couple who normally hosted in their home, and quickly knew we would need to go in two different directions after summer. We started a group in Hillsboro, and they moved to one that met at the church. They would meet on Monday nights, and we were asked by church leadership to meet on Tuesday nights.

Then bitterness started to seep in. I had already let it take root a bit, when I had to miss out on a women's Bible study the church was holding the same evening we were leading house church, and I needed to take care of my twins while Nick led the group. I was frustrated and worn out from pouring out and not having anyone in my life pour into me.

When Nick moved to leading the group on Tuesday nights, I was bitter because the kids had to go to bed early on Tuesday nights, having school the next morning. Josiah was at the school that provided three days of private and two days of homeschool. I wanted to have a Monday night group, so we could attend as a family and the kids could sleep in on the homeschool day. But instead, for me to be able to participate, I needed to leave my kids with a babysitter. Then I ended up helping to watch the kids at the group, because we had a lot of kids and not enough sitters. Eventually we rotated through mamas taking turns, but bitterness was evident in my heart. I had lost all desire to do this for our church. I felt forced into a place that didn't work well for our family, and my heart was not right before the Lord in it.

About a year later, we stepped back from leading a group, when it needed to split once more. That happened at the time when Nick and I opened up our home to the family that lived with us, so we really were not able to do anything extra. We were so worn out, and I had lost my place in the body at church. I didn't know where I fit anymore. I was no longer the first church admin; I did not help on the worship team anymore; I was no longer the wife of a house church leader; I did not help with the children's ministry; I was no longer taking time to get mamas together to hang out and build friendships. The church was huge, and I felt small and unseen. I was just me.

My identity was tied to what I did, rather than to who I was—a child of God loved by the One True King. And the job I did have, being a mama of four small children, seemed so small compared to the "great" jobs that so many other people had. I kept trying to strive for something, longing to fit, to make pieces go together for a new role. Nothing worked. I began believing the lie that my time and life in that season with four small children was unimportant, which is the furthest thing from the truth. The role of shaping the next generation is one of the most valuable things I will ever do with my life.

Nick and I wrestled through all sorts of things. The church had transitioned to groups called Missional Communities. The model for a missional community when it was first rolled out was the idea of having your small group be right in the middle of where you lived. You would meet with people from the church that lived right in your neighborhood and find ways to reach out to the people who lived next door to you and show them Jesus's love.

We had many conversations at night processing what this would look like for us. We were building a great community in our neighborhood, but no one who lived in our neighborhood attended our church and could meet together for prayer, worship and fellowship in a small group setting. Being part of another group meant time away from our neighborhood. While trying to figure this out, we attended one missional community group 20 minutes away from us, then another 15 minutes away, and finally we ended up back with our original group, deciding it was okay to meet together and support each other in the places God had us. It was a very difficult ideal to figure out how to do well.

I was also extremely tired. I would find myself driving and hitting a wall where I could barely make it home so that I could get to my bed to lay down. I didn't know what was going on at the time. I found out later that I was borderline anemic, and it wasn't until I started taking regular iron for a good six months that I started to improve and see my energy level begin to climb. However, while I was struggling in the midst of it, I found myself so frustrated that I could not do things the way I once had. I felt discouragement when I couldn't accomplish all the things I longed to do each day.

Call it a mid-life crisis a few years earlier than expected. A loss of identity in how I once defined myself as having it all together. No longer the supermom who found time to run, homeschool her kids, and blog about all the amazing things God was doing in my life. I had nothing. Glimpses here or there, but mostly a complete collapse of everything I once was.

But once again, there is goodness in all of this. It was humbling. Stripping. Peeling back all the twisted pieces that had become entangled with the goodness of what God was doing in and through my life. Removing me and putting my reliance solely on Him. I had lost myself, all of what I knew myself to be.

We decided to try going to a different service for a while at our church. Our church was huge—and the service we went to was always overflowing. We felt we should try to go to the later service. We did this for four weeks. I would look around and see no one I recognized. I couldn't see a single face I knew, which added to my feeling of being unseen. Unknown. Alone.

After four Sundays of attending this later service, my feelings of loss and missing identity were bubbling to the surface. As I stood in line to pick up my children from Sunday School, a familiar face, a pastor's wife, Britta, turned around and smiled at me. And with such a tender tone, she looked into my eyes and said, "How are you doing, Kari?"

I burst. I broke. I fell apart all over her, silent tears streaming down my face, filled with longings to be known, longings to be seen just for a moment. She took me into her arms and held me. She prayed over my soul and said these words that only the Holy Spirit could have given her: "Help Kari know she is seen by You—that You are a God who sees her…"

How did she know? How did she know that the deepest longing of my soul in that moment was to be known and seen—to not feel lost in a crowd of people in a church I had helped plant years ago? She could not have known on her own, but maybe through her own brokenness she might have had some intuition. Spirit-led intuition. In that moment I was told that the God of the Universe still saw me, and He still knew me, and He loved me.

Comfort poured into the cracks of my heart that felt so broken and lost and alone, and the Holy Spirit brought little parts of me back to life. It was raw, and painful, and beautiful. I knew that I was seen by Him, and that was all I needed to know. He is a God who sees me.

Dear Children,

You may find yourselves in seasons when you feel unseen. Being unseen can come in many different forms. Maybe finding yourself as a wallflower at a party or a big public event. Serving in the church doing what may seem like unimportant tasks without a stage to praise your work. Perhaps working at a job that you are faithful every day to go to, where someone else takes credit for your work. Or being in a marriage where your spouse doesn't see who you really are, doesn't see your heart.

People may not always see you. That should never be your goal. As followers of Jesus, self-glorification is not something we should ever aspire to. The things we do absolutely matter. They are important. But we take those things and lay them before Jesus's feet. He is the one we seek to glorify. He is the one that brings great purpose to what we are doing.

And He is the One that sees you. Every day, as you work at being faithful in what is placed in front of you, He sees you. He knows you. And what you are doing matters so much to Him.

Keep being faithful. Faithful to seek Him, to serve Him, to love Him.

You are loved deeply by Him.

Always,
Your Mama

Genesis 16:13 (ESV)

So she called the name of the Lord who spoke to her, "You are a God of seeing," for she said, "Truly I have seen Him who looks after me."

Psalm 139:3 (ESV)

You search out my path and my lying down and are acquainted with all my ways.

Revelations 4:10b–11 (ESV)

They cast their crowns before the throne, saying, "Worthy are you, our Lord and God, to receive glory and honor and power, for you created all things, and by your will they all existed and were created."

☙ HOLY SPIRIT, COME ☙

In the middle of my survival moments, I would have very difficult days. This particular Wednesday was right up there with the roughest I had felt in a while. Not in the way a typical rough day would be. Nothing hard happened to me on this day. Of course, it didn't help that I had struggled a bit with insomnia the night before. It hadn't been as bad as other times in the past, but definitely not enough sleep...But for me, this particular time each month my emotions ran high, hormones were raging, and my ability to handle normal tasks became very difficult.

Tasks such as taking my kids to school and ballet. Coming home to a house to clean—but before I could start on that I needed to fold clothes in the hall, empty the kitty litter, and take out all the garbage, to prepare the way for a clean house. A clean house that would only stay clean for an hour before someone needed to pee in the toilet, or eat lunch at the table, or heaven forbid, color with crayons and leave a few on the ground...You know, pretty much every mom's job.

The little list of to-dos piled up as I remembered I was making a crockpot dinner, and I needed to get that started as well. I cleaned up the bathrooms, cleaned the floors, did another load of laundry...and I hadn't woken up at 5:30 to run, so I wanted to fit that in, preferably before I ate my lunch. And of course, I would love to spend time taking the girls outside in the sun before we picked up Josiah and Ava for school.

At 11:30, I headed upstairs to throw on running clothes. Lunch was served for the girls, movie started. Two minutes into walking on the treadmill, the phone rang. It was Nick. Ava had spilled some stuff all over herself at school, and I needed to take her a change of clothes.

That was the straw that broke the camel's back. I threw on my regular clothes, had the girls load up in the van, and headed back to the school. But not before losing it on the phone with my poor husband and getting extremely upset, saying awful things I really didn't mean about being fed up with being a mom, and just being nasty. Oh, I regret those things— "put a guard O Lord over my mouth..."—especially at this time of the month.

I managed to regain my cool enough not to express my frustration towards Ava when I dropped off the clothes at school. I just ran in quickly and gave them to her and asked if she needed a change of shoes, but she was good there. It wasn't Ava's fault. She was just a kid that had an accident, and she needed her mom to bring her clothes. But my heart attitude was way off.

I made it back home, and as I pulled into the driveway something caught my eye on my doorstep. Something big and yellow.

At church the day before, a pastor from the UK spoke about the Holy Spirit. It was a great message, sharing about what the Holy Spirit does: The Holy Spirit empowers us to do what Jesus did; He directs and leads and guides; He confirms the love of the Father for us; and He fills us continually.

How can we be filled by the Spirit? Continue to chase after Him; eagerly desire His gifts. Ask, and receive in faith. At the end of the message, we asked for the Holy Spirit to come fill us, as He did at different times for the church in the New Testament. I was aching for it and raising my hands asking, but nothing happened. The pastor said to wait for it—that it was not our timeline, but His. And I waited, but left church not having experienced anything different than in the moments prior to asking for it.

Now back to the porch and the yellow something on my doorstep. I unloaded the car and walked to bring our garbage cans in. I saw that someone had brought me flowers and a note. I started shaking a little as I walked towards them. It was a bouquet of beautiful, bright, big sunflowers. The note read: "Come Holy Spirit, come...Encourage Kari's heart and may Your presence be ever present in her home. Psalm 121."

In my home...in my home that I had just yelled at my husband in, been irritated with all my children in, thrown a very unroyal hissy fit in...

At that moment, the Holy Spirit broke into me. I started crying and crying, knowing that whoever had done this had been listening to the Lord and took the time to go out of their way to be Jesus to me and show His love to me in a tangible way that told me I was important to God. I was valued by God. And God was calling me to respond so differently than the way I had that morning. I had failed, but He still loved me and He wanted to make sure I knew that.

Sometimes I forget those things. I have had the thought, "Well, I had my vacation with Nick last week, so now I don't deserve anything else for a long time. So many people gave so much for me to be able to do that." Or thoughts like, "Kari you are being such a consumer right now; you don't give to people and you have so many people that have helped you out so much in the last few months. You need to be careful so others don't think you are taking advantage of them." And thoughts like, "How can I care for those that mean so much to me, for those that do so much for me and my family, when I can barely handle the daily tasks of caring for my children right now?"

But God used this person to burst through all those thoughts and tell me *His* truth: I mean so much to Him, and I have His Holy Spirit inside of me. It broke me in a way I needed to be broken and put me back together in a way only *He* could do.

I am praying that I can keep my heart open to His leading, even when I have hard hormonal days. I think that day was an example to me, and I hope it can be an example to you of how important it is to listen to the Spirit's leading when He impresses something upon your heart. I don't know how my day would have turned out if that hadn't happened. But I do know how it turned out because that person listened and obeyed what the Holy Spirit asked them to do and became the love of Christ in my life when in my weakness I needed it the most.

Dear Children,

One of the best parts of being in a church is getting to be part of the body of Christ. Being able to care for one another and serve and love each other well. I was having a bad day, and as you know sometimes your mama does have those from time to time. God knew my heart, and He spoke to a friend of mine to reach out to me and pour His truth into the midst of it all. She was obedient to it, and went out of her way to act upon showing His love and speaking that truth into my life.

There will be times in your life when you are asked to be obedient in reaching out in His Spirit's power to touch the life of another. And there will be times to receive it. God's gift to us is His Spirit, which Jesus left with us to be our Counselor and Helper. I want to pray for you, Children. Holy Spirit, throughout my children's lives, would you please speak into them Your truth, with Your power, into the deepest and darkest of days, when things are falling apart? Show them also when they can be a helper and reach out and do the work You call them to. May my children learn to be sensitive to Your leading and direction in their lives.

I Love You!
Mama

Psalm 121 (ESV)

I lift up my eyes to the hills. From where does my help come? My help comes from the Lord, who made heaven and earth. He will not let your foot be moved; He who keeps you will not slumber. Behold, He who keeps Israel will neither slumber nor sleep. The Lord is your keeper; the Lord is your shade on your right hand. The sun shall not strike you by day, nor the moon by night. The Lord will keep you from all evil; He will keep your life. The Lord will keep your going out and coming in from this time forth and forevermore.

2 Timothy 1:14 (ESV)

By the Holy Spirit who dwells within us, guard the good deposit entrusted to you.

John 14:26 (NASB)

But the Helper, the Holy Spirit, whom the Father will send in My name,
He will teach you all things, and bring to your remembrance all that I
said to you.

⚘ TAKING A SABBATH ⚘

I want to share a little about a lesson God taught me during this season about taking time to rest with Him. As I was walking these deep waters of depression and brokenness in my life, there were a lot of changes that needed to take place for the health of my family. I had a very dear lady look into my eyes and tell me that God was going to be bringing me into a time of taking a break from being a Martha, and learning to be a Mary—to stop doing and start sitting at His feet once more.[32]

In the middle of all the loss, I was still trying to do all the right things. I was reading my Bible every day and praying, going to church each Sunday. However, when summer break began with the kids all at home, there came a point when I realized I couldn't keep heading down the path I was on anymore. I knew I needed someone to give me godly counsel and pray with me about everything. I met with Diane, the leader of ministry to women at church at the time, and after patiently listening to my story, she pointed out the obvious.

I had nothing left in me. I was completely drained. And those weeks when I thought I was doing okay, I was actually just surviving. I remember once when our church first started, I was at a Bible study where Diane had a tea cup and saucer that she used as an illustration to us women. She took a teapot and poured water into the empty cup. As it filled up, it began to overflow onto the saucer. The water represented the Holy Spirit pouring into our lives, and as we were filled up to the brim, what came splashing over was what we had to give to those around us: our husbands, our children, our family, our friends, the people we served, our ministries.

I was an empty tea cup. I had been striving and working without taking much time for rest for several years now, and the time had come to fix that. Diane shared some wisdom with me, so that when I left our meeting I was equipped with a plan to talk with Nick about. The first thing on the list was to take some time away to sort through everything that had broken our home, and work through all of it with the Lord, just me and Him. Secondly, I needed to figure out a time each week to Sabbath. In that season with all the littles at home, it couldn't be a rigid Sunday Sabbath rest, because every day with little children, no matter how hard you try, you are constantly needed for the care of your family. The purpose of the Sabbath needed to be a break from the responsibilities of my children, to take time to find things that would be life-giving to me. I needed to think of this as dates with Jesus.

As I ran through all of this with Nick, he was extremely supportive and we booked a hotel for me to get away for a night. When that day came, Nick confidently said he had the kids, and told me to leave whenever I wanted. I grabbed my stuff, loaded up the car, and drove to the beach. On the sand under the summer sun, I laid out on a blanket with a notebook. Some of the time I closed my eyes and rested and just listened to God and His truth wash over me. Then I would grab my notebook and begin writing out everything I needed to give to Him. Things I needed to forgive others of, things I needed to repent of. I repeated this several times. I also started writing out subjects for which I wanted to hunt for verses in the Bible, in order to replace the things I was surrendering to Him with His truth.

After a few hours, I knew it was time to go. I picked up my blanket and as I walked to the car, I knew what God wanted me to do next. I drove down the road to a more private beach and parked the car. I ripped out all those pages from my notebook of things I had repented of and things I had forgiven. I tore them in shreds and bundled them up tightly in my fists. I walked out to the ocean and looked out at the waves, pausing for just a minute. At first, I thought of throwing them into the waves, but it was a windy day and a picture of the pieces of my releases and repents landing all over the sandy shore for anyone to see entered my mind, so I chose option B. I got my feet wet, and as a wave came I put my hands deep in the water and released all those pieces. The wave took them out to the ocean, then another wave took them further out, and I turned and walked away. God had taken all those things, and I didn't need to go back to them or keep living in them anymore. For the first time in a long time, I felt free and fresh and light.

I drove back into town and spent the rest of my evening looking up Bible verses at the hotel, meeting with a supportive friend for dinner, and wandering through Barnes and Noble. I woke the next morning to a quiet time, opening up my Bible in fellowship and communion with Him. I followed that with taking a run outside. I tried a Starbucks Refresher Valencia Orange Coffee drink, then I went and got my hair done.

The next step for me was to figure out how to take a Sabbath each week. Obviously, a mom can't escape to be by herself every weekend. That would be very expensive and really impractical for my family. The best way I can explain my ultimate goal for Sabbath is this: taking time each week to be alone, sometimes outside in the sun resting on a blanket, sometimes curled up in my bed with the door closed. It's time without interruption from my littles to read my Bible and pray, to be silent and listen to the Holy Spirit, to address things with me. This is not time spent praying for my kids and my husband or the rest of the world, but time when if there is anything during the week that I didn't handle quite right, or I need to forgive, I can spend with the Lord processing that.

I have a theory on this. Speaking as a wife and mom, our lives are constantly being interrupted by our children and husbands. All the time. My brain may be thinking of a shopping list, then it's diverted to cleaning up a mess in the bathroom. I may be thinking of something I want to talk about with my husband tonight, and suddenly I find myself in the middle of a war between my two children and their much more urgent crisis. Pieces of my brain slowly get left hanging throughout the day. Computers undergo fragmentation that makes them do extra work and slows them down. They need time to be defragmented, to rearrange the fragmented data in order to work more efficiently. As women, we need that too. Time to turn on a defragmenter and put all the pieces of our brains back into a more efficient working order.

When I take that time with the Lord, He helps me defragment and get back to a whole, healthy, productive working order. He is my personal

Counselor during the moments of quiet, and He brings to light little things that I can be growing and changing in my life. I read in a book something that explained so clearly my failure over those last few years: I wasn't giving God time to speak to me personally. I was so busy doing all the right things that I missed out on what is best. I had become a Martha instead of a Mary. But in this new season I was now entering, He invited me to be a Mary once more. He began to take my dry bones and breathe new life during those Sabbath times. It was a beautiful gift to experience. I was beginning to see glimpses of hope, and I began to smile at my future once more.

Dear Children,

Your dad and I have stumbled through this, figuring out how to create time for a Sabbath for our family. We actually faced a bit of spiritual warfare in the midst of figuring it out. I don't think Satan likes the idea of having us take time to listen to Jesus and be refreshed and filled by the Holy Spirit, so that we can begin to pour into those around us again. However, it is extremely important to make sure we fight that battle and make it a high priority. Cover the time in prayer. Finding weekly rest with the Lord should definitely become a spiritual discipline in your life.

It is so important in the middle of all the doing to take time to focus on becoming more like a Mary. To start smiling at your future. To sit at His feet. To love Him and listen to Him. To allow Him to work in you. And then as you continue to be filled once more, you will get to see His Spirit splash out of your cup and fall onto the lives of other people He places around you. When we take that time to rest, we can be restored to the fullness of all He has to give and do in our lives.

I Love You, Children,
Your Mama Always

Luke 10:39–42 (ESV)

And she had a sister called Mary, who sat at the Lord's feet and listened to his teaching. But Martha was distracted with much serving. And she went up to him and said, "Lord, do you not care that my sister has left me to serve alone? Tell her then to help me." But the Lord answered her, "Martha, Martha, you are anxious and troubled about many things, but one thing is necessary. Mary has chosen the good portion, which will not be taken away from her."

Hebrews 4:9–11 (ESV)

So then, there remains a Sabbath rest for the people of God, for whoever has entered God's rest has also rested from his works as God did from His. Let us therefore strive to enter that rest, so that no one may fall by the same sort of disobedience.

Jesus said to him, "Get up, take up your bed and walk." And at once the man was healed, and he took up his bed and walked. Now that day was the Sabbath.

ꙮ A BIRTHDAY TATTOO ꙮ

I was about to turn 35. To many this represents just another year older. To me, as a teenager this represented a big year: the year I could get my ears double pierced! My dad had told me when I was a teenager that if I wanted to get my ears double pierced, I would need to wait until I was 35. I know he was just saying a "dad thing" and teasing me. I always told him that when I turned 35, I would go get it done. When I became an adult, he said it was up to me of course, and I could do it if I wanted to. But I decided to wait just for the fun of it.

As 35 began to creep up on me, I started to evaluate my big statement that "when I turn 35, I am going to get my ears double pierced." Being a busy mom who sometimes doesn't even find time to put earrings in her single pierced ears, I questioned the idea of dealing with two holes that needed earrings. When I was a teenager, I envisioned hoops and studs—I thought it looked so cool.

It's funny to think that now I could walk into Claire's anytime I want and get my ears double pierced. Now that I am standing on the doorstep, I am okay with maybe not following through. Who knows—I am open to it, but it's not something I desperately want to do like I did when I was a teenager.

Instead, I started thinking about something else I could do, equivalent to piercing my ears—something a bit out of character for me. I began considering a tattoo and what I would want it to say, how it would represent me. If I could put my life story into one word, what would it be? I knew right away.

Hope.

Hope is something God has taught me all along my life journey. Hope in Jesus is the main thread that runs deep throughout my life. Hope in Him when I struggled with depression as a young teenager. Hope in Him when I knew Nick and I were someday going to get married, but in the midst of waiting six years, Hope stayed with me.

Hope that when we got married, we would have a family. Hope that when we didn't get pregnant, we would have a family differently than planned. Hope that when we started the adoption process, it would end with a baby in my arms. Hope that when we started the adoption process a second time, we would add another baby to our family. Hope that when we tried in vitro, I would experience pregnancy.

What is odd about the list I just wrote is that all those things are great things, but as I walked through them I always learned again and again that hope is not based on circumstances, it is based on hoping in God, who knows better than I do. Even if I didn't get those things I wanted, I would be okay, because I always have Him.

Hope is something weaved into my soul. And it is something I have been struggling with not having as much of this last year.

It's easy to lose hope when you start focusing on the negative circumstances—the hard-to-understand tragedies of the world or the ones that hit closer to home. Hearing the news of a cousin who committed suicide; watching a friend's marriage break apart and not understanding why it didn't get fixed; living day-to-day in the same routine of caring for my little ones, questioning if I am really showing them Christ's love or if I am messing up their lives when I yell or say hurtful things I really don't mean; and personal hormone imbalance struggles that make me feel so discouraged and depressed that it's hard to keep going...

Again, I am placing my lack of hope on the wrong thing, so I battle to find the one true thing I know to get me through my days: placing my hope in Christ. When I come back to that place, I know that's what I can stand on. This world is *not* eternal, and my life here one day will end.

I watch my little 87-year-old Japanese grandma care for my grandpa after he had a heart attack the day before Easter. The hard work she puts in each day helping him get what he needs for basic functions, from eating to cleaning to getting stuck in a position that he can't get out of...it just shows me that getting old is not going to be easy. It's probably going to be one of the hardest journeys to end my life here on earth. For someone like me who does not like the idea of being a burden to someone else or having to depend on others, it will be very hard. Will I have the stamina to keep going to the end?

Hope. It's what I will need to carry with me for tomorrow, and for as many tomorrows as I am given. Hope is knowing that someday, at the end of this life, I may hear those promised words in Matthew 25:23 (ESV), "Well done, good and faithful servant! You have been faithful over a little, I will set you over much. Enter into the joy of your master." To enter into His joy someday—my heart thrills at the thought!

Every time I look at my wrist, I will remember the faithfulness He has shown me in times when I hoped through hard circumstances—and I will keep hoping in Him in the hard times to come. I will lift my hands to sing and praise Him with hope at church, and I will use my hand to pray for others and have hope *for them* in the trials they are going through. We all need that reminder to hope. But hope is nothing without Christ.

My Dear Children,

A tattoo is nothing to take lightly. It is a permanent mark on your body speaking a message. The bigger question is what type of message do you want your life to speak?

That is the story I want my life to share and the message I want my tattoo to communicate as I walk through this life. One that communicates our hope in Christ. And my prayer for you is this:

Romans 15:13 (NASB)

Now may the God of hope fill you with all joy and peace in believing, so that you will abound in hope by the power of the Holy Spirit.

Love You Always,
Mama

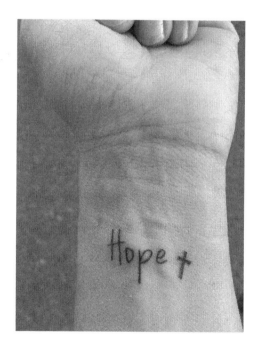

❧ NIGHT OF PRAYER ❧

Our church hosted a women's night of prayer every year. We met at midnight, and through the hours of the early morning we would go through the Lord's Prayer verse by verse.

When we reached "Hallow the Lord's name," we were each given a verse card that listed one of the attributes of God, with a few Bible verses describing His name. As a small group leader, I was asked to spend the month prior going through the verse cards, praying over the Scriptures, and asking God to speak to the women coming and reveal His attribute in their lives when they received the card laid on their seat.

I was usually a group leader for these prayer nights, but the year all the pieces of my world started to fall apart, when I was asked to lead I knew I needed to say no. I hated saying no, but I was not in a healthy place to be leading anything.

As the evening approached, I started feeling apprehension about going. I didn't want to go and be around a group of women who were praying. I had all of my walls up, and that environment felt so unsafe to me. Open up about my life, and how I was feeling like everything I ever stood upon had crumbled beneath me? No thank you.

I debated about going the whole evening. I was signed up—there was a place reserved for me, but I heard it was going to be a crowded evening with no room for any extra women. I reached out to my sister, who had also signed up to go. She debated about it as well, and we sat in my living room unsure of what the night would bring. My neighbor Maddy contacted me that evening and asked what I was up to. I told her I was supposed to go to a night of prayer at the church, but I was having second thoughts.

I was being *that* person. When you are a leader, you take time to pray for those coming who might be having second thoughts. For those who were afraid, that they would come anyway. For those who might be prevented in one form or another, that God would pave the way and get them there safely in one piece. Satan is not a big fan of prayer, so as leaders, we would have all sorts of stories about how one leader almost didn't get there because of a fluke stomach bug that happened that night, or another who had a crazy day leading up to it, fighting a spiritual battle to get there.

There was a spiritual battle going on over me that evening.

Maddy was a safe person to me. She was someone who had walked alongside our family the last year in all shapes and forms. I felt secure with her. I asked her if she would be interested in coming with me and my sister, and to my surprise she said she would love to.

That hadn't been what I was expecting or hoping—I had thought maybe she would say that she could just come over and watch a movie with us.

Then I reached out to my friend Alisa, who was leading a group, and asked if there was enough room for me to bring a friend. I figured this would be a no-go since I was told the sign-ups were all closed. However, that did not stop my friend from asking the women's ministry leader if they could make extra room for my friend.

Alisa texted back, "Room in my group for all of you—checked and it's fine to bring Maddy. Come."

Again, not what I hoped or expected. But with my Maddy and my Abbie by my side, arriving at the church into the safety of my Alisa leading our small group, I bravely went with a lackluster desire to be there.

And then God. We got to the card time to read the Name of God given to us, and the verses that are part of that, and I read:

"Holy One of Israel"

Isaiah 48:17 (NLT)

This is what the Lord says—your Redeemer, the Holy One of Israel: "I am the Lord your God, who teaches you what is good for you and leads you along the paths you should follow.

Isaiah 43:1–3a (NLT)

"But now, O Jacob, listen to the Lord who created you. O Israel, the one who formed you says, 'Do not be afraid, for I have ransomed you. I have called you by name; you are mine. When you go through deep waters, I will be with you. When you go through the rivers of difficulty, you will not drown. When you walk through the fire of oppression, you will not be burned up; the flames will not consume you. For I am the Lord, your God, the Holy One of Israel, your Savior.'"

Tears started streaming down my face. God had done all of this work to get me to the Night of Prayer, so that He could tell me that He would teach me what is good for me and lead me along paths that I should follow. When I walked through difficulty and oppression, I would not drown or be consumed. He was my Holy One, My Savior—I did not need to be afraid. He called me by name. I am His.

I rested in that truth over the following year. A friend sent me the song, "Oceans,"[33] which includes that same verse. I had been confused on my path, confused about things that had happened, but He was still going to be faithful. He continued to meet me where I was all that year. He used songs written by Kari Jobe about His role as Healer,[34] and how He is for me.[35] Truth was sung over me at a Women of Faith conference, the tears streaming down my face. The first year of that brokenness was so hard, yet so good, as He slowly began a restorative work in me. He was so patient and kind to help me sort through my struggles.

The next year, I was back at Night of Prayer. God still had so much work to do in my life, but this time, I was ready to lead once more. As I handed out the verse cards I had prayed over, I pulled one out for myself:

"Redeemer"

Job 19:25–26 (NLT)

"But as for me, I know that my Redeemer lives, and he will stand upon the earth at last. And after my body has decayed, yet in my body I will see God!"

Isaiah 41:14b (NLT)

"...O Jacob, don't be afraid, people of Israel, for I will help you. I am the Lord, your Redeemer. I am the Holy One of Israel."

Tears came to my eyes once more. I glanced across the circle and stared into the eyes of my friend Tanya. She had been a faithful friend who had walked through the fire and stuck by my side in all of this. When she heard me read "Redeemer," she knew it was for me. I knew God was promising me His hope—that He was going to teach me about Redemption.

The rest of that year, He taught me all about the redemption and restoration of physical earthly things. It started with a bedframe. And then night stands...followed by a hope chest. Then it moved into my living room...then to a dining room set. Little by little, piece by piece, I looked at the furniture I had used in my home for years. I studied it in its present form and struggled with the way I hoped my rooms to feel. I took apart my furniture, carried it out to my garage, and sanded away at the old stain or paint. I put on primer, then waited for it to dry. I added the color I had chosen. Two coats of that, then I finished with a sealer to protect it. I had two couches that were salmon colored. I had never liked the color, from the moment we brought them into our little townhome. I repainted a wall several different shades to try to match this couch set. I researched online a way to stain couches. I went to the hardware store and picked up some stain, followed by the fabric store, so that I could sew new pillow covers. I spent several days and nights primping and stitching and getting things just right. In the end, I had recreated my salmon couches, making something "new" and usable and beautiful out of something that was downright ugly, and which most would have advised me to just get rid of. Start over.

God was teaching me illustrations of His redemption. As I worked on each piece, His name, Redeemer, resonated in my soul. Restoring my furniture took patience and time. Much prep work and planning needed to be done.

As I redeemed and restored my furniture, He continued to do a new work of redemption and restoration in my heart. There were still lessons to be learned, healing to take place, and rough places to be sanded and smoothed. But I was beginning to see glimmers in my life of what He desired to do. Hope was building in my soul. And it was beautiful!

Dear Children,

There are many names and characteristics that describe our God. I challenge you to take time in your moments in the Bible with the Lord to do a word study on His name. It is a name we are to hallow. To honor, to make holy, sacred, sanctify, consecrate.

I want to give you a list of the names of God that we would remember on our Night of Prayer. A place to start in your search of God's names.

The Lord is My Rock, Lion, Prince of Peace, Strong Tower, Lord, The Word, Light of the World, My Husband, Immanuel, Physician, Daddy/Father, God Almighty, Mighty Creator God, The God Who Sees Me, Jealous God, Child, My Master, Bread of Life, Most High God, Everlasting God, Redeemer, Lord of Hosts, Hope of Israel, Friend, Holy One of Israel, Teacher, Judge, Lord Our Righteousness, The Lord Who Provides, The Lord is My Shepherd.[36]

There are so many other names and descriptions of our God.

He wants to be all of these things to us. We have access to this rich, amazing God!

Be encouraged and strengthened, Children. He is a BIG God. One BIG enough to walk with us through all of our seasons.

Respect His Name. Honor His Name. He is Holy.

Love You Always,
Mama

Matthew 6:9 (ESV)
Pray then like this: Our Father in heaven, hallowed be Your Name.

Luke 11:2 (NASB)
And He said to them, "When you pray, say: 'Father, hallowed be Your name. Your kingdom come.'"

Psalm 140:13 (NASB)
Surely the righteous shall give thanks to Your name; the upright shall dwell in Your presence.

Psalm 115:1 (NASB)

Not to us, O Lord, not to us, but to Your name give glory, for the sake of Your steadfast love and Your faithfulness.

Psalm 45:17 (NASB)

I will cause Your name to be remembered in all generations; Therefore the peoples will give You thanks forever and ever.

Psalm 63:4 (NASB)

So I will bless You as long as I live; I will lift up my hands in Your name.

❧ RALEIGH, NORTH CAROLINA ❧

A few years ago, Nick and I sat next to each other by his computer, and he told me about a job possibility that he had just heard about in Raleigh, North Carolina. It piqued my interest in the conversation. A year and a half prior, our church had started a new church plant out there. It was something that had intrigued us at the time, but we were in the middle of caring for the other family living in our home at that time. Our plate was full and we didn't consider it. I had several friends move out with the plant, so I was always vested in knowing how the church was doing.

We decided to research this job a little more. It turned out that an old co-worker of Nick's had switched to this company, and he had written the job requisition for it. We prayed about it, and Nick decided to send an inquiry to his friend. Immediately, his friend jumped on it, and Nick was scheduled for phone interviews that Friday. Everything started moving fast.

Paul and Rachel, the couple who adopted our remaining baby embryos and at the time had twin boys that are full biological siblings of our twins, had moved out to Raleigh a year prior. Nick and I talked and prayed about what the implications of taking a job close to them might be. We decided to ask them how they would feel about our living close to them before we went any further. Nick and I felt that if they would not feel comfortable with our making a move like that, we would stop the process of pursuing North Carolina immediately.

On Thursday evening, I wrote a Facebook message letting Paul and Rachel know what was going on, and asking them how they felt about it. That night, sleep was sparse for me. I was anxiously awaiting their answer and thinking about Nick's scheduled interview the next afternoon, wondering what was going to happen.

By 4:30 the next morning, I surrendered to the fact that I would not be getting any more sleep and quietly made my way downstairs to read my Bible.

Curiosity got the better of me, and I checked my phone prior to reading my Bible. There was no message from Rachel; however, there was a message from one of my forever mama friends, Becca, who had moved with her family to Raleigh and was part of the church plant.

The message was a cry of sadness. She had just learned that their dear friends, the couple who helped pastor the Raleigh plant, were being called back to Oregon to pastor Westside AJC, the church we attended, and they were going to be bringing a new pastor to Raleigh.

My heart skipped a little quicker..."Lord, is this You, moving in a crazy way?" I held my breath. Deciding not to share with my friend quite yet, I prayed for words to encourage her and point her back to Jesus. When Nick woke up that morning, I showed him the message. It seemed to us like this was from Him. No better time than now to go help at a church plant in the midst of transition. We received more confirmation when Paul and Rachel gave their blessing for us to move forward.

That afternoon, Nick had his phone interview, and the next week, they called and scheduled a flight for him to North Carolina for an all-day interview.

At this point, we were telling friends and family what was going on. It was heartbreaking to think of leaving them all behind. At church, our leadership brought up the new pastor that would be headed to Raleigh with his family of six, and we got to meet him and his wife while they were in Portland for the month of June.

Every Sunday we heard about things God was doing in Raleigh, and our hearts were stirred over and over. It truly felt like a calling from the Lord.

We also loved the idea of being on the east coast. Nick and I have only ever lived in Oregon, other than the first few months of my life. We began to dream of all the little adventures we could take with our family if we moved there. Excitement began to build.

Nick flew out for the interview, and I prayed and tried not to be a ball of nerves. I wish I could say that throughout the whole process I was a "super spiritual wife," even taking time to fast on the day he was there. But the reality was more a continuous curling up in the fetal position, crying out in prayer, and struggling with anxiety and doubt and fear whenever I took it before the Lord.

I was walking through the Rose Gardens with a friend and our little girls when I received the call from Nick after his interviews. He had six total, and he thought all went well, with the exception of the last one—he felt he might have tanked it. I did not feel the peaceful hope I was anticipating to follow the interview. He got on a plane home with no answer other than that he was still being considered, and they would get back to us.

We held our breath for three weeks. Our emotions wavered, and we wondered how this was all going to turn out. Nick felt a lot of doubt in his last interview, but still the company would not release him. "Still considering you..." was the answer we were given during the waiting. I half-jokingly told Nick that if Raleigh didn't work out, I got a trip to New York City (New York being a dream of mine for years).

I remember a pastor's wife from church coming up to me and saying, "Sometimes when we are supposed to go, it doesn't always work out." Her words didn't make complete sense to me, but I decided to ask friends to pray that if God wanted us there, Satan would not thwart His plans.

The weekend before the Fourth of July, I went into the prayer room at church and a couple covered me with His peace and prayers for answers. The three weeks of waiting had wreaked havoc on me. My biggest struggle, my lifelong learning lesson, is waiting. That night, Nick and I talked. We debated about going even if Nick didn't get the job, acting in faith.

The next day the Lord answered. It was a "no."

I was shocked. For the last month, our plans and the trajectory of everything we had been hoping for was leading us to Raleigh. There were so many things around us confirming this to us. I didn't understand. I thought we had heard from the Lord telling us to go.

The next few weeks we kept looking online for any other job possibilities that might pop up in Raleigh. There was nothing. Nick didn't feel peace about moving without a means to provide for his family. My heart was breaking inside. I would go to church and feel hard-hearted, questioning once more all these doubts that were surfacing.

Anger and bitterness toward God started to seep into my soul. "We were supposed to go!" I would cry out to God.

After several weeks, I sat in church, and I was at the point of the bitterness becoming something scary. God spoke to me through the sermon and laid out two paths before me. One required letting go and surrendering into His arms; the other turned the bitterness into a seeping, continuous drip that would eventually harden my soul.

I went to the prayer room, once more. My faithful companion and friend, Tanya, followed me in and sat next to me as I laid it all out. Silent tears of release streamed down my cheeks as prayers were spoken over me and my broken dream, a healing balm to my heart and mind that could only come from His Spirit. I let go of all bitterness and chose to hope in Him once more. Even in the midst of this broken dream, I decided to believe that He had purpose in all of it.

Moving forward, I bought some plants for my yard to settle back into my home. My beloved neighbors, Josh and Maddy, and my dad came over as I was trying to dig holes. Seeing my struggle with the clay soil, Josh and my dad took over and dug the holes I couldn't dig on my own. Once more I was reminded of all I had in my life to be grateful for.

That Friday evening, as I was getting ready for bed and about to turn my phone off, my curiosity was piqued by a notification of an email that had just come into my box. I don't usually get new emails at 10 at night, so I decided to take a peek. As I read through it, my heart began to stir with a new hope.

Remember how I told Nick that I got a trip to New York if Raleigh didn't work out? My friend Emily was planning a trip to New York in October, and she wanted to know if I could go with her. I decided to let my sleeping husband continue sleeping so that he would be well rested when I showed him the email the next morning. In the meantime, I prayed and dreamed my way to sleep, anticipating what he would say.

The next morning, I received a "yes" from my husband.

The most humbling and amazing part about all of this is God's timing. I didn't get offered this trip while I was dealing with bitterness. He gave me room to choose to let it go. In His grace, He provided me time to release all the heartbreak and brokenness from an unfulfilled dream. Then, in spite of my struggles with all of it, He pulled out a new, beautiful dream that had been tucked away in the corner of my heart, and, unblemished, untarnished by any of my former bitterness, I was able to openly receive His gift with a joy in my heart only from the Lord.

Dear Children,

I want to encourage you in reading this. At the time, I didn't understand why we didn't get to go to Raleigh. Many things in life will come your way that you may not understand in the moment. You may not ever know the reasons in your lifetime. Once again I want to remind you that He has a much bigger, broader view of what He is doing. His gospel story goes way beyond anything we could begin to write for ourselves. Here is some real truth for you to rest in. He knows us so much better than we know ourselves, and He does want to pour His love into us. He is so patient for us that He gives us time to work through our grief, and then piece by piece, He continually restores and brings about new dreams that are so much better than anything we could have controlled or orchestrated.

That doesn't mean that there will be New York trips awaiting us on the other side of every disappointment. But it does mean, don't get stuck in bitterness. It scares me to think about where I would be right now if I hadn't gone to the prayer room at that time to lay down my bitterness and pride. So I plead and fight for you right now: In those crossroads of choosing bitterness or release, I promise you, God is big enough to take on the hurt you might be feeling towards Him over something not going how you hoped.

He wants to meet you in all of life's joys and disappointments.

He loves you so much.

Always,
Mama

Proverbs 16:9 (NASB)

The heart of man plans his way, but the Lord directs His steps.

Proverbs 14:10 (NASB)

The heart knows its own bitterness, and a stranger does not share its joy.

Hebrews 12:12–15 (ESV)

Therefore lift your drooping hands and strengthen your weak knees, and make straight paths for your feet, so that what is lame may not be put out of joint but rather be healed. Strive for peace with everyone, and for the holiness without which no one will see the Lord. See to it that no one fails to obtain the grace of God; that no "root of bitterness" springs up and causes trouble, and by it many become defiled.

Proverbs 19:21 (ESV)

Many are the plans in the mind of a man, but it is the purpose of the Lord that will stand.

Visiting Statue of Liberty & views at night from Rockefellar Center

Emily my companion for the trip & taking a bike ride around Central Park

My first New York Pizza & a Picnic in the middle of Central Park

NYC skyline views from the top of the MET & taking a pause at Grand Central Station

An amazing meal of fresh pasta from the Eataly

Eating our "Razzles" on the Brooklyn Bridge (think "13 Going on 30) [37]

My hope is built on nothing less than Jesus' blood and righteousness.

I dare not trust the sweetest frame, but wholly lean on Jesus' name.

On Christ the Solid Rock I stand, all other ground is sinking sand.

All other ground is sinking sand.[38]

✌ ANGER, ANXIETY, AND MENDING THE SOUL ✌

After I returned from New York, there were many things I was reflecting on in my life. I remember sitting in church on Sunday, and during a sermon given by Pastor Dom, I heard God very clearly speak to my heart, asking me if I was ready to get back into being part of His Big Gospel Story and stop sitting on the sidelines in my struggles of depression. I knew I wanted that badly.

God had work to do in me. He had brought me to a place where it was time for His healing work to take shape in the remains of the broken pieces of my soul.

It started with going to a women's brunch. After several years of almost non-existent women's ministry, God was starting to birth something new at the church. At the brunch, there was discussion and information about upcoming events. I was intrigued by a class entitled, "Anger and Anxiety." Not knowing what to expect, but knowing I had struggles I needed to sort through, I signed up.

This class was four weeks long, and on the first night, we received our official assignment. We were to create our own form of "Stones of Remembrance." In Joshua, the Israelites carried stones across the Jordan river and set them up to be their stones of Remembrance, so that when they saw them, they would remember what the Lord had done in bringing them out of Israel and into their promised land.

It was to be a visual reminder of all the ways God had been faithful to us, and with each "stone," there would be a word to represent that part of our story. I had a collection of stories I had already written, and I thought if I put them into a box, the kids could read them as they got older and remember His faithfulness to our family. But Vickie, the leader of the group, encouraged me to come up with something simpler and more tangible. God gave me a picture of a tree firmly planted by the water. It was bearing fruit, and each fruit had a word on it, representing a story of His faithfulness.

I purchased a large art board and some good quality colored pencils, then I came home and drew my tree, planted by the water, bearing fruit. I added my favorite verses and a song of faithfulness the Lord gave to me. Then I framed it.

As I wrote a word on each fruit, I was reminded of how faithful God has been in my life, and how His faithfulness had not ceased even in the dark parts of my life. Just because there were broken pieces did not mean He couldn't cause fruit to grow there. I realized I needed to keep myself planted next to His stream, and He would grow the fruit in my life.

As I opened up and shared my "Stones of Remembrance," I knew I was on the right track to healing.

A few months went by and I was approached by Vickie. She was looking to lead another class called "Mending the Soul." This was a class to help women walk through and find healing from abuse in their past. She shared that her purpose was to walk through it with about six women, and she hoped other leaders would emerge from the group to facilitate their own "Mending the Soul" classes. She asked if I would pray about being part of that. I was thrilled with the idea of finally having a role[39] at church again—a place to serve, to be part of the Big Gospel Story. I talked to Nick about it, we prayed through it, and we decided to make the time for me to take the class.

As I talked through the class a little more with Vickie, she mentioned that not everyone would become a leader. Sometimes God had different purposes for the class. But I was confident that this did not apply to me. I did not have much abuse in my childhood. There were only a couple minor incidents, but I knew my story was not filled with it. Not like so many others. I was doing this so I could be equipped to help others.

I was wrong. Very, very wrong. We started going through the curriculum, and I learned pretty early on that there are many forms of abuse other than the obvious sexual and physical abuse. God started bringing to mind events that had taken place a few years back. He helped me start to put names to the things that had been done—the spiritual abuse, the forms of manipulation, and the verbal abuse that had occurred and taken deep root inside me. Gently, God started bringing those realizations to the forefront through this class, bringing me to a place where He could begin to heal and restore me.

When I reached the pages on Isolation, I hit a huge wall. That was about all the processing my heart could take in that season. Isolation, guarding my heart and protecting myself, was exactly what I had been doing these last few years. And in protecting myself, I had hurt new people who had tried to get in. I wasn't able to get much further in the book. Vickie said that was normal, that often women get to a certain place and that is all they can do. Then maybe they take the class another time and get a little further, or find healing in a different part of their life. I knew by the end of the class that I was not ready to lead a group. God's purpose had not been for me to have some high calling to help abused women—at least not at that time. It was for Him to heal me.

I now understand in part why we didn't go to Raleigh. If we had gone, I would not have had that next year, when He was able to help me sort through and heal from all the broken things that had happened in my life. Raleigh had represented a fresh start to me, a "do-over" after all the loss and hurt I had experienced. It was an easy way out. But it would not have been easy, because there were steps God still needed to take in my life that would not have taken place if we hadn't stayed that year in Oregon. We may not always understand in the moment, but I now know very clearly one of the main reasons why we didn't go to Raleigh is because God was not done working things out in me. Out of His mercy and kindness, He said no.

Dear Children,

One of the best gifts God gave me in this year, as He continually worked to bring healing to my heart, was a reminder of His faithfulness. Walking through the Stones of Remembrance and listing out all of the ways He was faithful helped me rebuild some foundational pieces that had cracked and been broken. Spending time to refresh and renew my mind with all He has already done in my life was key to begin to rebuild.

Taking that class stirred the reminder in me of the story that I had stopped writing. This book I am finishing the final pages of as we speak, was brought back to life from the Lord, when He showed me once more that I needed to write this for you. He showed me that it would speak into your lives the times He has been faithful to me, to our family.

His ways are so much better than ours. He had things He was asking me to do. I had been paralyzed by my mind for three years. It was now time to pick up my mat and walk, to rejoin His Big Gospel Story and the part He was asking me to play.

I love you, Children. In the areas where you have been broken, where you have walked through difficult times, I pray right now that the Lord will bring the healing you need in the right time, to bring you to a place of wholeness with Him. We live with broken people, we as broken people are hurt by people, and we hurt people. But don't allow that to define who you are, because He wants to take those weaknesses and make beautiful things out of them.

Pick up your mats, and follow Him. Time to join in His Gospel Story.

I Love You,
Mama

Matthew 9:6–8 (ESV)

"But that you may know that the Son of Man has authority on earth to forgive sins," He then said to the paralytic— "Rise, pick up your bed and go home." And he rose and went home. When the crowds saw it, they were afraid and they glorified God, who had given such authority to men.

John 8:12 (ESV)

Again Jesus spoke to them, saying, "I am the light of the world. Whoever follows me will not walk in darkness, but will have the light of life."

Joshua 4:20–24 (ESV)

And those twelve stones, which they took out of the Jordan, Joshua set up at Gilgal. And he said to the people of Israel, "When your children ask their fathers in times to come, 'What do these stones mean?' then you shall let your children know, 'Israel passed over this Jordan on dry ground.' For the Lord your God dried up the waters of the Jordan for you until you passed over, as the Lord your God did to the Red Sea, which He dried up for us until we passed over, so that the peoples of the earth may know that the hand of the Lord is mighty, that you may fear the Lord your God forever."

⚜ STUCK ⚜

While I was in the middle of Mending the Soul, I had a breakdown when my Josh and Maddy neighbors announced they were moving. Then our beloved extra grandma neighbor also shared that she was moving. My stable neighborhood was changing, and people I loved and cared about were not going to be a constant in my days anymore. One night I drove home from my class in tears after receiving a text from a different neighbor letting me know that Josh and Maddy had put a realtor's lockbox on their home. It hurt so badly, and I hated it.

I started to feel antsy over my life. Over things to come. I felt stuck in this house that reminded me so much of the brokenness that had taken place when we opened our home to another family for a time. I felt frustrated that we hadn't moved to Raleigh. The class had hit a huge nerve of loss of control over change in my life. I always felt like everyone else left, while I got left behind. Suddenly, I didn't want to be in that neighborhood or in our home on the hill anymore. I begged and pleaded and cried with Nick. I told him I didn't want to be there anymore. I didn't want to stay and remember how that family had left us, and now our Josh and Maddy were leaving us too. I kept using the word stuck—I felt so stuck.

Nick prayed much for me during that time. And then he shocked me. He told me we could move. The market was booming. Josh and Maddy had sold their home within three days of listing it. We needed to handle things differently, though. We would look and see what was available, then once we found a home and our offer was accepted, we would put our house on the hill up for sale. This involved a little risk, but it was riskier to do it the other way.

Nothing about the move was easy for me. In fact, I felt huge regret over our decision after we sold our home. It did nothing to bring me the peace and resolution I had hoped for. I wanted to run back the other way and take back all my decisions. But Nick, like a rock, said, "Nope, we have made our decision.

We are moving." I dealt with a lot of doubt—it was the first time in my life I didn't have peace from the Lord about making a decision to move.

Honestly, it was not the wisest financial choice long term, either. I couldn't see what lay ahead of us in the coming year. However, what I do know is this: In our new home, God brought more healing into my life. He brought me to a place of refuge with Him like I had not experienced for a long time. It was my first year with all my children in full-time school, and I was not sure what He wanted me to do with my time. That year at the Night of Prayer, I received the card, "The Lord is My Shepherd."

I experienced having everything I needed in that home. Not because of the home, but because He set me free, and He gave me everything I needed. I started to dream again and make plans for things to come with Him. I was ready to engage fully and completely in the Big Gospel Story that He was creating. It was no longer a time to live in fear, but to be at rest with Him and let Him lead me and guide me on paths of righteousness for His name's sake. I didn't know what it would look like, but I knew that He would be with me in any and every circumstance.

I want to share something I have witnessed over and over in my life and in the lives of those around me as I get older. There is no end to brokenness on this side of eternity. Things change, people get hurt, or hurt people, sin happens, and there is a constant battle between what God intended this earth to be, and sin and Satan and fallen things destroying it.

But God. But God is continuously faithful. He is good. He is our Shepherd. He is everything we need. Those are words of truth to rest in. When we can live in a constant state of remembrance of all He has done in the good seasons and hard, broken places, He fills us up with His hope. He is constantly fighting for us and desiring to bring His redemption and beauty into our lives.

Rest in that and stand in His truth.

Dear Children,

This was a time when I wanted a change in our family's circumstances to bring healing to my broken heart. I couldn't handle being left by people I cared about so much. Of course, other people's choices to move and change their lives are just a natural course of life—change is something that continually takes course throughout our days—but this particular change felt like the last straw. I had felt a safety net with our Josh and Maddy neighbors, and now it was being taken away, and the feeling of being stuck had reached a point I was not able to cope with.

I felt a complete loss of control, and my plan was simply me grasping at anything I could to mend it. Instead of surrendering this change to the Lord, I decided to try to control the change by making change myself. After we decided to list our home, I felt regret over the decision because I hadn't made it with a right heart before the Lord. My heart tailspinned to a new level of loss of control. Taking charge didn't fix the problem. It complicated it. When I finally arrived at our new landing place, I saw truth that brought my heart to a place of peace.

I badgered my husband to sell the house. I may not have had the right intentions behind my request, but my husband prayed for me. He prayed over the decision, and God gave him peace to move forward in selling our home, which meant that even though I was struggling with leaning into the Lord, my husband was not.

And what I witnessed in those days was nothing short of incredible. Your dad stepped into a role of caring for our family like never before. During the next few months as we transitioned into our new home, Nick gave of himself to me through his actions. We bought a home that needed fixing, and Nick labored to make it a beautiful place for us to start fresh.

At first, I dealt with feelings of guilt that it was all my fault we had made this move. This did not bring encouragement to my husband. He took my fretting as complaining that he wasn't doing a good enough job. Once I realized what I had been doing to him, God shut my mouth and helped me come to a place of contentment. I found a new role in supporting my husband with my words and encouragement. And I found a safe landing place, knowing my husband was leaning into the Lord, leading and taking care of me and our family.

Children, sometimes in life, we make mistakes or choose to solve problems on our own, instead of surrendering to the Lord. That is a scary place to be. It's not a wise way to handle anything.

I am so grateful for your father, who loved all of us well through it and took us to a place where we could find refuge. I know it was hard to leave our neighborhood that we had loved being part of. I am sorry my struggles took us to that point.

What I want you to remember is that just like you have an earthly father who loves you so well and fights to take care of you, you have a Heavenly Father who, even when we try to take control of our lives, still loves us and wants to bring us back to peace and contentment with Him, and longs for us to find our refuge in the one thing that is constant and never changing. He is our Refuge. No matter what the circumstances, we can always be at home with Him.

I Love You Always,
Mama

Mark 14:36 (ESV)

And Jesus said, "Abba, Father, all things are possible for you. Remove this cup from me. Yet not what I will, but what you will."

Psalm 52:7–9 (ESV)

See the man who would not make God his refuge, but trusted in the abundance of his own riches and sought refuge in his own destruction! But I am like a green olive tree in the house of God. I trust in the steadfast love of God forever and ever. I will thank You forever, because You have done it. I will wait for Your name, for it is good, in the presence of the godly.

Psalm 57:1–3 (ESV)

Be merciful to me, O God, be merciful to me, for in You my soul takes refuge; in the shadow of Your wings I will take refuge, till the storms of destruction pass by. I cry out to God Most High, to God who fulfills His purpose for me. He will send from heaven and save me; He will put to shame him who tramples on me. Selah. God will send out His steadfast love and His faithfulness!

The School Paths

⚜ SCHOOL DECISIONS ⚜

Our school decisions have always been something we have taken to the Lord and spent much time praying over for our children. Our decisions have not been lightly made, but have involved much researching and wrestling over options and seeking wisdom and opinions from others who have gone before us. It is something we have poured much time into. And when you make a school decision, you don't make plans in order to change them every few years. But God has placed us in different schools in a variety of seasons of our lives. It's not what I would have chosen if I were planning it all myself, but that's why I'm not in charge. He does know best, and I figure it is wise to go with His leading on things. I wanted to take some time to reflect on the way He has led us through school situations.

When looking at preschool options for Josiah, we enrolled him at preschool in Tigard for a three-year-old class where my mom was teaching. We thought it would be a great experience for Grandma to get to be his teacher for one year. However, I felt a lack of peace over the summer prior to school starting. God laid it on my heart to keep him home one more year, to work on school with him at home, and to enroll him in sports classes through the rec center instead. I never regretted that decision, never looked back. I loved having that year with him. That was the year I also got pregnant with the twins.

In December of 2008, we started thinking about options for Josiah again. Would I homeschool him? We really felt like he was learning a lot, but that he could also use an education in how to socialize with other children. We looked into preschool options and couldn't find anything that fit the bill. He was already doing a little bit of kindergarten math and knew all his letters and the sounds they make, so we wanted something that would be challenging for him if we were going to pay the money.

A few people started mentioning preschool at a church in Beaverton. We looked into it a little more. It was close to our home, and it offered an extended program for four-year-olds to stay an extra hour and a half and be challenged if they needed it. We were sold—it sounded like it would be perfect for Josiah.

I showed up early for enrollment the day they opened it to the public. We snagged the very last spot for Josiah in the extended class. I was overwhelmed by God's provision, and super nervous about having my oldest boy head off to preschool the coming fall. Over the summer we found out I would have to be on bed rest right when Josiah's school started. I wondered if we should keep him home, but friends and family stepped up to take Josiah to and from preschool.

His preschool was a perfect fit for him. His teacher was really top notch. She was very patient and kind with the children. She looked at her job as a ministry, and she did it well. It was nice to be set for preschool, but right around the corner the school year was fast approaching, and we needed to make a decision about kindergarten. We thought we knew where we were going to send Josiah, but when the kindergarten teacher there told us she didn't know how she would keep him challenged, we were stumped.

We had some good talks with Josiah's preschool teacher, and she was so insightful. We agreed that typical homeschooling would be amazing for Josiah except for the social aspect, and in his case, we felt a school setting would be good as well. She asked if I would consider an alternative option. She then shared about a unique school that offered three days a week of private school, and sent schoolwork home on Tuesdays and Thursdays so that you could homeschool those days.

This was a school I had heard about when Josiah was a baby, and I thought it sounded like a great concept for our family someday. At that time Nick was unsure about it, so I didn't push. But now our beloved preschool teacher was suggesting it as something to consider. All of the sudden, my heart started to wonder if maybe it would be a good fit. Nick and I had a lot going on during this time of decision making. We had baby twins at home with two-year-old Ava, and we were trying to sell our townhouse and keep it clean all the time. It was a very busy season.

One morning I woke up early to read my Bible, pray, and exercise—a typical morning routine for me. Nick was on a business trip. I emailed the principal at the school, just to see what the situation was for enrollment in the kindergarten class next year. He emailed right away and told me there was one spot left. Nick and I hadn't visited the school yet...but we had talked about our thoughts on if it would be a good place for Josiah to excel. Not wanting to push Nick, I emailed him the information the principal had given me and then went about my early morning doing an exercise routine and trying not to think about that last spot. I carried out a continuous prayer for God to lead us in that decision. At 7:30 a.m., Nick called me and said, "Enroll him, Kari."

I emailed the principal back and told him we would like to register Josiah and hopefully do the follow-up interview and tour later. I also told him that I would not be able to drop off the forms and check until I took Josiah to preschool, so it would be after 9:00 a.m. He wrote back right away and said he would hold the spot for Josiah, and to bring in the paperwork as soon as I could.

When I arrived at the school, I found the principal in his office reading his Bible. Peace filled my heart from the Lord. In the core of my soul, I knew this was a good choice. As I sat down in his office with the paperwork, the principal shared that it was a good thing we had emailed this morning, because right after he promised the last spot to Josiah, another family came through the doors to register their child. We had gotten the last spot. Again. My heart filled with humility and gratefulness to God, not because we had snagged the last spot and someone else hadn't gotten it, but because God knew exactly where Josiah was supposed to be and had provided in a way we would not forget.

The following year when Josiah entered first grade, once again God gave us an amazing teacher who helped us figure out that having him skip a year of school would help put him in a place where he could be successful. When it came time to register Josiah for second grade, the school opened up a spot so that he could go straight to third instead. That year, Josiah thrived so much at school. The boys in his class were a great fit for him. It was so cool to see his excitement in learning about rocks and minerals and studying animals. It was clear this was a good decision for Josiah.

God has worked in ways with Ava, too. We put her in three-year-old preschool at the same preschool Josiah had attended, and she loved it. But then we began to think about logistics for four-year-old preschool and the distance it was from our new home. I would need to pick her up during the middle of the twins' naps, so we decided to look for another school. One of the moms from the preschool got wind of it and told me she would bring Ava home every day for the school year, so she could stay with her friends. I was blown away by her kindness. I just get so amazed at how caring and thoughtful people can be. It was such a good example of Christ's love in my family.

When Ava moved into kindergarten, the Tuesday and Thursday homeschool days became a struggle between us. She did really well learning in a social environment, but on our days at home it sometimes felt like pulling teeth to get her to do school. And while she was working on something, I had to keep Josiah focused on his schoolwork and help him with any direction he needed. The twins would enter the mix and tear apart the house unsupervised, or take turns throwing tantrums because they "wanted me." I started feeling spread very thin.

This was the year we walked through the fire in our own home, when we had the extra family living with us for five months, and when I entered my battle with depression. The pain and loss we were witnessing sometimes felt too heavy to bear. We talked for a while about how our children might need different things in education. Right after the New Year, when we had our first full homeschool day—complete with a kitchen faucet breaking off and leaking water underneath the sink, me getting frustrated and yelling at my children, cats throwing up on carpet, working on getting food made for the day, and Ava trying to read a page of words with her concentration constantly interrupted by the twins—I was spent trying to divide myself up.

I realized I couldn't do it all anymore. I was dreading Tuesdays and Thursdays. I was not being Christ's love to my children. It was heartbreaking to me. I thought I could handle it, but it just was not going well anymore. Nick and I started talking about it that night, which turned into a week of staying up in the evenings, talking and praying through what we should do. We first thought maybe we should keep Josiah at his current school, and move Ava into a five-day-a-week school—a place where she could be successful—and I could take on the role of cheerleader and move out of the teacher role.

As we talked more, we knew we wanted a school that Josiah could transfer to in fifth or sixth grade. This was something we planned to do when the kids got older. I did not feel equipped to teach middle school and above. Josiah was doing so well, and we had just skipped him up a grade into a new class. But then we started contemplating if it was time to consider moving him with Ava. The idea of switching things up again for him did not sit well with me at first.

We realized that it would still be a stressful situation to have me divided between two schools, trying to be involved in two places, having two homeschool days, trying to pour into Mallory and Lena, who were getting the short end of the attention stick so often...this is where it got hard for me. We looked again at the big picture and realized that it would be much more difficult to change Josiah's schooling in middle school than if we were to do it going into fourth grade. If we made this earlier change, it could help him get roots in where he would—Lord willing—be attending the rest of his primary school years through high school. As we prayed more, we realized that God was not just leading us to move Ava to a five-day-a-week school, but also Josiah.

We visited a full-time private school just a short drive from our home. As we toured the halls of this new school, everything inside me wanted to cringe. I didn't want to be here. I didn't want my children here. Not because it was a bad school, but because it wasn't my family. My community. But deep down, I had a peace that surpasses all understanding that it was where we were supposed to move our children. I knew that when we came home and Nick and I discussed our options, in the end the decision was going to be to send Josiah and Ava to school here.

We told Josiah that night, and at first he seemed fine with it. But after the kids went to bed, he came downstairs and was having a difficult time sleeping...then he burst into tears and cried for us to not take him out of his current school. We talked and prayed and cried with him that evening. My heart sank as I began to think of all that we were going to be giving up, starting with the amazing community of families there—we had been so blessed by them all. He begged a few more times for us to change our minds. After we sent him to bed, Nick and I talked some more. Nick reaffirmed to me that it was the best decision. It was a great opportunity for us to walk Josiah through a difficult change and show him, when he looked back on it a few years down the road, God's faithfulness and provision in it all.

My heart still was not sold on the decision, but as we went to meet the principal at the new school the following week, and the first thing she wanted to do was pray for our time together, God's peace flooded my soul. As she covered us in prayer, the Holy Spirit confirmed to me that this was going to be our kids' new school home. For the sake of our children, we knew we had to do it, so that we could make sure our children were taken care of while I got better.

We filled out our admission papers, and on March 1 of that year, we received official confirmation that we made it into the school. They would start at the new school in the fall. We started saying goodbye over the next few months to those families and teachers we loved. I hated it. I knew I had to do it for my children. I knew I could not do homeschooling in this season anymore, and that it was the right decision. But my heart broke over the loss. It ached over watching my son, who didn't want to leave our school, learning to say goodbye. Finishing his third-grade year, he was the most affected by the loss and change.

One gift of hope in the middle of this transition was that I was going to have more time to pour into Mallory and Lena. For the first three years of their lives, they had been carted around to wherever the bigger siblings needed to go. That would now change. I would get to give them a year of, "What would Mallory and Lena like to do?" I could also focus on some much-needed training with hopes to curb the tantrums that were very prevalent in that season.

We made the decision to enroll them in the same preschool Josiah and Ava had attended. They were so cute—they thought they started school the day I dropped off enrollment forms. They packed up their backpacks and walked into the office with them as we dropped off their registration. It was hard to explain to these three-year-olds that they would have to wait seven more months. I started to dream about taking them on field trips, watching them make little friends for themselves, and seeing God develop character in their lives.

I clung to the words the kindergarten teacher at the school we were leaving covered me with when I talked to her about our decision. She asked me if I remembered why the Israelites were going to leave Egypt. I did not have an answer. She said God called them out because He wanted them to worship Him. God was calling our family out of the homeschool role, so that I would no longer live a life of checklists, being a very good Martha. Instead, He was going to provide a little more time for me to be a Mary and sit at His feet and worship. I never could see through the business of it all how much that was missing in my life.

Honestly, once we started at the new school, our schedule did not slow down to give me the real chance to be Mary at Jesus' feet right away. It shifted to being busy in different ways. It was definitely a healthier environment for everyone in our family, but I was still scurrying about to get my children to where they needed to be. I knew my year to be a full time Mary was coming soon. I did my best to cherish the days my twins were not at preschool and was grateful for the release of the pressure of being responsible for my children's home education.

That summer was a dread for Josiah. He was unsettled and anxious, and we all felt that turmoil inside of him. It was a long-drawn out summer filled with the unknown of what the new school year would bring. We prayed much over him and for him. We found out that more than half the students in Josiah's class would be new to the school, which brought a little peace to me, knowing he would not be alone.

Then that first day of school came. I walked them to their classes in the unfamiliar territory before me and new faces that I didn't know. Some of my anxious thoughts were relieved that night, when my son came home all smiles, saying, "I had no fun at all!" He was very loud and hyped up, partly from the Dairy Queen Blizzard my husband had given him on his way home. We knew he was settled and that both Josiah and Ava would be okay.

However, I had more loss to grieve that first year. Waves of sadness washed over me when I sat at school soccer games watching Josiah, with no one to talk to, feeling so lost and alone. I remember coming home and crying for half an hour one time after I picked my children up in carline from school. I had gotten reprimanded because I had not done carline correctly, and I was so embarrassed and confused. I felt completely awkward as a mom at this new school. I kept the tears hidden behind my sunglasses to keep my children from seeing my sadness in the midst of the light they were starting to see at their new school. I would not squelch their hope of new adventures in this place. The continued waves of feeling lost and unseen rolled over me, humbling my once elevated identity into new forms of identity theft. I didn't know who I was anymore. I didn't place my identity where it needed to be.

I thought I would get more involved that year at the school, but it quickly became evident that both Josiah and Ava were taken care of. I needed to pour some time and love into Mallory and Lena, who had taken a bit of the brunt of being dragged around everywhere their older siblings needed to go in the years prior. I let go of the hopes of volunteering and instead attended the occasional class party, putting my focus on my twins' preschool experience and the time I had at home with them on their days off.

I slowly began to heal and process through the loss. God continued to show me the redemption He was performing in the midst of those dark moments when I struggled with so much hopelessness and loss. And He taught me that my identity is in Him. Period. He was once more speaking into my life that He is a God who sees me. He is my Redeemer who makes beautiful things out of brokenness.

Dear Children,

Your dad and I have been put in the position, as your parents, of making decisions for you while you are young. What I hope and pray you see in all of this is the time we took in praying through those decisions. We sought the Lord as we weighed our options. And when the timing was right, He showed us what to do, and we had His peace covering our decisions.

It got harder to navigate as you all started to reach school age and we needed to think through what would be best for each person, and overall the wisest for our family. It is a hard balance to figure out. Even some of the best-made decisions, when walking through the results, didn't always turn out the way we hoped.

Our prayer has been and will continue to be that in walking through these decisions with schools, our stability would never rest in a place, but in Christ alone. Our identity isn't found in where we go to school, where we work, who our friends are, our church body, or even the family we have. All of those things can change or get taken away from us. But when we set our anchor of hope on Christ, He will never leave us, never forsake us. He is our hope.

I love you, Children. May your identity always rest in Him alone.

Love,
Your Mama

Romans 15:13 (NASB)

Now may the God of hope fill you with all joy and peace in believing, so that you will abound in hope by the power of the Holy Spirit.

Hebrews 6:19–20 (NASB)

This hope we have as an anchor of the soul, a hope both sure and steadfast and one which enters within the veil, where Jesus has entered as a forerunner for us, having become a high priest forever according to the order of Melchizedek.

Psalm 40:4a (NASB)

How blessed is the man who has made the Lord his trust.

﹌ HE IS MY SHEPHERD AND EVERYTHING I NEED ﹌

In the middle of our second year at the school in Aloha, we spent a good month praying about what we should do for Mallory and Lena as they were getting ready to graduate from preschool. I didn't want them to go into full-time kindergarten. I wanted them to go to the original school we had left, so I could do part-time private, part-time homeschool with my babies of the family, who were growing up way too quickly. Nick and I took a date night to pray at both campuses and seek the Lord on what we should do. After taking the time and doing a little more inquiring, it became evident that God wanted all of our children together at the same school. We enrolled them at our older children's school.

As we entered into our third year there, I started to feel settled. The horizon of the future sat broadly before me, and I could picture our family at this school until they all graduated high school. I had dreams of my kids maybe marrying high school sweethearts someday... For Josiah, the teachers were so great at working to keep him challenged. This being his first year of middle school, he was thriving and it was a joy to see. Ava was plugging along doing well in her class, social as ever. I began volunteering at the school, specifically in Mallory and Lena's class. I fell in love with these beautiful kindergartners and pictured getting to be "Mama Kari" to these kids as they grew older. I hoped they would find a safe place with me, as I was making long-term plans and dreams to stay committed to this class all the way to graduation. I started to get to know the staff and build relationships with all of these people who had been caring for my children. For the first time in three years, I was finding my own sense of belonging in this place.

Yet there were some sad, dark things stirring and lurking under the surface. In January of that school year, on a Sunday afternoon, my friend drove me home from our weekly ritual of eating out after church with our family friends. We talked a little bit about school decisions. I talked through something that God was showing me. I had been struggling with a tighter budget this year for extra yearly expenditures, and although we had enough for our children's upcoming school expenses, I wondered if we should pull our younger girls out and I should homeschool them, to save money. I had this stipulation that I wanted to guarantee we could afford private school when we got to high school. Since I didn't know and couldn't control what the future held, I wanted to control it now, and in my bubble of control I wanted to make sure we would have our savings. Nick was sure we should keep our kids all in school, so I let go of that.

The realization hit me. I was trying to control things that had not unfolded yet. I wanted to manipulate the future to guarantee the things that I, Mama Kari, wanted for my children. There was no surrender there. Realizing the sadness in this choice, I had to let go once more. It was a good revelation for me. Once more Pastor Phil's words he had spoken on the day Josiah was born came back to me. That even if things worked out and we were given Josiah, he didn't belong to us. He belongs to the Lord. Was I really giving the Lord my children completely, laying down my Isaacs before the Lord in complete surrender?

Monday morning of that week came. I looked ahead at my Bible reading: Job and James. You know, there is something about both of those books that—when it comes time to spend reading them—you realize there is just no guarantee of what could get shaken, right? Monday afternoon, we received an email from our principal at our children's school. She was resigning.

We were shocked and concerned. There was no explanation. We started to pursue and pray for answers. Her heart and passion for the school, the vision and direction she was bringing about, was the reason we wanted to be there. When we started to unravel some disagreement between our principal and the leadership over the school about where she was taking it, our concern elevated. What were those differences? And if they were big differences, what could we expect for our children the next year? A meeting announcement went out for Thursday night, when they would discuss what was going on.

On Wednesday, a night Josiah normally has youth group, he came home sick from school. It was a weird sickness—we thought he was going to get the stomach bug, but instead he just rested and read books the rest of the afternoon, so we kept him home from youth group. This ended up being a big, unexpected blessing, because it gave Nick and me a chance to process. Nick and I talked about and prayed through what our options would be if things fell apart—what we would do. We decided to make an appointment to tour a different school the day after the big meeting was scheduled to share the new direction at our school. We were hoping to cancel that tour, that our fears would be relieved once we went to that meeting, and it would just be some minor changes that we could handle.

We started to get the feeling something big was about to happen. In the middle of our prayers, our principal responded to an email we had sent her regarding why she had resigned. She was very vague, but she said that she and her husband had prayed and fasted over this decision, and she used the word "clarity" in her message to us. When I read those words, a weird peace fell over me. God was showing me something very clearly. Nick and I could not put our stability in our children's school situation. It needed to rest in God alone. And no matter how this turned out, He would be with us. I fell to my knees, and we prayed for clarity over the situation and rested that night knowing He was with us in this.

Thursday night came. All of us parents filled the room, unsure of what was to come. If I think through what I was looking for that evening, I hoped for answers about simple questions...like if their vision was different than our principal's, would they still keep the same form of testing that we appreciate? How would the offering of classes look like for the next year? What would they do with technology, and would my children continue to be challenged in the areas God has wired each one of them? Simple questions like that.

As the meeting began, and speaking and questions and answers began, we saw something deep and dark and unexpected. An understanding of the foundation of the school and how it was operated was revealed to us. And as the meeting progressed, our hearts slowly began to break, yet we hoped that light might still be found. Sadly, by the end of the meeting, we knew. Our prayer for clarity was answered. Nick and I drove home in tears, filled with sadness, and I realized the one thing I never, ever wanted to do again to my son—to my children, but especially to my son—we were going to need to do.

We came home to Josiah, who we had asked for the very first time to babysit our girls. He is growing up so fast. Sitting down with him, we told him that we were going to have to look for another school. We could not put our children under the leadership that was left at the school. Unless something drastic changed, we would be finishing out our year here, and then moving ahead.

It's so hard to see your children, who you love and want to protect from pain like this, walk through the hurt of it. But it's an opportunity, a chance for us to trust our children and their life circumstances to the Lord. It's a chance to walk alongside them when they are young and show them that we are there to help them navigate through all the hurt and pain they might be feeling, to pray with them, and to show them that in this life, things do fall apart. Not everything goes the way we plan.

The thing I have learned and seen in my years of walking with the Lord is that if we didn't have these trials, and everything went perfectly in our life, it would be very easy not to see our need for Jesus. I know I need Him, and I know my children need Him, and even though I hate that Satan brings darkness which looks to kill, steal, and destroy, I believe with all my heart that it is where God does His greatest works in redeeming the yuck and making beautiful things from the dust. It's a chance to find hope in Him once more, to lean into Him when it hurts, and to find our comfort in Him, believing Him to be faithful, and believing that someday we will be able to praise Him for what He did in the midst of the brokenness.

As the weeks progressed, I watched all these families that I had more fully opened my heart up to over that school year. There were many broken hearts, dreams that were crashing and hopes that would not be fulfilled at this school.

You know what I found? First, that all four of our children were definitely supposed to be at this school this year. We needed to be there, to be fully present for all of our children, so we could support them and walk through this together.

Second, that God had prepared me for such a time as this. My years of grieving and losing our first school had shown me how to have empathy and love for those that had been so deeply vested in this school for many years. He showed me how to pray, how to be quiet, and how to lean into Him. There were many days that followed that were not easy for many of the families, including ours. He made it evident inside of me that it was an opportunity to show them that He loved them, and He wanted to take their dreams and hopes and broken hearts, and pick up the pieces to begin new works in all of this brokenness. Satan wanted to mess up and cause division—he is good at that—and sadly, there was much of it, but our God is greater and He is the Master Creator of new things. I rested in the truth that it was not finished yet. Jesus would take victory once more. We may not see exactly what that looks like in the moment, but I am confident that looking back, we will see His Redemption stories in many families.

My Beautiful Children,

I am so sorry. I know that the road we had to walk through from this brokenness has been so hard for you. You have had to sacrifice much of the things you loved, the relationships you loved, and in a very difficult way, you have had to start over from scratch. That is such a hard thing to do. The brokenness caused by change, and also by sin, is not without hope. We have a Redeemer God who is always at work making new things. I am confident that God will use this in Mighty Ways in your lives, if you let Him. There is always temptation to turn these hurts into bitterness and doubts, but that is exactly what Satan would want you to do. Take the bitterness and hurts back to Jesus. He understands the deep pain that you carry, and He wants you to give it to Him, so He can make new things out of the loss.

There will be many things like this in your life as you grow up. I pray that you can learn how to walk with Jesus in the suffering and in the season of joy. May His will be done. Always. In all circumstances. I pray that each of you live this way, no matter what other people have done. I love you so much. You are all incredible.

Your Mama Always,

Kari

James 1:12 (ESV)

Blessed is the man who remains steadfast under trial, for when he has stood the test he will receive the crown of life, which God has promised to those who love Him.

Isaiah 43:19 (NASB)

Behold, I will do something new, now it will spring forth; will you not be aware of it? I will make a roadway in the wilderness, rivers in the desert.

Jeremiah 17:8 (ESV)

He is like a tree planted by the water, that sends out its roots by the stream, and does not fear when heat comes, for its leaves remain green, and is not anxious in the year of drought, for it does not cease to bear fruit.

Philippians 4:11–13 (NASB)

Not that I speak from want, for I have learned to be content in whatever circumstances I am. I know how to get along with humble means, and I know how to live in prosperity; in any and every circumstance I have learned the secret of being filled and going hungry, both having abundance and suffering need. I can do all things through Him who strengthens me.

He is Our Stability...He is Our Home

MEMORIES OF MY HOMES

Years ago I had the privilege of attending a Mary Courson retreat—twice. Even though it was the same story both times, I was so blessed and encouraged by her way of sharing her life so beautifully and the ways God has worked in it. It truly is an example of older women teaching younger women and I loved it! She wrote a book that was just more details of what she shared at her retreats: Fragrant Pathways.[40]

One of the topics she wrote about was homes. She wrote about all the different homes she lived in, the memories she cherished from them, and the time spent in them. I am going to pull a copycat, and do that myself. I think it is a beautiful way to end this book that the Lord has given me to share.

In my room there is a framed picture—it's really a puzzle Nick and I put together one Christmas break—of a Thomas Kincaid painting, a beautiful home with lights glowing on the inside. I picture that as my home that God is preparing for me someday. It is a simple little cottage with beautiful flowers outside, and it just seems homey and inviting, a place where others could come and be blessed. So that is my heavenly home someday that I look forward to.

The first home I remember was my childhood home. It was an old farmhouse, now over 100 years old. I loved that house. There was a garden that my parents planted each summer. My dad built us a very cool tree house in the back in one of the apple trees, with a homemade swing. One year he had a bunch of friends come and help pour concrete in the back to make a patio, and we all got to put our handprints in it, even Pooh Bear, the kitty. My dad also turned the attic upstairs into three bedrooms. My bedroom had a curtain closet that I made into my little writing room, where I would make up stories and dream about things. I was given a typewriter by a friend's mom, which I put in there, and I would type out stories and I even typed out a newspaper for a while. This was the home of my dreams, where I was allowed to be a dreamer. I would look outside my window and watch people go by and dream.

I was going to be the next L.M. Montgomery or Louisa May Alcott—I was sure of it.

The downstairs floor was hardwood, and it made great floors for "ice skating" in socks. That was the house my parents brought my baby sister home to. It gave me a beautiful picture of a mom who would spend her afternoons sewing clothes for us kids while watching us play from her bedroom window, and a dad who could do anything in the way of fixing and constructing things. He even put in a basketball court where we would shoot hoops together in the evenings sometimes. It was the home where I learned my love of music. It was a great house.

It was old, though, and I remember carpenter ants that would show up every year—those were really gross. One year right after Halloween, I had a bunch of candy wrappers in my garbage can, which they found and crawled around on. As I started killing them, they started crawling on me. I developed a deep dislike—no, a deep hate—for ants that day.

When I was in middle school, my parents decided to sell that house and move into a newer home that had more basics, such as more than one bathroom for our family of five. This was the home where I finished growing up. My dad put a wall up in the family room downstairs and created a room for me with glass closet mirrors and double doors. It didn't have carpenter ants, which made me very happy. My parents purchased a trampoline at this home, which after many years of jumping with friends and family on, recently reached the end of its springing days. That was the home where I spent my last night as a single woman, before I said "I do." And it is a home where my children all love going to spend time with their Grandma and Grandpa Ray, who have generously watched our children for us many times.

There was my first apartment home, where Nick and I spent our first half-year of marriage at the Verandas. That was the home where we got a kitten, Katie, and used our wedding money to pay for the pet deposit. That was the home where we walked through the doors and were greeted by a huge pile of wedding gifts and confetti and balloons and roses *everywhere*, thanks to loving friends and family—especially my brother, who snuck my keys away and had them copied before I got married.

Then there was our first "real home." It was a four-bedroom house with a little yard that backed up to a busy road. There was a palm tree, given to us by our dear college group friends Nathan and Michael at our housewarming party. It now grows over the fence, and you can see it as you drive by on the main road. That was the home we dreamed of starting a family in. It was a home that got toilet-papered by high schoolers from our youth group one weekend. (Thank you, Eric, for giving us the list of everyone involved!) That was the home we brought another kitten into—Lucie—when I was getting the pregnancy itch and needed something to practice my maternal instincts on. That was the home where I would cry on my bed after spending days with my friends and their children, aching uncontrollably for the desire that this home would someday be filled.

It was a home that held an empty room, which I kept the door closed to, with a few baby items in the closet, hoping maybe someday I would get to fill it with a baby. It was a home that we gave up, so that we could move closer into Beaverton to help start a church plant and take money from the proceeds to start the adoption process. It was a home that was never filled with our children, but jump-started that dream for us.

Then there was the summer apartment—a place we lived interim while our new Beaverton townhome was built. A place where dreams were starting to move forward—a home where we filled out adoption paperwork. The home I would come back to after working at the church as a secretary for three days a week. A home with sidewalks we would walk on in the evenings and talk about our new church and dreams of starting our family. A home we knew was only for a short season and so full of hopes and plans and excitement.

In October of 2004, we moved into our townhouse, the home we would settle into for the next five years. This is where we brought all four of our children home from the hospital—Josiah, Ava, Lena and Mallory. A home where I repainted a purple wall many times to get the colors just right to match my "salmon" couches. A place that was close to the MAX station, which would take me and Josiah and Ava on little adventures to the zoo or downtown. The perfect location for walking to and from, with a patio where I planted climbing hydrangeas on the rock wall that grew beautifully. A place where I watched my busy little boy run circles.

There are memories in that house of deciding to pursue adoption again, telling Nick that I was okay with it as we looked at the picture of me and Nick and Josiah over the mantle, when I knew we were not done with just one. Memories of hearing about birthparents changing their minds and deciding to keep their child, and coming back home to Josiah, feeling *so grateful* for our little boy. Memories of getting to bring Ava home to her brother, and later getting to decorate a baby girl nursery because of awesome friends who bought me the bedding I had dreamed about a year before...That was the home where I watched Josiah and Ava take two Easter eggs down the hall to the front door and hand them to Nick to tell him I was pregnant.

There was a couch where I sat for eight weeks while I was on bed rest with the twins, and I watched the blessing of the Lord pour out on me. Friends and family took care of us and provided for us while I sat and carried my babies to 38 weeks. That was a home which was not empty for very long and was suddenly filled beyond max capacity. One we chose to put on the market a month after Lena and Mallory were born, when I kicked into "super-cleaner mom," and thankfully, we sold it six months later.

Then came our home on the hill. A home we settled into within a 24-hour period with all of our children. A home where the bedrooms' white walls stayed that way. As my children grew older, I was able to fill them with color, room by room. It was a place where I enjoyed seeing my husband and Josiah create a garden and plant things and find joy in watching them grow. A home with four bedrooms, so Josiah and Ava could each have their own space to be themselves, and a home with plenty of room for friends and family. A place where I got to watch the neighbors down the road do their annual illegal fireworks show on the Fourth of July, shooting them right over the roof of our home (thankfully we had a rainy June). It was on a hill, so it was a home that taught me, with my running, how to run up hills at the end.

It was a place my kids broke in with a year of sickness, starting with Mallory's mystery infection, then the "100-day" cough, stomach flu, ear infections (10 total), and Scarlet Fever. It was where I came home each day after being "commuter mom" for my two older children, driving them to and from their different schools.

It was a home where we took in another family that had lost their own place to call home. We had seven children and three adults living in our home for a season. Markers were colored on everything by three rambunctious toddler girls. It was a home where we learned sad news and experienced brokenness. A place where, after brokenness affected our lives, I fell into depression and struggle. A home that reminded me of the losses that had taken place, the grief I felt when forced to sever a relationship without any other option, feelings mirroring a divorce from someone I once called my best friend.

And then, it was a home where He began to show me what Redemption looks like through the physical experience of staining my salmon couches and learning how to sand and paint furniture, turning old things into new treasures. And where He showed me what Redemption looks like through the spiritual healing of my heart, after separating out the abuse that was not from Him, and learning the truth that was there all along, searing into the depths of me and making all things new.

Still, in this home, even after the paint had covered all the marks on the walls and the furnishings had been restored, constant memories of the past flooded me. Then we lost our two cats, Katie and Lucie, within two weeks of each other, and a few months later our neighbors who had walked through fire with us, announced they were moving away.

In all the loss this place reminded us of, we finally said goodbye to it, and at a great cost, my husband willingly moved his family from our home on the hill and took us into a new home. This became my husband's gift. Instead of taking his eight-week sabbatical to rest and refresh, he worked his way through it, fixing up and selling our home, and finding a new home that also needed much fixing and restoration.

And he gave selflessly the gift of his time to me, to create a place of refuge, a home not associated with the past. A renovation project that made him better than Chip Gaines, and gave me the chance to wade through the waters of Joanna Gaines. We took our time, talent, energy, and money, and made this home beautiful. We painted walls, fixed doors, replaced appliances and light fixtures, remodeled the kitchen, and installed new carpets and hardwood floors. I had money to decorate and find pieces to fill this home with lovely things, reminders of beauty and celebration and life. And a neighborhood where we could take walks with our children as they rode their bikes and scooters. A home we finally thought we would settle in for good.

But then, life got messy. Brokenness happened once more. Our kids' school, where I anticipated watching all of my children graduate, fell apart. A few months later, things at Nick's work began to unravel, and we were faced with the reality that he needed to look for a new job. That job would not be local, which meant listing the home we had poured so much into, and saying goodbye to the beautiful custom things we had fingerprinted on this home. This refuge we had created was not meant for our family anymore. The short time we lived there was a blink of an eye.

During the time we lived there, God taught me the ability to rest before Him again. To close my eyes on my couch and pray for those around me, as this time the brokenness was shared in the loss of school, and what I had walked through before prepared me to encourage and walk beside those also walking in brokenness. To take time to read through His word, journaling deeper than I had in a long time, to breathe in the fresh air of His Spirit. To dream dreams and visions of plans for things at our church. And then to surrender those dreams into the hands of others, because I knew we would probably not be in Oregon when those dreams came to fruition. To let go of the plans I had made for my children and come back to surrender before the Lord.

Our next home is to be a rental, to care for someone else's home for a season. This was a huge fight of mine with the Lord. Because, see, I should get my own house to nest in if I am giving all of my family and friends up. Yet in that story, I find *my* brokenness is not worth complaining about at all. I learned that a man bought this home for himself and his wife, but something fell through with her work visa. She was sent back to her homeland, and he has to stay here. He has this huge house now just for himself, so he is giving it into our care while he rents a small place and works hard for the day he can bring his wife back to live with him and start their lives together. While we live in this home that does not belong to us, I think God has brought us here to pray for them, and to hopefully get to celebrate with them when she returns to him. Maybe they will find Jesus in this time apart. There is so much more in the bigger scheme of things, in the Grand Gospel Story that He is writing, and I know He wanted to show us that again. It's not about us, it's about *Him*.

And one more time, He reminds me the truth that continuously rolls around in my mind as I walk this bumpy road ahead of me. He soothes my soul and keeps my hope in the knowledge that He is our Home. This is Home because He never stops teaching me what it means to live now, between today and eternity, and being at Home with Him no matter what.

Dear Children,

I am reminded once more of what we eagerly long for. We were created for the perfect world before the fall, but sin changed everything, and so we live in these earthly bodies with souls longing for eternity with our God. Our earthly homes are temporary and changing. No home stays perfect forever. Within a few weeks they need cleaning; over the years, new paint needs to be applied, and tiles need caulking. A roof can only handle so many rainstorms, and even the foundations do not last forever.

These temporary things in our life push us to the eternal longings we have for eternity with God. We are left in the here and now, learning to be content and at peace with where God has us, in all circumstances of life. These homes are witnesses to what God is doing in our lives. But they cannot speak. So we find contentment with God and wrestle in a healthy way with our longing to be with Him. It's really a beautiful thing to contemplate. I love you, Children.

Your Mama,
Kari

Hebrews 13:14 (ESV)

For here we have no lasting city, but we seek the city that is to come.

Philippians 3:20–21 (ESV)

But our citizenship is in heaven, and from it we await a Savior, the Lord Jesus Christ, who will transform our lowly body to be like his glorious body, by the power that enables him even to subject all things to Himself.

Philippians 4:11–12 (ESV)

Not that I am speaking of being in need, for I have learned in whatever situation I am to be content. I know how to be brought low and I know how to abound. In any and every circumstance I have learned the secret of facing plenty and hunger, abundance and need.

Matthew 6:33 (ESV)

But seek first His kingdom and His righteousness, and all these things will be added to you.

Romans 8:22–25 (NASB)

For we know that the whole creation groans and suffers the pains of childbirth together until now. And not only this, but also we ourselves, having the first fruits of the Spirit, even we ourselves groan within ourselves, waiting eagerly for our adoption as sons, the redemption of our body. For we hope we have been saved, but our hope that is not seen is not hope; for who hopes for what he already sees? But if we hope for what we do not see, with perseverance we eagerly await for it.

❧ OUR FAMILY NOW ☙

As I conclude writing this book, our family life has taken quite the turn. After our children's school fell apart and walked through a split, Nick's work also began to show signs of trouble. Things started to come up that he was struggling with ethically. People he respected left the company. Then layoffs rolled out and new precedence for review and rating procedures were put in place. My husband started wrestling with his job. His job is very specialized, so to leave his company wasn't a simple consideration, but would require looking outside of the area where we have lived our whole lives.

With those two changes, we fell on our hands and knees. Our stability was completely shaken and rocked by things we once thought secure. Dreams for the future began to fall at our feet, and we started to go before the Lord and ask Him, what did He have for us next? We wanted to be paying attention and seeking the Lord in all things.

Nick started pursuing different jobs, mostly in Texas. And then one morning, someone pursued him for a job in Seattle, just three hours away from our family. By the end of June, Nick had interviews scheduled with two companies, one in Austin and the other just outside of Seattle. Both interviews went well, and by the middle of July, he had two job offers which we prayed over. In the end, he accepted the job in Seattle.

At the end of August, we said our goodbyes to the church we helped plant, the family we love deeply, and the friendships that are like family to us. It was heartbreaking.

We have begun a new chapter in the Adams family. It is a lot to wrestle with and pray through. The Lord has been showing us that He is Provider in new ways—not in the ways we would plan, but in ways that are teaching us not to put our stability in anything but Jesus. There is much we are grieving, and at the same time many new things He is starting. There are highs and lows of emotion, yet His constant peace remains steady and secure.

Maybe 15 or 20 years from now, I will need to write a second installment of the stories of God's faithfulness in our lives, because the truth is, it does not stop. Over and over again, He is faithful. Even when we struggle with our doubts, He is full of mercy and patience. I am already starting to build a list of all the ways He has provided, and I know in the coming days there will be more to add.

So far, here it is, my praises to remember:

o   *A job provision for my husband*

o   *A rental home seven minutes from my children's school that allows three pets*

o   *A school that I wouldn't have given a second glance at, until I received an email from a person I knew years ago who happens to be the Director of Admissions*

o   *A robotics class that my son gets to take part in*

o   *A gymnastics gym close to the school and home with a sibling discount*

o   *A welcoming community at the school*

o   *The opportunity to pray with other women who love Jesus at MIP*

o   *A church to start building community with*

This is just a start. Lord, You are so faithful to our family. May we share of Your faithfulness with all those You place in our life.

Dear Children,

I invite you to join me to search for things to praise God for. They are there if you look for them. It may be joy in the little things, like getting to take a walk outside and breathing in fresh Northwest air. It may be the way someone showed you love, or perhaps the opportunity you were given to show someone else Christ's love today.

Write those moments down. Start a journal. Make your own stones of remembrance to show you what a faithful God we have, so that you will never forget the stories He writes in your lives.

This book is my gift to you—my stones of remembrance—to praise God for the faithfulness He has shown to our family. He is the one that grew our quiver full. He is the one who chose each of you to be part of our family.

I love you, Children. You have a Father who loves you more than I am ever capable of. Look to Him. Invite Him to be your Faithful God. You all hold my heart.

Your Mama Always,
Kari

Joshua 4:21–24 (ESV)

And Joshua said to the people of Israel, "When your children ask their fathers in times to come, 'What do these stones mean?' then you shall let your children know, 'Israel passed over this Jordan on dry ground.' For the Lord your God dried up the waters of the Jordan for you until you passed over, as the Lord your God did to the Red Sea, which He dried up for us until we passed over, so that all the peoples of the earth may know that the hand of the Lord is mighty, that you may fear the Lord your God forever."

References

[1] Genesis 1-3. *NASB*.

2 Joshua 4. *NASB*.

3 *Anne of Green Gables*. Directed by Kevin Sullivan, Performances by Megan Follows, Colleen Dewhurst, Richard Farnsworth, Patricia Hamilton, Marilyn Lightstone, Schuyler Grant, and Jonathan Crombie, CBC, 1985.

4 Montgomery, LM. *Anne of Green Gables*. Boston, MA: L.C. Page & Co., 1908. Print.

5 Alcott, Louisa May. *Little Women*. Boston, MA: Robert Brothers, 1868. Print.

6 Harris, Joshua. *I Kissed Dating Goodbye*. Sisters, OR: Multnomah Books, 1997. Print.

7 James 1:13-17. *NASB*.

8 Genesis 37, 39-48. *NASB*.

9 Mullins, Rich. "Awesome God." *Winds of Heaven, Stuff on Earth*, Universal Music-Brentwood Benson Publishing, 1988.

[10] Proverbs 27:15-16, Proverbs 19:13-14. *NASB*.

[11] Philippians 4:4-5. *NASB*.

12 Gunn, Robin Jones. *Christy Miller Series*. Sisters, OR: Multnomah Books. Print.

13 Barry, Jeff, Ellie Greenwich and Phil Spector. "Chapel of Love." Performed by The Dixie Cups. Red Bird Records, 1964.

14 Watson, Wayne. "Somewhere in the World." *How Time Flies*, Word Records/DaySpring, 1992.

[15] Matthew 1:5. *NASB.*

[16] Genesis 2:18-25. *NASB.*

17 Hughes, Tim. "Here I Am to Worship." *Here I Am to Worship*, EMI Gospel, 2001.

18 Psalm 37:3-7. *NASB.*

19 Arterburn, Stephen, and Fred Stoker. *Every Man's Battle*. Colorado Springs, CO: WaterBrook Press, 2000. Print.

[20] Arterburn, Stephen, Brenda Stoeker, Fred Stoeker, and Mike Yorkey. *Every Heart Restored*. Colorado Springs, CO: WaterBrook Press, 2004. Print.

[21] Warren, Rick. *The Purpose Driven Life*. Grand Rapids, MI: Zondervan, 2002. Print.

[22] Psalm 37. *NASB.*

[23] Hughes, Tim. "Everything." *Holding Nothing Back*, Sparrow Records/Survivor Records, 2007.

[24] Wells, Christa. "Held." *Awaken*, Natalie Grant, Curb Records, 2005.

[25] Boynton, Sandra. *What's Wrong Little Pookie?*, New York, NY: Robin Corey Books, 2007.

[26] Shust, Aaron, and Dorothy Greenwell. "My Savior, My God." *Anything Worth Saying*, Brash Music, 2006.

[27] *Sisterhood of the Traveling Pants.* Directed by Ken Kwapis, Performance Leads by Alexis Bledel, America Ferrera, Blake Lively, and Amber Tamblyn, Distributed by Warner Bros. Pictures, 2005.

[28] Bunyan, Paul and made by Oliver Hunkin. *Dangerous Journey, The Story of Pilgrim's Progress.* Grand Rapids, MI: Wm B Eerdmans* Publishing Co., 2010.

[29] *Tangled.* Directed by Nathan Greno and Byron Howard, Performance Leads by Mandy Moore, Zachary Levi, and Donna Murphy, Distributed by Walt Disney Studios Motion Pictures, 2010.

[30] Fraser, Brooke. "None but Jesus." *United We Stand*, Hillsong Music Australia, 2006.

[31] McKeehan, Toby and Mark Heimermann. "Jesus Freak." *Jesus Freak*, ForeFront/Virgin, 1995.

[32] Luke 10:38-42. *NASB.*

[33] Crocker, Matt, Joel Houston, and Salomon Ligthelm. "Oceans (Where Feet May Fail)." *Zion*, Hillsong Music/Sparrow Records, 2012.

[34] Guglielmucci, Mike. "Healer." *Kari Jobe*, Integrity Media and Gateway Create Publishing, 2009.

[35] Jobe, Kari. "You Are for Me." *Kari Jobe*, Integrity Media and Gateway Create Publishing, 2009.

[36] Isaiah 26:4, The LORD is my Rock. Revelation 5:5, Lion. Ephesians 2:14, Prince of Peace. Proverbs 18:10, Strong Tower. John 9:38, LORD. John 1:14, The Word. John 8:12, Light of the world. Hosea 2:16, My Husband. Matthew 1:23, Immanuel. Luke 8:45, Physician. Mark 14:36, Daddy/Father. Isaiah 51:15-16, God Almighty. Genesis 1:1, Mighty Creator God. Genesis 16:13, The God who sees me. Exodus 34:14, Jealous God. Isaiah 9:6, Child.

Psalm 22:30-31, My Master. John 6:35, Bread of Life. Psalm 91:1-2, Most High God. Isaiah 40:28-29, Everlasting God. Isaiah 41:14, Redeemer. Isaiah 44:6, Lord of Hosts. Jeremiah 14:8, Hope of Israel. Luke 12:4, Proverbs 17:17, Friend. Isaiah 48:17, Holy One of Israel. Psalm 32:8, Isaiah 2:3, Teacher. Psalm 94:2, Isaiah 30:18, Judge. Jeremiah 23:6, Lord our righteousness. Philippians 4:19-20, The Lord who Provides. John 10:14, The Lord is my Shepherd. *NASB.*

[37] *13 Going on 30.* Directed by Gary Winick, Performances by Jennifer Garner, Mark Ruffalo, Judy Greer, and Andy Serkis, Distributed by Columbia Pictures, 2004.

[38] Mote, Edward. "My Hope is Built on Nothing Less." *Melody* by William Bradbury. Published 1837, Composed 1863.

[39] Tracy, Steven R. *Mending the Soul.* Grand Rapids, MI: Zondervan, 2005. Print.

Tracy, Celestia. *Mending the Soul Workbook Fourth Edition.* Grand Rapids, MI: Zondervan, 2012. Print.

[40] Courson, Mary. *Fragrant Pathways.* Print.

Made in the USA
Middletown, DE
04 December 2019